THE WHITE HOUSE DOCTOR

THE
WHITE HOUSE
DOCTOR

My Patients Were Presidents: A Memoir

DR. CONNIE MARIANO

THOMAS DUNNE BOOKS

ST. MARTIN'S GRIFFIN

NEW YORK

THOMAS DUNNE BOOKS.
An imprint of St. Martin's Press.

www.thomasdunnebooks.com
www.stmartins.com

Photos courtesy of Connie Mariano

The Library of Congress has cataloged the hardcover edition as follows:

Mariano, Connie, 1955–
  White House doctor : behind the scenes with the Clinton and Bush families / Connie Mariano.—1st ed.
      p. cm.
    Includes bibliographical references and index.
    ISBN 978-0-312-53483-7
    1. Mariano, Connie, 1955– 2. Clinton, Bill, 1946——Friends and associates. 3. Bush, George, 1924——Friends and associates. 4. White House Medical Unit (U.S.)—Biography. 5. Women physicians—United States—Biography. 6. Physicians—United States—Biography. 7. Filipino American women—Biography. 8. Filipino Americans—Biography. I. Title.
  E886.2.M366 2010
  610.92—dc22
  [B]

                                                                  2009039260

ISBN 978-0-312-53484-4 (trade paperback)

First St. Martin's Griffin Edition: June 2011

10 9 8 7 6 5 4 3 2 1

With love and gratitude to Andrew, Jason, and Richard

CONTENTS

Acknowledgments   ix

Foreword by Former President Bill Clinton   xiii

ONE: Sweet Dreams   1

TWO: Destined for Duty   13

THREE: The Steward's Daughter   26

FOUR: The President Will See You Now   43

FIVE: One of the Guys   60

SIX: The New Face of the White House   72

SEVEN: Change Is Our Friend   85

EIGHT: The Presidential Road Show   103

NINE: Life in the Kill Zone   122

TEN: The King and I   135

ELEVEN: The White House Bag Lady 156

TWELVE: The House of Sorrow 174

THIRTEEN: Rough Seas Ahead 191

FOURTEEN: Eye of the Storm 208

FIFTEEN: It Takes a Village 223

SIXTEEN: My First Family 244

SEVENTEEN: A Star Is Worn 260

EIGHTEEN: Doctor's Progress Notes 278

ACKNOWLEDGMENTS

I never planned to write this memoir. Instead, I was interviewed frequently by others who went on to write and publish their own books about what I said and did. . . . Always the interviewee, never the author. So my competitive nature compelled me to tell my own story in my own words.

My first thanks go to bestselling author, physician, and dear friend Michael Palmer, who showed me how to make "rhino stew." Without him I would have never had the courage and insanity to put thoughts to paper.

To my First Patient, former President Bill Clinton, thank you again for your trust in me and for the kind words of this Foreword.

To my agent, Susan Crawford, my thanks for your courageous spunk in taking care of me. Nobody climbs mountains better than you.

To my word guru and mapmaker, John Nelson of Bookworks Ltd., thank you for your brilliant editing, brainstorming, wise counsel, and for those inspirational kicks in the ass when I needed it. You made this book a lot more fun to write.

To my wonderful editor, Marcia Markland of Thomas Dunne Books, St. Martin's Press, my appreciation for your sage guidance. You can lead the dance anytime.

My thanks to Jim "Mac" McLeod, my former "black cloud" medic who became the "white cloud" office manager of my private practice. Thank you for your patience and encouragement as I balanced clinic and chapters. Thanks for the memories!

My gratitude to my patient patients for allowing me to share my dreams of writing this book. I hope you all buy several copies and continue to eat in moderation, exercise regularly, and continually ask yourself, "What would make my life better?"

Thanks to my assistant, Lisa Hebestreit, for her research assistance in the writing of this book, and to my clinic concierge coordinator, Rachel Leonard, for keeping the clinic appointments moving on my schedule.

My thanks to White House alumni Steve Bachar for rekindling my memory of that night in the Imperial Palace. A platter of bananas to you. Thanks also to Dr. Jeff Eschbach for travel reminders and allowing me to tell the world we called you "Doogie Howser" at the White House, and to Bill McGee for reminding me of the details.

Many thanks to Dr. Richard Tubb for his kindness, humility, and inspiration. You will always be "number one" in my book.

To Dr. Richard "Dick" and Leslie Ridenour, thanks for letting me stay at your house in Fond du Lac. It was the perfect setting to get the news about my promotion.

To my dear friends and "Sedona Sisters": Maddy Williams for your loyal support and encouragement, and Georgia Bunn for your laughter and creative spark. To Lecia Scaglione, who candidly warned me when I told her I was contemplating writing this book, "Remember when you write a memoir, you piss off two groups of people: the ones you mention and the ones you don't mention."

For the people I do mention, I hope you agree I got it right. And to those I did not mention, please forgive me, and realize I could not name you all.

And, finally, to my "favorite president," John H. Weber, for your constant encouragement, protection of my writing time, and gentle, loving reminders to "write the damn book, darling."

Well, here it is!

FOREWORD

By Former President Bill Clinton

Dr. Connie Mariano held many titles during her nine years at the White House: White House doctor; Physician to the President; Director of the White House Medical Unit. Rear admiral. In each case, Connie was the first: the first military woman to become a White House physician, the first woman director of the White House Medical Unit, and the first Filipino-American in American history to become a Navy rear admiral. For the daughter of a former Navy steward from the Philippines, this particular distinction awarded during my presidency meant a great deal to her and her family.

Throughout my entire presidency, Connie was at my side making sure I stayed healthy. She was with me during the happy times and the sad times, as well as in the historic and private moments. I trusted her with my life and the lives of my family. She bore up to the task with tireless patience and good humor. My family, staff, and I referred to her affectionately as "Dr. Connie."

Dr. Connie took care of the White House cooks and cleaning staff the same way that she took care of presidents and world leaders: with straightforward honesty, compassion, and wit. The organization she directed for seven years, the White House Medical Unit, owes significant improvements to Dr. Connie. She transformed her medical organization into a state-of-the-art responsive medical team that brought twenty-four-hour on-site medical coverage to the presidency. She also created the specialized practice she termed Protective Medical Support that maps out the team's emergency-response plans.

The story of Dr. Connie Mariano began in humble circumstances, moved by struggle, faith, and courage, and resulted in great achievement. A little girl from the Philippines became the physician to the president of the United States; Dr. Mariano's life indeed recounts a wonderfully American success story.

THE WHITE HOUSE DOCTOR

ONE

Sweet Dreams

1.

I never slept with the president. I did sleep with the former president. In fact, I slept with three of them, all at once, on Air Force One. Actually, it was more like a slumber party, which sounds even more bizarre. This all started on a very typical White House day that ended up as anything but typical.

"Hey, Doc, we've got a tourist down in the State Dining Room."

I looked up from my computer on the mahogany desk in my office on the ground floor of the White House. The tall dark-haired man standing in my doorway was a Uniformed Division officer of the Secret Service. I recognized the guard's face, but his first name escaped me. Even after seven years at the White House, I couldn't remember the names of all the guards who sat in a post outside my office, the doctor's office, across the hallway from the president's private elevator.

"Do you want me to call over to the clinic for the duty nurse to respond?" he asked tentatively.

I stood up, clipped my Secret Service radio to my belt, and inserted my earpiece as I walked around the desk, grabbing the AED, the automated external defibrillator, and my medical bag along the way. "He can back me up, but presidents, visiting dignitaries, kitchen help, and . . . tourists get the same treatment."

Taking care of an ill or injured tourist is one of the first duties a White House physician assumes, even before meeting the first patient, the president of the United States. It was one of the first things I learned to do after arriving at the White House in 1992 as the Navy physician to the White House. It wasn't the first time I had taken care of someone who had passed out. Years of working as a Navy doctor in emergency rooms, clinics, teaching hospitals, and onboard a destroyer tender in the Pacific made me an expert in critical care. What was special this time was the setting: the grandeur and elegance of the State Dining Room of the White House.

Please don't let anyone die on my watch, I prayed as we rapidly ascended the marble staircase to the State Floor. The medical bag and defibrillator I was carrying were quite heavy. This was going to be my workout for the day: stair climbing and lifting medical bags. No chance for a run on the Mall. I was scheduled to leave in one hour with the president and first lady for an overseas trip.

I entered the State Dining Room where the line of tourists weaves its way from one end of the room to the other. A gold cordon separates them from the formal dining table in the center of the room, resplendent with a large floral centerpiece, with the chandeliers glittering overhead. The fallen tourist was an elderly, frail woman sitting in a chair in the corner of the room. A woman guard stood beside her. The Secret Service first-aid and trauma—FAT—kit was already on the scene, and the guard was waiting for my cue to administer oxygen. I squatted down beside the woman, looking at her eye to eye. She was approximately eighty years old, wearing glasses, hearing aids, and was sweating profusely. I took her hand in mine and squeezed it gently. It was cold and clammy. My index and third fingers planted themselves on her radial pulse, which was rapid and strong, not thready. I began my routine.

"Hello, ma'am. I'm the White House doctor. How are you feeling?"

She looked at me and blinked. "Are you the nurse?" she drawled. Her voice was soft, sweet, and fresh from West Virginia.

I smiled. "No, ma'am. I'm the doctor, and I'm here to help you. Are you having any chest pain?"

She squinted behind her glasses. "You're not the nurse?" She examined me closely, trying to comprehend how someone who looks like Connie Chung could be a White House doctor. I suppressed the urge to tell her, "Welcome to the Clinton White House," as I wrapped a blood pressure cuff around her arm.

"Ma'am, are you a diabetic?" I asked as I pumped the blood pressure cuff.

"No, no diabetes."

Her blood pressure was 110/60 and her pulse was 80 and regular. Respirations were 20, unlabored. I looked up to a woman in her fifties standing behind the chair, who had identified herself as the daughter of the elderly tourist. "Does your mother take any medications for blood pressure, diabetes, or heart disease?"

She shook her head. "No. No medications at all."

"What happened to her this morning?" I asked.

"She was so excited about coming to see the White House that she skipped breakfast. Then we waited in line for an hour. By the time we got upstairs, she said she was sleepy and then she broke out in a sweat."

I looked at the guard and before I could say "OJ please," a White House usher had brought a glass of fresh orange juice on a silver tray.

"Ma'am, we're going to give you a sip of orange juice, okay?"

She nodded, accepting the glass and drinking it quickly. She patted her lips with a napkin the usher had handed her. She then noticed the embossed gold presidential seal on the napkin, and placed it surreptitiously in her pocket.

By now the White House nurse on duty had arrived. It was tall, brown-haired, all-American Jim Hosack carrying his medical bag. He hunched down beside me, looking guilty, and confessed in a hushed tone, "Sorry, Captain, I was delayed. We were swamped in the clinic."

"I think our patient is going to be okay," I reassured him. "She's a little hypoglycemic. Blood pressure and pulse are stable. I'm going to turn her over to you."

Suddenly, my radio blared—I had taken out my earpiece to attend to my patient. "All points on Oscar . . . Eagle moving . . ." Eagle was the Secret Service code name for President Bill Clinton. Oscar was the name of the Secret Service frequency. The voice was one of the president's agents reporting Bill Clinton's movements on the White House compound.

Jim looked up at me. "The funeral?"

I nodded. Jim tentatively asked, "With all the presidents?" I smiled. I could see intimidation in his eyes. That was why I was taking Vince Starks, the senior White House nurse, with me. He understood: they were just patients. As I walked away, I could hear Jim introduce himself to our elderly patient.

"Oh, so you're the doctor?"

As I hurried back to my office, I checked my watch. It was twenty minutes before we were to lift from the South Lawn on Marine One. The helicopter had not even arrived. Then I heard over my radio, "Eagle moving." "Eagle moving" meant Eagle was on the move, going somewhere. But where? "Eagle moving to the residence," someone said over the radio, as though he had heard my question.

I now heard the muffled sound of Marine One's rotors as it touched down on the South Lawn. My ride had arrived. The helicopter would shortly take the president to Andrews Air Force Base. He was preparing to depart the White House and I, his physician, was to accompany him. As I approached my office, I asked the Secret Service agents across the hallway near the president's elevator, "What gives? Are we going early?" They smiled and shrugged their shoulders; so much for Secret Service intelligence.

I stepped into my office, wondering how soon before we would depart to Andrews. The president could be upstairs for a minute or he could decide to leave in an hour. The Secret Service doesn't know. How could I have not predicted that President Clinton would be true to form: predictably unpredictable!

But I had my own spy network: the president's Filipino valets. I went to my computer and text-paged Master Chief Joe Fama, one of the president's valets, with the message, "When is departure? Doc M."

No sooner had I struck the send key when my phone rang. I picked it up and it was Joe: "Doc, POTUS wants to leave in ten minutes," he announced, from POTUS's (President of the United States) lips to Joe's ears. The president's valet was among the most trusted and reliable of sources. Everyone at the White House knew it. Even Ken Starr knew it.

I walked out into the hallway, grinning like Socks the cat because I now had something that everyone on the eighteen acres of the White House coveted: the scoop. The military aide on duty had just arrived in the hallway now. We called him (or her) the "mil aide." One is assigned each day to follow the president and carries the black briefcase called the "football" that contains the nuclear codes.

The mil aide on duty today would also be accompanying the president on our overseas trip. He was in full dress uniform, perspiring and breathing rapidly. The military aide was not cool; he didn't have the scoop. I walked over to him. He greeted me formally, "Hello, Captain Mariano."

I smiled back and tested him. "Any word about departure?"

He wiped his brow with a white handkerchief and then answered, "No, ma'am."

"Oh," I remarked. "The president's valet just called me and said that POTUS wants to leave in ten minutes." The mil aide's mood brightened when he realized that I had just given him the scoop. You've got to have the scoop to be in the loop. And being in the loop is something military aides crave.

"Per the valet, POTUS wants to depart in ten minutes," he announced into his radio with an air of authority. The Secret Service, White House communications, Marine One pilots, and military personnel who monitor the Secret Service frequency heard the announcement. The Secret Service agents standing in the hallway beside us gave the mil aide the thumbs-up. The approval went to his sweaty head, and he began to strut around like he was the man. Then he caught himself as he saw me observing him. He whispered to me, avoiding eye contact, "Uh, thanks, ma'am."

"Don't mention it, Major," I whispered back to him knowingly.

2.

"Eagle and Evergreen. South Lawn," reported the SAIC, the president's special agent in charge, into his sleeve microphone as President and Mrs. Clinton stepped from the Diplomatic Reception Room onto the South Lawn. They were greeted by a thousand points of light from the camera crews positioned on the west side of the South Portico. I trailed behind them, trying to be invisible as I gingerly stepped onto the moist green lawn. Stay out of the shot and don't trip, I reminded myself. Stay out of the picture is what we are told on day one of our arrival at the White House. The commandment handed down from the White House Military Office is: Thou shalt be invisible. It was an easy edict for me to follow. Growing up as the Filipino daughter of a Navy steward, invisibility was embedded in my DNA.

The rear hatch of Marine One closed with a loud thump. I took my seat on the cushioned bench opposite the hatch, wrapping my woolen navy blue coat around me, shivering. The SAIC sat in the jump seat across from me. He slid on the headphones that allowed him to talk with the Marine One pilots in the cockpit. Looking in my direction, the SAIC must've noticed me bundled up in my coat. "Doc's cold back here. Can you turn up the heat?" he asked the pilots. In a minute, the compartment began to heat up as we lifted from the South Lawn.

I looked toward the front of the helicopter at the president and first lady. They sat facing each other in royal blue cloth seats each bearing the presidential seal, reading their respective briefing materials. The president's personal aide and the national security advisor were on the opposite bench, each reviewing the trip books that outline the president's itinerary. I gazed out the window as Marine One lifted from the South Lawn. It was twilight now, and the red lights from the top of the Washington Monument blinked in a pulselike beat. As Marine One banked south, we flew close enough that I could almost touch it. I realized how very few people had the privilege of seeing this structure so close in the air and from the presidential helicopter no less. A sense of awe and appreciation overcame me as the helicopter made its way across the Tidal Basin.

I gazed out onto the Potomac as we flew toward Andrews Air Force Base. I thought about how quickly this trip had been scheduled and arranged. King Hussein of Jordan had just died and as it's often said at the White House: you die, we fly. This meant Air Force One was prepared to fly the president to the state funeral in Amman, Jordan. Onboard the presidential aircraft would be President and Mrs. Clinton, senior White House staff, State Department officers, Secret Service, White House press, and members of my White House Medical Unit. This journey was particularly special because of three additional passengers: the former presidents George H. W. Bush, Jimmy Carter, and Gerald Ford. I was looking forward to seeing President George Bush, who had been my first "first patient" when I arrived at the White House in 1992. I had also previously met President Carter during one of President Clinton's trips. And I had dined with President Ford at a symposium at Wake Forest University a few years ago.

Fifteen minutes after leaving the White House, Marine One touched down at Andrews. President and Mrs. Clinton departed the helicopter from the front steps. The camera crew on the tarmac filmed the arrival and the president's dignified stroll to the 747's steps. Meanwhile, at the back of the helicopter, two Filipino valets, Fred Sanchez and Lito Bautista, were off-loading the president's and first lady's luggage. As I lugged my medical bag, defibrillator, and briefcase off the chopper, I patted Fred and Lito on the back. They smiled at me.

On the tarmac in front of Air Force One with the White House Press Corps in the background. I traveled to over 100 countries in my military career, most of them while at the White House. (OFFICIAL WHITE HOUSE PHOTO, JUNE 1994)

I evaded the camera lens as I briskly walked toward the rear steps of the plane.

I loved Air Force One, which had become my home away from the White House. As I moved forward toward the medical compartment at the front of the plane, I passed the press section and waved to the seated White House press corps reporters; several waved back. One reporter asked, "Hey, Doc, can we drink the water over there?"

"Bottled water and plenty of it," I advised him.

I walked past the compartment where the Secret Service detail sat and noticed an agent had fallen asleep in his chair even before we had taken off. This hastily arranged overseas trip had everybody working late hours, especially the Secret Service. But once we were airborne, they would at least get a ten-hour break. Some sooner than others.

In the next compartment that manifested the White House staff, one of the advance office staffers asked me for a sleeping pill. I advised her to see me in the medical compartment during the flight. As I passed each compartment, I reviewed the passenger manifest in my mind. All the people onboard were also potential patients for me.

When I reached the medical compartment, Timmy Kerwin, the chief flight attendant, stepped over. Cheerful in his blue vest with flight wings insignia and his name engraved in gold on the front, he was youthful in appearance despite his twenty-five-plus years in the Air Force.

"Hello, Doc. We got everybody onboard, including the three presidents. They're in the senior staff compartment." He nodded to the next compartment down from us.

"Where are they going to sleep?" I asked. I knew that beds were at a premium on Air Force One. There were two beds in the president's cabin in the forward compartment. The only other decent beds were here in medical, two single-mattress bunk racks folded into the wall. These were designed to fold out for a patient who needed to be monitored or treated. If there were no patients, I would usually sleep in one of them on long trips. But I was willing to surrender my bunk bed to a former leader of the free world.

Timmy responded, "I've manifested the three presidents in the senior staff compartment."

This space held three large-size reclining passenger seats. These leather chairs were comfortable but did not allow the passenger to lie flat. As I tried to visualize our distinguished guests trying to sleep in these seats, Timmy proudly added, "I also got three brand-new sleeping bags from Walmart just in case."

The image of a presidential slumber party on the floor of the senior staff compartment jarred me. "Timmy, I can't imagine them lying on the floor in sleeping bags. Say I'm offering them the two bunk racks and the reclining chair in the medical compartment."

Timmy smiled and ran off to inform the presidents of this invitation.

As I stepped inside, I was met by a tall, handsome African American man in scrubs. Navy Lieutenant Vince Starks greeted me with a tired

"Good evening, ma'am. I got the blood in the belly of the plane." For overseas trips, the White House Medical Unit carried several units of blood reserved for the president and first lady in the case of a medical emergency. This was stored in portable containers in the belly of the aircraft during flight.

Vince Starks, the senior White House nurse out of six, was the most experienced in terms of training and length of White House duty. Because of the short notice and our special passengers, I wanted Vince to assist me in case of an emergency in the air or in Amman.

"Get ready for some overnight visitors," I announced, as I put away my medical bag and sat down in the seat across from him.

"Let me guess," he said, smiling, his pearly white teeth contrasted against his ebony skin. "They all respond to the same first name: Mr. President."

"You got it." I nodded. "So let's make it special."

Vince leaped into action, folding out the two racks from the wall, and getting pillows and sheets to cover the thin mattresses. As an added touch, we prepared three place cards, each labeled "Mr. President" under the presidential seal. Like a five-star hotel concierge, Vince placed the name cards, along with a mint, on each of the pillows and in the seat across from mine. As an intensive care nurse prior to his assignment at the White House, I'm sure that Vince never imagined his duties would one day include bed preparation.

As we readied the compartment for our evening guests, Timmy had visited the three former presidents, telling them of the "doc's offer" to sleep on bunks in the medical space. The offer was greeted enthusiastically by all. The first president to enter was Jimmy Carter. He arrived smiling, his bright eyes twinkling, looking relaxed in a jogging suit. A former naval officer, he greeted me by requesting to "come aboard" the compartment. I offered him the first pick of the two racks or the reclining chair. President Carter went directly to the bottom rack and sat on the edge. He grinned and proclaimed, "Just like onboard a submarine."

"Sweet dreams, Mr. President," I said. I caught myself using the same bedtime "nighty-night" tone reserved for my children on those rare occasions when I was home to put them to bed.

President Ford then entered the compartment, tall and tired. He looked at the bottom rack where Jimmy Carter lay sleeping with a blanket covering him. I offered him the top rack or the seat opposite mine. "Oh, I'll take the chair," he said. "I'd be more comfortable in a recliner." We gave President Ford a blanket and dimmed the lights.

President Bush was the final guest to report for bedtime duty. "May I sleep with you, Connie?" he teased and winked.

"I serve at the pleasure of the president, Mr. President," I said and gave him a big hug. He was the first president I had ever met and he held a special place in my heart.

I then glanced down at his bedroom slippers and noticed the presidential seal embroidered on them. "Nice shoes . . ." I began.

"Don't give me a hard time about it," he warned. "Those jokers," he said, nodding at Presidents Carter and Ford, "were kidding me about my slippers." We both laughed.

"Oh, they're just jealous," I reassured him. He smiled. "Sir, we've got the top rack reserved for you. Need any help climbing up?"

"No, ma'am." President Bush glanced over at Vince, who was ready to jump to his aid. The seventy-five-year-old former president placed a steady foot on the bottom rack, careful not to disturb the sleeping Jimmy Carter, and hoisted himself up and over onto the top rack. Vince and I almost applauded the effort. He pulled the blanket over and was soon in presidential dreamland.

I sat back in my seat, dimmed the lights further, leaving only the floor lights aglow. Vince settled into the remaining seat and was soon asleep. As the night wore on, I had trouble sleeping. This was often the case when I flew on Air Force One. While others slept I lay awake in my seat doing inventory—I was mentally reviewing the checklist of preparations before we landed in Amman.

Because this trip had been scheduled at the last moment due to the king's untimely death, the usual preparations for a foreign presidential visit, which often took months, were now afforded only hours. We had dispatched our senior White House medic to Amman less than twenty-four hours ago; he was to inspect the hospital chosen should the president become ill or injured. The White House advance staff in Amman had arrived two days earlier and fortunately none of them was ill from the water or the local cuisine. The medic would meet Air Force One upon its arrival and would ride in the motorcade with me and Vince. The three of us would take care of the president in the event of an emergency. But we also had to respond to any health issues involving the first lady or any of the former presidents. It was understood that I could never leave the side of the president, and that Vince or my medic would have to take care of other injured patients. These scenarios tumbled in my mind as I sat in the darkness.

As I looked around my compartment, all I could see in the dim light from the muted orange-colored floor lamps were the shadows of three softly snoring elderly statesmen snuggled in their blankets. Keeping watch over them this cold February night were an African American male nurse and myself, a Filipino-American female physician.

A few hours later, President Clinton poked his head into our compartment. His thick, wavy salt-and-pepper hair was slightly tousled and the bags under his eyes more prominent with the long hours he had recently kept. He glanced at his sleeping guests and smiled at me. I nodded silently to him. Despite all the pressures of his office, President Clinton was ever the gracious host, checking on his guests before catching a few hours of sleep himself.

After he left, Vince shuddered and then woke up. His first instinct was to gaze protectively at our three charges. I whispered to him as I closed my eyes, "Just make sure they keep on breathing."

And "keeping them breathing" is what I did for nine years, twenty-four hours a day, home and abroad. How did I become the keeper of the presidential pulse? I was destined to become the first doctor of the United States of America.

TWO

Destined for Duty

1.

When I became a White House physician, I embarked on an incredible journey after which my life has never been the same. In fact, most people who have worked at the White House in any position tend to tell their life story as "pre" and "post" White House years. I am no different; the only difference was that I never expected to be appointed. While I was qualified, a commander in the Navy with decent medical credentials, even this military assignment went to those with the connections. I was the daughter of a Filipino steward; what chance did I have?

It was the fall of 1991. I had been in the Navy for ten years and was stationed at the naval hospital in San Diego. One of the largest military hospitals on the West Coast, the hospital was located in beautiful Balboa Park. It was a bustling, major medical center where the internal medicine department was continually challenged with the care of the large active duty and retiree military population of San Diego. I was the division head of the department as well as the director of the internal medicine clinic. My days were long and hectic, starting off at 7:30 A.M. with morning report or what we called "morning distort," as the young interns went over the night's events: who was admitted with what and their treatment, any emergency procedures, and so forth. This was followed by the "morning retort" by the senior staff, who would lecture on what diagnosis was missed or what tests should have been ordered. Since this was a teaching hospital and our department had a rigorous residency program in internal medicine, we kept the horseplay to a minimum, unlike shipboard deployment when such reviews could get rowdy.

An hour later, I would be off doing my rounds with my ward team, and then back to the clinic to see a full load of retired geriatric patients with their annual checkups for diabetes, hypertension, coronary disease, pulmonary disease, depression, and the usual mix of chronic diseases that characterize a busy internal medicine practice. Then there was the administrative paperwork for a division head, endless reports in triplicate. I loved the doctoring, hated the desk duties. My days were long, and by the time I got home at 6:00 P.M., I was exhausted but had to rally for my "second shift": two hungry young sons and a husband. After dinner, there was playtime, bath time, and then bedtime. And then it all started again at 6:00 A.M. I lived in a state of peripatetic exhaustion. But my boys were happy living two doors down from their grandparents, and my husband was an associate at a prestigious law firm and enjoyed his work. As for me, I was getting restless, wanting to move on to something more challenging.

Something was indeed missing in my professional life. I was moving up the ladder as they say, but command and its responsibilities didn't have the same excitement as shipboard deployment or a triage unit in a war zone. Maybe it was the routine nature of internal medicine; maybe I needed a transfer to an ER? But as the pressure built up inside me, something interesting began to happen, what I later realized was a premonition of sorts. Each day at the hospital, I would hear the rotors of the helicopters as they prepared to take off from the helo pad across the street. *Thump thump thump* the rotors began to spin, ready for wheels-up. I felt that the helicopter was summoning me: the medevac helicopter, my old friend. When I was three days old at the Sangley Point Naval Hospital in the Philippines, I developed complications in the nursery. The doctors airlifted me by helicopter to Clark Field Air Force Base and their neonatal care unit. I owe my life to that helo ride. Now at the naval hospital in San Diego, I couldn't shake the feeling that somehow a helicopter again would figure prominently in my life. Little did I know that the helicopter calling me was Marine One.

As I longed for change, I took into consideration that my service obligation to the Navy was almost complete. As a 1981 graduate of America's military medical school, the Uniformed Services University School of Medicine, I incurred a seven-year payback commitment. In 1991, I was a year away from completing that obligation to the Navy and eligible to be released from active duty. This meant I would be free to leave the Navy. No more regulations telling me what to wear, what to do, what to say. It would be a dramatic change for me, since the Navy life was all I had known. My father was a career enlisted man. I started life in a naval hospital, grew up as a Navy brat who moved every two to three years, dated my future husband when he was a midshipman, and became a naval officer when I entered the military medical school. Was I ready to "jump ship"?

I mulled over this decision for some time. My husband was all for it. In private practice, I could be a 24/7 mother and wife, and we wouldn't be threatened with another tour of duty and have to move from our beloved San Diego. So, after a weekend of rest and reflection at my husband's law firm retreat in Palm Springs, I went into work one Monday morning and marched down to the administrative office. I requested the papers for release from active duty, which would take effect in one year. I brought the papers up to my office to look them over.

On my first day of medical school at the Uniformed Services University (USU) School of Medicine. Wearing combat fatigues and helmet, I inspect my M-16. (FAMILY PHOTO, AUGUST 1977.)

As I sat at my desk reading the forms, I realized that these were like divorce papers. I was divorcing the Navy. Meanwhile, in the background, I could hear the haunting *thump thump thump* of the helo rotors coming from the hospital landing zone. My concentration was then broken by the buzzing sound of my pager. Before digital pagers, we had voice-activated ones at the hospital. These devices were particularly annoying because the voice was simultaneously loud and garbled.

I could barely discern the message from my pager and when I did, my heart skipped a beat: "Commander Mariano, please call Captain Mitas STAT." This call somehow seemed connected to the helo rotors, which faded out when the pager blared. Maybe there was an emergency that required my attention across town at one of the Navy's many training facilities. And while I was concerned for a

Left: As a first-year medical student at USU, wearing the short white coat that medical students are privileged to wear on our clinical rotations. (FAMILY PHOTO, OCTOBER 1977) *Right: At graduation, promoted to Lieutenant in the U. S. Navy Medical Corps.* (FAMILY PHOTO, MAY 1981)

patient who needed such immediate care, I was also glad to be lifted out of my life, if just for the morning.

Captain John A. Mitas II was the chairman of internal medicine and my boss. Since I was the division head for internal medicine, I was almost certain the captain was calling me about a problem. What was it this time? An intern caught kissing a nurse in the stairwell? Another scheduling snafu at the clinic? A complaint from an admiral's wife who had to wait in line in the ER? Anyway, there was no helo ride this morning. I quickly dialed the captain's office and his secretary connected me to him.

The captain's voice was smooth and his words were crisp. "Connie, I'm looking over the message traffic from Washington today. There is one particular message that caught my attention. The detailers are requesting that the Navy nominate six candidates for the position of White House physician. It's a two-year assignment. I looked over the qualifications and I think you'd be a good candidate. I'd like to nominate you."

My heart rate started to drop to normal. Relieved that this was not another administrative fire to put out, I began to focus on what the captain had just told me. "Thank you, Captain," I responded, taken aback by the timing of his call in the midst of my pending divorce from the Navy. "I've never heard of the position."

"Not many people have, since we keep it low-key. Each of the armed services—Army, Navy, and Air Force—sends a physician to serve in the White House Medical Unit, which is made up of military doctors, nurses, PAs, and medics. Their mission is to take care of the president, vice president, and their families. They also take care of the military personnel on the White House compound. The assignment does involve a lot of travel since the doctors accompany the president." Captain Mitas paused. "And I know how much you hate to travel." The truth was quite the opposite, as he well knew.

"Reminds me of deploying to sea," I said, "taking care of the crew while you are underway in foreign ports." I reminisced about my two years as ship's doctor on the destroyer tender USS *Prairie,* my best time in the Navy. "Sounds like a great job, Captain. But I'm sure there are some better candidates out there."

"Connie, listen to the requirements," Captain Mitas

Receiving my first medal, the Navy Achievement Medal, as a Lieutenant ship's doctor on USS Prairie. *Taken in Subic Bay, Philippines, during my ship's six-month deployment in the Western Pacific in 1983.*
(CHAPLAIN TIMOTHY C. SIMS)

countered, reading them off, "Board-certified in internal medicine, shipboard and deployment experience, clinical acumen, interpersonal skills, and leadership abilities. And no skeletons in the closet to hold up the security clearance. You're the perfect candidate."

"Sir, I'm very honored and flattered. May I get back to you on this? I should talk to my husband before I give you an answer."

"Sure, run it by your attorney," he said with a snicker.

I called Richard at his firm in downtown San Diego. His first reaction was expected. "What? Are you crazy?" Richard asked. "Why would we want to move back to the East Coast? It's hot, muggy, and crowded. And they don't even have decent Mexican food. We've got a house, kids in school, and our families live here. Plus, I've got a great law practice. And anyway, I thought you were going to sign the papers to get out?"

His litany of reasons was practical but not very uplifting. As I listened to his reply, I realized what was missing: I wanted to be inspired, I wanted to get up in the morning excited by the day's prospects, not bored by mindless protocol. "I don't know. It sounds exciting, not your everyday routine assignment."

My response stopped Richard cold. I could hear him take a deep breath. He knew how I felt about hospital work. More softly, he replied, "Do you think you have a chance?"

"Are you kidding?"

Richard laughed. "You know, even getting turned down would make a good résumé item."

I almost snorted. That was Richard, always the practical one. "Well, let me think about it." I hung up the phone, sat back in my chair. It sounded glamorous, but did I really want to prolong my time in the Navy by two years? It was interesting that this should come up the day I started filling out my release papers. I stood up and walked over to the window, gazed out at the helo pad. The chopper was still deployed. The phone rang. It was Richard.

"Hey, I was just thinking. You deserve this; it's a great way to go out. That is, besides the résumé item," he added with a chuckle.

"You're right. My twenty-one-gun salute." I paused, getting a shiver up my spine. "I'll tell the captain to put it through."

2.

When the White House calls, everyone jumps. In my ten years of military service, I'd never seen the administrative machinery work as smoothly as it did for my nomination to the White House. Within a few days of the nomination package being submitted, I met with the security officer to prepare the paperwork for my top secret security clearance. The interview date at the White House was set for December.

As I prepared for my interview, Richard did a literature search on my prospective boss, J. Burton Lee III, who was the personal physician to President George H. W. Bush. Dr. Lee held the political appointment of physician to the president. If I got the job, Dr. Lee would be my new boss. He was to interview me during my visit to the White House.

I read the newspaper interviews that Dr. Lee had granted in the past, and what I sensed from the interviews troubled me. I got the impression that Dr. Lee was not in favor of women physicians, in or out of the military.

"Oh, great," said Richard when I shared my initial impression of Dr. Lee. "With that attitude, you two should hit it off just fine." He paused, and then added, "But like we said, it's a résumé item; you're not expecting to get the job anyway."

The White House in December is a magical and beautiful place. The State Floor is decorated with colorful ornaments, lines of tourists weave their way through the mansion to view the trees and decorations, musicians play traditional Christmas songs along the tour line path, and the household staff rushes about preparing for the evening holiday parties. The house hums like a beehive. Being born and raised Catholic, I love traditional Christmas festivities, especially in a winter climate. I was taken slightly aback by my initial White House reception. I expected cold and political, but walked into a warm and very human climate. This was more inviting than I had expected.

This was my second visit to the presidential mansion. The first time I set foot in the White House was through the kitchen door. My father's cousin, Marciano "Rocky" Mariano, was a Navy steward stationed at the White House in the 1960s as a valet to President John F. Kennedy. At that time, my father was stationed at the admiral's quarters at the Navy Yard in nearby Anacostia. I was in the third grade, and my parents had asked my uncle to set up a tour of the White House. My uncle arranged to have his wife, Diane, escort my parents, siblings, and me onto the compound. We didn't enter with the tourists. We came in with the kitchen staff, through the back door.

Thirty years from the time I first set foot in the president's house as an eight-year-old Navy brat, I returned as a Navy commander in my dark blue winter uniform to be interviewed for the job of a lifetime. A job I believed I had no chance of getting. Wrong sex, wrong color, even wrong height. I didn't look like the stereotypical White House doctor: male, Anglo, graduate of the military academy, member of the country club set. And the decision on my appointment would be made by the most aristocratic of them all. This could be the shortest final interview in the medical unit's history.

The first part of the process went smoothly. I met with the military security officer, who reviewed the information for my security clearance. He was particularly impressed that my uncle had worked for President Kennedy. I was then interviewed by the White House doctors, who consisted of Army Colonel Larry Mohr, Air Force Lieutenant Colonel Tom Koroscil, and the incumbent Navy physician, Commander Al Roberts. I had never met any of these officers during my military career. I knew of Al Roberts from my friends at the naval hospital in San Diego where he had trained in pulmonary and critical care before going to the White House. I also heard that one of the other candidates being interviewed that day was a good friend of Roberts. *Great*, I thought, *how can I compete with that?* I wondered if he had already promised his buddy the job. This was the rumored tradition of how previous White House physicians had been selected. The incumbent military doctor would nominate a friend, and then lobby for him to be selected. How could I be so naive as to believe it would be based on merit and qualifications alone? This was Washington, D.C., where people got jobs based on connections. *You are nobody if you know nobody.*

So I went into my interviews believing that I was a long shot and that I would never get the position. No old friends, no political connections. Who was I? The daughter of a Navy steward. Navy steward? You know, those nice, smiling Filipino men who quietly serve you your meals, iron your laundry, and keep your house clean. They are my roots, my people. I can hear the White House doctors thinking, "Okay, send in Mariano, the steward's daughter."

As I was sitting in the reception room with this tape running through my head, a male voice boomed out ominously from the adjoining office. "I'm ready for the next one."

Al Roberts had escorted me to the doctor's office on the ground floor of the White House. I had finished my interviews earlier with the three White House doctors, and the final interview and decision was left to J. Burton Lee III himself. Roberts poked his head into Lee's office to announce that I was here. I waited quietly in an armchair in the cramped front office where his secretary sat smiling at me sympathetically. She must have thought they were filling their minority quotient by interviewing me. The office opened up to the ground floor of the White House. Across the hall was the elevator to the second floor and the private quarters of the president and first family.

Al Roberts stood in the doorway. Kind, sincere, and pleasant, Al was a wonderful host during my full day of interviews. "I don't have her military records with me, Dr. Lee. They're in the Old Executive Office Clinic where we reviewed them," he told him.

"Well, never mind," the loud voice snapped. "I don't need the records. I'll make the decision myself." Then I heard what sounded like books being tossed onto a desk. "Send her in," he yelled from his office.

Al stood back, glanced at me apologetically and waved me inside. "Thanks, Commander. You've been great." I then took a deep breath and said a quiet prayer as I walked into the doctor's lair. *If this is meant to be, show me a sign.*

Dr. Lee was a tall, handsome, elegant man. Upper-crust. Sophisticated. A man befitting the "III" after his name. His ties with the first family went back many years. He was one of the few people at the White House who was close enough to the president and first lady to call them by their first names.

"Dr. Mariano, I presume." Dr. Lee extended his hand and smiled diplomatically, examining me from head to toe while he shook my hand.

"Dr. Lee, it is an honor to be here," I responded, looking up at him, searching for an answer. And then I saw something that made me smile.

Show me a sign. A Band-Aid.

There was a simple, tan Band-Aid across his forehead. It was what I would've put on my little boys' knees for their owies and ouchies. Dr. Lee had a "boo-boo." The sign was telling me that behind the gruff exterior the man had a soft heart and that I shouldn't be put off by his manner.

Then the mood shifted from diplomacy to interrogation. "Sit down," Dr. Lee barked, as he pointed to an armchair across from the seat at his wooden desk.

Okay, I said to myself, waiting for him to sit first, *but I've got your number, buddy.* I had met many arrogant men in my military career. Many of them would try to intimidate me; often I would have to bite the bullet, as most were as coldhearted as they were gruff. *This man is different*, I told myself. *Don't overreact.*

I did not become angry. Instead, I remained calm. In fact, I became almost Zen-like in my peaceful posture. I had nothing to lose here. Even better, I had been given a sign and should just let it unfold.

Dr. Lee noted that, in military fashion, I was waiting for my commanding officer to sit first. I could see that this had an effect on him. As a civilian, he apparently liked military discipline and formality, and probably didn't expect it in a woman. Dr. Lee sat down in his seat, and I took mine.

"Why do you want this job?" he fired off to me. The man did not believe in foreplay.

I sat back for a moment to absorb the impact of his aggressive posture. I didn't react angrily, but the anticipation of this interview over the past six months began to well up inside of me. I leaned forward in my seat, leveled him with a fixed stare. "Dr. Lee," I spoke in a clipped tone, my best Clint Eastwood, "it's payback time."

This caught the good doctor off guard. He looked puzzled. "Huh," he finally blurted out.

"I owe a lot to this country," I said, speaking from my heart in a voice I hardly recognized. "My father was a poor man in the Philippines, but with pride and character. He was accepted and joined the U.S. Navy in the 1940s, and the Navy gave him and his family a wonderful life here in the United States. My brother, sister, and I have all received scholarships for higher education. The Navy paid for my medical school. My family and I owe so much to America. So, if I can pay back this country by serving as a doctor to my commander in chief, then that's what I want to do."

Dead silence. Dr. Lee was a little taken aback. This was not what he had expected. And truthfully, me either. I didn't prepare this speech; it just came out of me.

"What can you do here?" he asked, now taking me seriously.

"You see these stripes on my sleeve?" I pointed to the three gold stripes of a commander on my Navy uniform jacket. "The longer I stay in the Navy, the more stripes I receive. The more stripes I receive, the more desks they put me behind." I pointed to the mahogany desk where he was planted. "Dr. Lee, I'm not a desk doctor. I'm a *trench* doctor. I take care of patients in the field, onboard ships, and in foreign ports. That's what makes my day." He nodded his head and gave me a stone-faced cool assessment. I couldn't gauge his reaction one way or the other.

Dr. Lee abruptly stood up. "As far as I'm concerned," he began in a solemn tone, "we can stop the process right now."

Oh no, I thought. *The most important interview of my life is also the shortest. He's going to throw me out now. Gone in sixty seconds.* I stood up to take the bad news.

"I don't care who they're interviewing today or tomorrow. You've got the job," he announced. "When can you start?"

Startled by this unexpected declaration, I blurted out, "Whenever you need me." Then I realized my security clearance had yet to be completed. He guessed as much.

"Security clearance? Don't worry." Dr. Lee finally smiled. "The boys in the military office will set everything up." Then a wise, sly smile wrinkled his face while the Band-Aid remained undisturbed. "I'm going to tell Barbara about you. We've got ourselves a live wire." He then quickly shook my hand and strode out of his office, through the reception room where Al Roberts and his secretary were standing in shock. Dr. Lee crossed the hallway, as we all watched, to take the private elevator to the second floor to inform the first lady of his decision.

I followed in Dr. Lee's wake and stood in the reception area. Al Roberts looked at me and asked sheepishly, anticipating bad news, "What happened?"

"I think I got the job," I confessed hesitantly.

Al did a double take, his eyebrows arched in disbelief. "I guess we'll just have to entertain the other five candidates." Al smiled, knowing his boss all too well. "When Burt makes up his mind, it's a done deal."

THREE

The Steward's Daughter

1.

How did I prepare for my new job as a White House physician? I didn't realize it until much later, but I was being groomed for this job from the moment I was born in the Philippines in 1955. My father was a U.S. Navy steward assigned to the quarters (military house) of Vice Admiral Hugh Goodwin and his wife, Eleanor, at Sangley Point Naval Base. Eleanor was the daughter of a prominent San Francisco physician. A genteel, elegant woman who married the roguish admiral from Georgia, Eleanor took an interest in the family lives of the Filipino stewards who served in her household. Birthdays and Christmas gifts for the children were never missed. My father so admired Mrs. Goodwin that he wanted to make her my godmother for the christening ceremony. But since Eleanor was not Catholic, our parish priest would not allow it.

Instead, to honor her, my father named me Eleanor and had the name added to my birth certificate. I was originally to be named Concepcion after the Immaculate Conception. My mother had wor-

*My father, Navy Third Class Petty
Officer Steward Angel C. Mariano.
Taken in 1949.* (FAMILY PHOTO)

shipped at the Shrine of the
Immaculate Conception in
the town of Cavite in the
Philippines a year before my
birth. Believing her chances
of fertility would be in-
creased, my mother would
sip the holy water from the
shrine. Moved by this beautiful icon of the Blessed Vir-
gin, my mother prayed that
if she ever had a daughter she
would honor her with the
name Concepcion. But when the birth certificate was issued, the
admiral's lady got top billing over the Mother of God, which was
relegated to a middle name. Typical of Navy life everywhere, the admiral's wife outranked everyone.

Shortly after I was born, the doctors at the naval hospital diag-
nosed me with severe dehydration. The nearest neonatal intensive
care unit was at Clark Field Air Base located forty-five minutes away
by air. I took the first of many helicopter rides on a medevac chopper
at the tender age of three days. As I mentioned earlier, the *thump
thump* of helicopter rotors was to play an important, and symbolic,
role in my later life. I of course don't remember the ride, but it
must've made an impression.

I was two years old when I flew with my mother and baby brother
to Hawaii, where my father, Angel Mariano, had been transferred.
My father had flown ahead of us to Honolulu to set up our new home
in a Navy housing project at Pearl Harbor. All I recall of the trip is
my mother later telling everyone how brave I was. At one point in

the journey, we refueled on the island of Kwajalein. As the passengers were returning to the plane from the terminal, my mother held on to my baby brother with one arm and my hand with the other. As the propellers started turning and everybody picked up the pace, I couldn't keep up with her and fell hard onto the tarmac, scraping my knees. I did not cry. I just picked myself up and kept moving toward the plane. My mother had turned back to watch my reaction, which in her two-year-old child both frightened and impressed her. Little did she know that this hardened reaction was to become my modus operandi for the rest of my life: fall down, don't cry like a girl, get up and move on.

One of my earliest memories was also emblematic as was my response: searing anger. I was three years old and my family had lived about a year in the Navy housing at Pearl Harbor. I recall sitting on the wooden floor in the second bedroom of our concrete and mortar row unit, which my father used as a study. A pink plastic rolling doll with its clownish smile was placed in front of me for my amusement, and it would roll forward and back, the sound of the jingling bell inside taunting me. The smiling face on the doll was oblivious to my need to hug it and the bell only rang more insistently as I batted it back and forth. I was angry because this cold plastic toy with its stupid expression remained fixed and unmoved by my entreaties. As I look back years later to those times when I've had a similar emotional reaction, found my anger rising, it was usually in response to "plastic" or inflexible people whom I'm unable to influence by logic, or unable to move with an emotional appeal.

Both sides of my family in the Philippines were what we would call today lower-middle-class, not impoverished but certainly not from the affluent class either, although my mother's family did put her through school in Manila where she became a dentist. Joining the U.S. Navy as a young man was certainly a step up for my father, even if the Filipino stewards, especially on shipboard deployment, were like glorified houseboys. Looking back at our family pictures, I cherish a black and white snapshot of my maternal grandmother, her black hair pulled

My maternal grandmother, Placida Jingco, stands proudly behind her grandchildren, from left to right: Tessie, myself (age two), Remy, and Jose Jr. Taken in 1957 before I left the Philippines for the United States with my parents.

(FAMILY PHOTO)

back into a bun, standing in front of a neighbor's thatched hut, arms lovingly enfolding her four grandchildren: three little girls and one boy. I'm in the middle, a little disheveled, my hair unruly. You could see the character and resolve in my grandmother's face; she endured with dignity whatever the circumstances. I see a lot of myself in her; that steady nature speaks to me, has helped to assuage my anger at times over the injustice in the world.

My life in color photographs, certainly symbolic, began in Hawaii: lush green plants, reddish brown earth, and pink glistening sand. The little waif with the grimy countenance has been transformed into a grinning, plump imp dressed in pink; I'm standing in front of a birthday cake with five candles, surrounded by four Caucasian girls close to my age. We appeared different in the slant of the eyes, the color of the hair, richness in skin color, and the propensity to freckle. I resembled a China doll at that time and spoke two languages: my parents' Pampanga dialect and my adopted English learned from the neighborhood kids and Nimitz Elementary School, but mostly from Saturday morning television cartoons.

When my family moved to Hawaii, I could only speak the Filipino dialect of my parents' province of Pampanga. I quickly picked up English; my early life in America was a series of attempts to assimilate with the children in my neighborhood and school. That was difficult when my name, face, and speech did not fit the American stereotype. I made a conscious decision in childhood to speak English exclusively, and to speak it distinctly and without a trace of an accent. I rejected my parents' dialect, and sadly their culture, when I witnessed them being treated as second-class citizens because they were not fluent in English. I resolved at a young age that if I were to succeed, I had to speak English better than any of my Anglo classmates.

As the child of a Navy steward, I knew my place—we were the military servant class. Whenever we would visit my father at the admiral's quarters, we would always enter through the kitchen. We were taught by our parents that it was our place: to go through the back door into the kitchen. Growing up with this tenet, the mantra implanted subconsciously in my mind was: *You are not good enough.* That mantra became the secret of my success in life, the rallying cry that would evoke my anger, my inner rage to prove myself. It would ultimately fuel the strength needed to overcome the doubters and all who would underestimate me, in school and in my military career.

At school my chosen arena of excellence was the classroom. I excelled in academics in elementary school and later graduated valedictorian of my high school class in San Diego. At Nimitz Elementary in Honolulu, I was quiet, obedient, and smart—the teacher's pet. Another symbolic event in my childhood was when I was selected to be a junior police officer, the elite group of students who raised the flag every morning, led the Pledge of Allegiance, and guarded the crosswalks. This didn't start out well, but I recovered and went on to become captain—the Navy rank I would later hold through most of my White House years. On my first day as a patrolman, I was assigned to hold the stop sign at a crosswalk. I heard the whistle from the lieutenant watching the traffic and signaling me to lower the stop sign in front of this crosswalk. As I was lowering the pole, a car sped by, almost striking a child about to cross the street. Although the child was unharmed, the incident shook me. If the car had hit the

Left: Giving the valedictory commencement speech at Mar Vista High School, Imperial Beach, in 1973. (MARIANO NARCISO) *Right: College graduation photo from the University of California, San Diego, in June 1977.* (FAMILY PHOTO)

little girl, there was nothing I could have done to help her. I think I resolved at some level never to be in a position of helplessness again.

I watched my parents suffer in timid helplessness many times; once, when my mother was unable in her broken English to correct a misdiagnosis, it almost cost my baby sister her life. I was six years old at the time and my little sister was a toddler. She had been sequestered in a playpen in the living room when a visiting aunt liberated her. My sister wandered unsupervised into the backyard where my father was applying liquid wax to his car. The phone rang, and he placed the metal container on the ground and ran into the house to take the call. My baby sister spotted the shiny container and proceeded to drink its contents. When I returned from the playground a few minutes later, I found her lying unconscious on the ground. I ran to get my parents, who piled the whole family into the car, and my father drove frantically to Tripler Army Hospital.

At the hospital, I sat at the foot of the exam table while the Army physician attempted to get the incident history from my mother. My father, feeling guilty about the mishap, sat in the waiting room with my brother. As my mother tried to convey what had happened, my sister had a grand mal seizure on the table. The doctor, unable to clearly understand her, told the nurse that my sister had epilepsy. At the age of six, I was twenty years shy of my medical degree so I didn't know about epilepsy, but I knew the doctor hadn't been told everything. I stood up and started pulling at my mother's skirt, yelling "Tell him about the poison!" This stopped the doctor, who turned back to us, and my mother confirmed that my sister had drunk cleaning solvent and didn't have epilepsy. My sister was admitted to the hospital where her stomach was pumped. She stayed for three days and survived to grow up healthy and feisty. But I found my voice that day, encouraged by the praise heaped on me afterward by my parents to speak my opinion no matter what my "place," and to help others whose voices are misunderstood or ignored.

But, by far, the single most striking impression from my childhood was spending Saturdays or Sundays in the admiral's kitchen. There was always something magical about these kitchens. The smell of food cooking, the chatter of the Tagalog dialect as my father and his fellow stewards conversed and joked with each other while preparing the meals for the admiral and his family. This was my introduction to the camaraderie of military life, of people working together for a single goal, even if it was just preparing dinner. One Christmas morning when my father had duty in the admiral's house, my mother and I visited him. I remember my father lifting me up to peek through the glass window in the swinging kitchen door that led to the dining room. We couldn't venture past that door into the admiral's dining room and the remainder of the house. Our only view was through a tiny glass window, a small portal that offered a precious glimpse into another world: a world of status, privilege, and authority. This was a world totally alien to my parents and to me at that age. Peering through the portal, I would behold a beautiful dining room with a chandelier, elegant china set on the dark, polished dining table, and in the distance a large evergreen tree decorated (by the stewards) for the holidays. I delighted at this glimpse into the life of the admiral and his family, for they were like royalty to us, with their glamorous life filled with luxury as well as tragedy.

My father would tell countless stories of the admiral and his family. They were like mythical characters in a storybook. My father's favorite admiral, as mentioned earlier, was Vice Admiral Goodwin, who in retrospect was a father figure to him. The Goodwin family was picture-perfect: the dashing, well-decorated three-star admiral; his sophisti-cated wife, Eleanor; their bright and articulate daughter, Sydney; and their handsome young son, Hugh Jr., a Navy pilot. Their perfect life, however, was shattered one evening at dinnertime when my father took a phone call from Navy headquarters. Hugh Jr. had been killed when his plane collided with another plane during operations off an aircraft carrier at sea. The tragedy was ironic in that the other pilot killed was also the son of a Navy admiral who, like the vice admiral, had flown numerous missions unharmed in wartime. Both admirals lost their only sons on a routine mission in peacetime.

My father whispered the tragic news to the admiral at the dinner table. The admiral sobbed bitterly as he told his wife and daughter what had happened. The family bowed their heads and wept over their empty plates as their Filipino stewards stood by helplessly. This story taught me in childhood that the power and privilege associated with rank offered no immunity against sorrow and tragedy. I would later learn this lesson again as White House physician taking care of the first family.

2.

Although I knew my "place" as a steward's daughter, I also believed that the "place" I inherited was capable of honor and dignity. My fa-ther, whose family was extremely poor, was ambitious and re-sourceful. The Navy rewarded his ambition by promoting him in the enlisted rank until he achieved the highest position of master chief.

My father was proud to be a steward, proud to take care of the admiral and his family. He didn't consider his rank as an indicator of his value as a human being. Instead, he viewed his station in the Navy as merely his job, not a sign of his worth. That attitude was very important in forming my opinion of enlisted rank in the military. Years later as a naval officer, working closely with enlisted personnel in my department onboard ship, I assessed each individual based on his or her expertise and never considered rank as an indicator of anyone's worth as a human being. That was often not the case among my fellow officers in the wardroom.

My parents taught me that hard work was a virtue equal in value to humility. They believed that anything could be accomplished through hard work. But once you achieved your goal, then you needed to be humble about it. They also taught me to respect my elders and that it was an honor to take care of your extended family. My parents would send checks monthly to their parents in the Philippines, which were used to support grandparents as well as aunts and uncles going to college in Manila. What sustained my parents throughout their years of financial struggle was faith—faith that God would ultimately provide for them and their family.

The irony of my upbringing is that throughout my childhood, I never fit comfortably into the Filipino culture of my parents nor did I feel totally secure in the American culture. I spoke the Filipino language at home, but when I went to school, I was an American girl in behavior, thought, and speech. I straddled both worlds in my teenage years, but at times I found myself feeling ashamed of my Asian roots. When I reported to the White House in June 1992, I was a decorated Navy commander who was eager to assume the position of White House physician. Although my medical training and military experience were requisite for my new job, surprisingly my Filipino roots more than any other factor were the biggest contributor to my early success at the White House.

On my first day, my predecessor, Dr. Al Roberts, the Navy physician I was to replace in the White House Medical Unit, gave me this sage advice: *approach this job with a servant's mentality.* I knew this attitude all too well, having had it ingrained in me during my upbringing. But I was not a servant; I was a naval officer and a physician who had graduated from an American medical school and was board-certified in my field. And above all, I had the gifts of courage and wit, which I had relied upon throughout my military career onboard ship, at the naval hospital, and in clinics. Many times I was the only professional woman in a particular department. I knew what it was like to stand out from the rest of the crowd. But I believed that when you stand out in gender and race, you need to be outstanding, for you represent more than just yourself.

During my first week at the White House, all eyes were on me as the "new doctor" in the house. I not only represented the U.S. Navy, but women physicians in general. The only other woman who had been a White House physician was Dr. Janet Travell, a civilian physiatrist and President Kennedy's personal physician. I had heard disparaging remarks about her by the male physicians in the medical unit. I was not surprised, since she had broken the traditional all-male physician's circle at the White House; she was not welcomed into the boys club and didn't care. I would follow her thirty years later and had prepared myself for intense scrutiny, testing, and possible rejection during these first few months. It was only then that I came to appreciate the wisdom of Dr. Lee's intimidating interview. If I could hold my own against Burt Lee, then I would be able to stand up to this kind of scrutiny as the new doctor in the medical unit.

What helped me to persevere in those first weeks at the White House were my "special" connections, but not to the mighty and powerful. Instead, it was my instant friendship with the people who took care of them: the housekeepers, cooks, ushers, and most of all, the military mess specialists who served as valets to the president. These were the members of the silent servant class at the White House; the people who every day attended to the leader of the free world in his private quarters, who woke him, fed him, prepared his clothes, packed his bags, and traveled with him. These were my influential White

House connections. My childhood spent watching my father take care of the admiral boomeranged back to me as a White House physician taking care of the commander in chief. History repeated itself in my family; this time it was on a higher level and only in America.

My introduction to Washington and the White House was also a great adventure. I would drive to work each morning on the George Washington Parkway along the Potomac, tree-lined with breathtaking views of the monuments. As I crossed over the Arlington Memorial Bridge with its golden statues, I solemnly passed the Lincoln Memorial and then the Vietnam Veterans Memorial. In a few minutes, I would be on Constitution Avenue, turning onto 15th Street to enter Pennsylvania Avenue. I was lucky to have a parking spot across the street from the White House complex. I entered the compound through the OEOB, Old Executive Office Building, waving my blue security badge to the uniformed guard at the gate. I no longer wore the usual khaki Navy uniform. Instead, the uniform of the day was now a civilian business suit, high heels, subdued makeup, and tasteful jewelry. The new work uniform satisfied my penchant for fashion. Later, I was given the sobering assessment that those in military uniforms were more likely targets on presidential road trips.

My routine was to arrive at the Medical Unit Clinic in the OEOB early in the morning to change into my running outfit and shoes. I would run three to five miles along the Mall across the street from the White House. As I ran, I took in the incredible picture-perfect views of the Washington Monument and Lincoln Memorial. This allowed me time alone to assess and adjust to my family's new life in D.C.

My husband, Richard, on sabbatical from his law firm in San Diego, was teaching evening classes at George Washington University Law School. During the day, Richard was a stay-at-home dad taking care of our young sons, driving them to and from their Montessori school in Alexandria where we were renting a modest townhouse. His days were full taking care of the children, preparing for his evening classes, and running our household. I realized years later how lonely his life had become. He no longer enjoyed the camaraderie of his law firm associates, or the frequent visits with his mother and siblings in San Diego. And with my long hours and frequent travel away from home, Richard had become a virtual White House widower.

We had rented out our house in San Diego, expecting to return in two years after my tour was completed. Although we missed our families and friends, we were resolved to enjoy life on the East Coast. Our sons looked forward to the change of seasons and especially to some snow days off from school.

One day, during my third week at the White House, I had finished my morning run and had showered and changed in the women's locker room in the basement of the OEOB. I arrived in the Medical Unit Clinic on the first floor, where I was assisted by a military nurse and Navy independent duty corpsman in seeing a variety of civilian and military patients working at the White House compound for ailments ranging from skin rash to chest pain. The patients moved quickly through our clinic with minimal waiting time. The nurse, corpsman, and I were taking a break in the now empty waiting room, when our lively conversation was broken by a phone call from Dr. Lee in the epicenter located just across the street. The nurse answered the phone and handed it to me.

"Connie, I've got a unit commander meeting at ten," Dr. Lee said, and, in his devil-may-care tone, added. "I'm too busy to stay for the whole meeting, and I want you to cover for me."

I looked at my watch. It was already 10:08. "I'm on my way, sir," I said and quickly headed over to the East Wing. When I got there, Shirley Kelly, the longtime medical unit admin assistant, escorted me to the bomb shelter and then into the Presidential Emergency Operations Center, the PEOC, where the meeting of the unit commanders of the White House was in full swing.

As I entered through the vaulted door, I heard raucous male laughter, reminiscent of a shipboard wardroom. A Supply Corps officer greeted me at the door and then introduced me to John Gaughan, who was the civilian head of the White House Military Office. As I was led to Dr. Lee's empty seat, Gaughan introduced me to the group of twenty unit commanders, mostly senior military officers. He then asked each of them to introduce themselves. During my three weeks of orientation, I had already met half of the group, each with an impressive background and military bearing. And they were also very friendly and highly spirited. There were only two other women in the room: one was an Army major and the security officer, and the other was a young Navy lieutenant junior grade in charge of the White House television unit. Both appeared a little uncomfortable amidst all this male camaraderie. For me, it felt like being on my old Navy tender at a wardroom meeting of department heads. Instead, these participants were senior civilian officials, full-bird colonels, Navy captains, and the pilots of Air Force One and Marine One.

During the introductions, one of the unit commanders said to me, "You remember me? I'm the one who showed you my chest in the clinic." The whole room erupted in laughter.

I responded without missing a beat: "I'm not sure; so many men try to show me their chests at the clinic." That got an even bigger laugh from the men while the two women junior officers silently blushed.

After the introductions, we watched a video on the closed circuit TV about security. As the video concluded, Dr. Lee entered the vaulted room. Upon seeing him, I stood up to relinquish his seat, and he motioned for me to sit down. He came over and whispered into my ear, "I want you to stay and watch a high-level meeting about low-level things." He then winked and strolled out of the room; no one commented about his brief appearance.

After Dr. Lee left, the room became quiet, awaiting the arrival of Tim McBride, the assistant to the president and the senior civilian in charge of the White House Military Office. I was expecting a gruff, mature politician, but was surprised when the roomful of officers stood up for a tall, blond, all-American hunk. An officer beside me, noting my surprise, whispered, "They say McBride started in politics at age twenty."

McBride made a few comments about working as a team and ensuring good communications. I had heard this speech throughout my military career; it was the generic top dog pep talk. Now I was hearing it from a senior aide to the president. I was a little disappointed. During the brief break, when coffee and pastries were served by a Filipino mess specialist who made fleeting eye contact with me, McBride came over and introduced himself. He mentioned that he had spotted me on the South Lawn during the arrival of Russian president Boris Yeltsin the previous week. "I noticed you had brought the defibrillator," he said in jest, apparently referring to Yeltsin's heart condition.

Actually, the nurse was holding it, but I just played along. "Why, do you have a broken heart?" He smiled, a glorious smile, and I could feel the heat of this man's charisma. I would've voted for him in a heartbeat, except I was a closet Democrat in a Republican White House.

After the break, McBride departed with all the military officers standing at attention as he left the room. We then continued with the three-hour meeting. I found the group to be interesting. The political appointees were smooth, highly educated, and cultured—elitist in dress and manner, with embroidered dress shirts. The worker bees were thirty-year career Army men from the South. Navy Captain Jay Yakeley, soon to be a one-star rear admiral, was the senior military officer. He was a "down South homeboy," who spoke more candidly when the civilian boss had left the room. "I'd rather be dead than look bad," Captain Yakeley drawled to the group, referring to looking good for the press. "Remember, when you wrestle with a pig, you both get mud on yourselves, but the pig has a good time." Eloquent words from the military boss at the White House.

Other topics discussed at this high-level meeting were the ongoing Tailhook investigation and the president's upcoming horseshoe tournament. The secretary of the Navy had just turned this investigation of sexual harassment at the Tailhook Convention over to the Defense Department's inspector general, which didn't bode well for the Navy. Possibly due to the presence of military women at the meeting, none of the male officers expressed an untoward opinion about Tailhook. Although I was the senior-ranking military woman in the White House Military Office, no one sought my opinion nor did I offer it. It was with some relief that the topic switched to the horseshoe tournament that was scheduled for that afternoon. High-level meeting about low-level topics—Dr. Lee was right. Years later, when I would view the television drama of the Situation Room depicted in the *West Wing*'s version of the White House, I would remember my first unit commander meeting as well as many other "high-level" meetings I attended over my nine years. I developed a growing cynicism about leadership and organizations sitting at meetings considered by some to be at the pinnacle of the military and government hierarchy. Much of what I observed was sheer performance, jockeying for position, stroking of the ego, and simply more fluff than stuff. I understood then why Burt Lee ditched the meeting and had me, the junior doctor in the medical unit, fill his seat. There were more important things to do than sit for three hours talking about a horseshoe tournament.

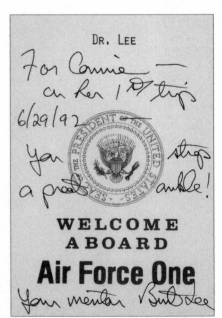

Welcome praise from Dr. Lee, who autographed his Air Force One seat card, congratulating me on completing my first Air Force One trip with George H. W. Bush. On this trip, I took care of a staffer who twisted her ankle and Burt writes: "You strap a great ankle!"

3.

After the meeting, I returned to the clinic, which was now quiet. I was starving, having missed lunch, and was pleased that no new patients were waiting for me so I could grab a quick bite. There was only one person in the waiting room. It was presidential valet Master Chief Joe Fama.

"Commander Mariano," he said, pronouncing my last name perfectly, "the master chiefs at the White House want to meet you."

"And I want to meet them!" I replied happily, relieved that I was done with the grueling unit commander meeting. "But may I pick up a sandwich from the cafeteria first? I missed lunch today."

"Doc," the master chief chided, prolonging the word into a chastising tone. "You know us Filipinos. When we invite you, that means we feed you. Please come with me."

Master Chief Fama escorted me into the bowels of the OEOB. This was my second trip to subterranean level in one day. This time, I was struck by the familiar aroma of sautéed garlic, onions, and shrimp. The smell reminded me of my mother's kitchen, but even more—it took me back to the admiral's kitchen where my father had worked. This time I was in the master chiefs' mess surrounded by ten Filipinos who were the senior-enlisted assigned to the White House. I looked around me at these men, all of whom could have passed as my relatives. We were all brown-skinned and black-haired with easy smiles and humble natures that camouflaged our fierce dedication and pride.

Master Chief Bayani Nelvis had prepared a meal of Filipino soul food consisting of the traditional noodle dish we call pancit, lumpia or Filipino eggrolls, and chicken adobo stew and steamed white rice. After a morning of sipping black coffee with upper-crust military officers in the PEOC, I was now eating home cooking with my Filipino brothers. Many of the master chiefs had been at the White House for the last six years. Master Chief Lito Bautista had served three previous presidents before President Bush. I learned that the master chiefs accompany the president when he travels, preparing his clothing, packing his bags, and arranging his meals, ensuring that his food is not contaminated or adulterated. They will even sample the food if there is any threat of poison or possible harm to the president.

When I asked one of the master chiefs to name his favorite president and first lady, he remarked, "The Bushes. They are so nice to us. They acknowledge us." Then he quietly added, "We were not very happy with the Reagans." He chose not to elaborate. It is not the Filipino way to whine or to criticize the people they serve. Just do your job and be quiet. I learned more about service to your country that afternoon sitting with the presidential valet master chiefs than I did attending my high-level meeting about horseshoe tournaments.

"Ma'am, how come you're not stuck-up like some of the other officers?" one of the master chiefs candidly asked an hour into my visit with them.

"Master Chief, it's because I know where I came from. My roots are the same as yours. My father was a master chief steward like you," I confessed to these men, who looked like my uncles from the Philippines. "We're all here to do the same job. And that is to take care of the president."

It was during that simple home-cooked meal that the president's valets pledged to look out for me. I, in turn, promised to be a good student and to learn from them, dubbing them my "godfathers." I also told them if they ever became ill, I would take care of them and be their doctor as well.

So on that summer afternoon in 1992, while Washington groaned in the sweltering heat, I savored the warmth of kinship and kindness in the chiefs' mess of the Old Executive Office Building. Little did the president know that a special alliance was being forged between his valets and his new doctor—between his kitchen and medicine "cabinets"—one that would elevate the care of both.

FOUR

The President Will See You Now

1.

"Doc, we have a situation," said the Navy military aide, listening to his earphone. I looked up expecting to spot enemy aircraft overhead. The aide turned to me and barked, "The president needs a Band-Aid!" as if he were still on the bridge of a destroyer in the Indian Ocean. Instead, we were sitting side by side, avoiding conversation, in a golf cart on the fifth green at Holly Hills golf course in Frederick, Maryland. President George H. W. Bush had just putted and was now examining his heel. It was July but the weather was unseasonably cool and rainy. We had taken Marine One from the South Lawn this morning, a day before the Fourth of July weekend.

This was my first golf duty covering the president and I was nervous. I had been at the White House a month, and the only advice I had received for golf duty from the other doctors was to stay out of the path of the president's golf ball. I did not feel fully prepared to follow the president around while he played a round of golf. I didn't even know what the game was about. Unlike many of my fellow physicians,

I never had the time or inclination to learn the sport. I knew what to do medically if the president had an emergency, but felt uneasy about the proper social protocol.

Although I felt out of place, I looked like I was part of the president's entourage. I wore a discreet dark blue jacket with the WHMU hard pin on the collar, long-sleeved light blue blouse, and dark slacks. I was supposed to blend in with the security detail of tall, beefy Secret Service agents who donned blue jackets, tan Dockers, and earpieces. I was definitely the runt of the lot. They likewise were trying to look and act naturally, as if this were a fraternity outing at the country club, shadowing the president on this OTR—"off the record"—presidential movement. There were about ten golf carts in the president's entourage. It was difficult to be inconspicuous when you traveled with such a large posse.

This was the first of many firsts for me as the new White House physician. And everyone at the White House knew it. I was the rookie doctor and all eyes were on me as I negotiated the White House rites of passage: the first meeting with the president, the first motorcade, the first in-town event, the first off-the-record event, and now the first golf event. The military aide who sat beside me was a seasoned veteran of two years at the White House, and at the end of his tour would be returning to sea where he belonged. He had no intention of sharing any words of wisdom and experience with me at this point. Instead, he was expecting me to earn my stripes, as he no doubt had before me.

As I sat watching President Bush on the green, I reflected on my first meeting with him just a few weeks earlier. On the evening of my second day at the White House, my predecessor, Al Roberts, called me at home around dinnertime. I was startled to hear the "drop line" phone ring. The White House Communications Agency had installed a phone line in my house, a requirement for all White House doctors. The drop phone had a distinctive, gnawing ring. The sound sent my heart pounding with simultaneous excitement and dread. My family knew when that phone rang, I would abandon whatever I was doing. It became a family joke that whenever the drop line would ring, I would literally jump out of my seat and grab the phone, fearing that one of my patients had dropped dead.

"Your presence is requested tomorrow at 0645 in Dr. Lee's office in the residence," Al announced with suppressed vicarious glee. "Something bad?" I asked, automatically assuming the worst as I clung to every word, wondering if our conversation was being bugged.

"One of your patients wants to meet you. Dr. Lee will do the intro. Be there or be square." Click, dial tone, and panic on my part. I almost expected Al to give me a code word to authenticate the covert nature of his cryptic message.

The next morning, I took the Metro to the White House and reported for duty at 0630. I stood in Dr. Lee's office waiting to find out who my patient would be; I assumed it was the first patient himself. The nurse on duty that morning was Navy Lieutenant Mary Jackson, who noted my tense, quiet behavior. She tried to reassure me saying, "You know, President Bush asked about you a few weeks ago, when he knew you were going to report for duty."

Instead of reassuring me, her words made me slightly more anxious. "He asked about me?" I was surprised. Surely the man had a lot on his mind, such as Iraq, Libya, and his upcoming reelection campaign. "What did he want to know, Mary?" I prodded gently, trying not to appear overly anxious. "My credentials? Where I'd gone to medical school? Previous military assignments?"

Mary chuckled, almost snorting when she said "Heck no! He just wanted to know if you were athletic and if you had a sense of humor." I sensed then, even before meeting him, that President Bush was a wise man. I would learn after my nine years at the White House that physical endurance and the ability to laugh were essential to survival.

"Is this your first time meeting the president?" The query came from a cheerful Navy captain, Dr. David Corbett, who was in the adjoining examination room. Dave was the head of dermatology at Bethesda Naval Hospital and had been summoned that morning to see the first patient. Cool, calm, and confident, Dr. Corbett had an easygoing nature. I instantly liked him and felt more relaxed.

My mischievous sense of humor also returned. "Yes, this is my first time. I hope he'll be gentle." Both Mary and Dave laughed and exchanged looks. I could hear them thinking, "Yes, she's one of us."

"Oh, everyone remembers the first time they . . . meet the president!" Dave retorted.

Dr. Lee arrived a few minutes later. He greeted Mary, nodded at Dr. Corbett, and ignored me as he placed his briefcase on his desk.

Then, precisely at 7:00 A.M., we heard the three bells that signaled the presidential elevator moving from the private residence to the ground floor. The announcement came over the Secret Service frequency, "Timberwolf on the ground floor." This was the Secret Service code name for President Bush. I could now hear the sound of dogs barking in the hallway. Then I heard the sharp whistle of their master, rising above the dogs' yelps.

In a few seconds, the president entered Dr. Lee's office, took off his coat as he walked in, and handed it to his personal aide, a handsome young man who shadowed him silently. George Bush was six foot three, larger than life, with brilliant, clear eyes. He was the epitome of dignity even as he started disrobing. Dr. Lee greeted the president and escorted him into the exam room, where Dave, Mary, and I stood at attention.

President Bush surveyed the faces in the private exam room. All were familiar to him except for mine. Handing his shirt to his aide, the president muttered to Dr. Lee, "Burt, what a way to meet your new doctor. Taking off my clothes like this! Is she married?" he asked, smiling broadly and pointing to me. I stood silent, waiting to be introduced formally.

"Don't worry, she's married," Burt snapped back at the president, surprising me in the abrupt manner in which he spoke to the chief executive. "Just treat her like another technician," Burt told the president. He then formally introduced me to the president, who extended his hand.

"I've heard a lot of good things about you, Doctor." The president spoke softly as he sat down on the exam table. As the president spoke, Dave Corbett went into action, examining the skin on the president's back and then rapidly applying liquid nitrogen to several skin lesions he had identified.

"Thank you, sir. It is an honor to meet you," I responded as I shook the president's hand. I was simultaneously flattered by the president's compliment and deflated by Dr. Lee's comment about treating me like a technician.

The president winced slightly from the application of the cold solution onto his skin. "Take it easy back there, Doc," the president complained.

Dave Corbett laughed softly. "Sorry, sir. This may smart a little bit, but it will take care of the early skin cancers on your back."

After Dave had finished his treatment, President Bush stood up and his personal aide instinctively handed him his shirt. As he buttoned the long-sleeved shirt, the president wandered into Dr. Lee's adjoining office, examining the framed photos on the wall. He called to me, "Connie, have you met General Scowcroft yet?" President Bush was admiring a photo that featured his national security advisor, Brent Scowcroft. "He's a wonderful fellow."

I went to the president's side. "No sir. I look forward to it." Then I recalled how much the president loved his dogs. "But I would like to meet Millie and Ranger."

The leader of the free world perked up. "Oh! They're right outside in the hallway. They hate coming into this office, which is where the veterinarian draws their blood and gives them shots. They don't have a good feeling about it. I don't blame them."

Sitting in the golf cart, I smiled as I recalled that first meeting with President Bush and his dogs. The fastest way to the president's heart was through his dogs I learned early on.

"Band-Aid, Doc!" the Navy commander nudged me, snapping me out of my reverie. He then clicked his radio and spoke to the agent who had radioed in the "distress call."

What is it with this administration and Band-Aids? I wondered, as I recalled my interview nine months earlier with Burt Lee, who had sported a tan Band-Aid across his forehead. Once again, this most innocuous of first-aid basics was going to determine my fate as White House physician. I opened the newly packed medical bag that sat between me and the military aide. The blue canvas satchel that served as my doctor's bag was planted beside the black leather case that carried the nuclear football. One of my first assignments in the White House Medical Unit was to stock and pack my personal medical bag, which I would carry with me on presidential movements such as today's.

There was no special inventory or standardized list of items for what to carry in the bag, as I was to learn—a year later I created a standard list for the medical unit. I followed traditional White House doctor folklore by packing those items I would need for any worst-case scenario, such as a gunshot wound, cardiac arrest, or chemical or biological attack. I hadn't anticipated that I would be treating presidential boo-boos.

I rummaged through my bag for a Band-Aid. I found the Bristojets of cardiac medications, pocket mask, laryngoscope, tongue blades, epinephrine, and bretylium. Band-Aid? I started to sweat as I dug deeper into the abyss of my medical bag, only to turn up some high-tech medical device or cardiac medication. I violated the credo I was later to drum into my staff—"Never let them see you sweat." The mil aide looked askance at me, no doubt wondering about this new doc.

"Doc's locating a Band-Aid now," he murmured nonchalantly into his radio, demonstrating his own coolheaded control, to inform the agent standing beside President Bush on the green and looking back at us impatiently.

I glanced up to see President Bush strolling over to our golf cart. My heart started to race, and I frantically started to toss items onto the seat of the golf cart as the mil aide looked on in amusement. This was the end of me. My first golf outing with the first patient, and I was going to fail him miserably for lack of a simple Band-Aid.

Running with President Bush in Louisville, Kentucky, with his Secret Service detail, military aide, and nurse Deb Beatty in 1992.
(WHITE HOUSE PHOTO)

Then suddenly something caught my eye at the very bottom of the bag. A single, crumpled Band-Aid that may have been left by the previous owner of the bag, or in my case most likely placed there by divine intervention. At that moment, I didn't care where it came from. I was just happy and grateful to find it.

As I pulled out the Band-Aid, President Bush stepped over to our golf cart, planted his foot on the fender, and pulled down his sock. I jumped from the seat with the Band-Aid in hand and went to my first patient's side. He pointed to the abrasion on his heel from the chafing from his new golf shoe. I pulled off the adhesive and placed the dressing over the wound, patting it gently. The president smiled, blue eyes twinkling, and patted me on the back. "Thanks, Doc. Let's hope this is the worst it gets."

I went back to my seat on the cart where the military aide sat grinning. "Welcome to the White House, Doc. Where little things are big things," he said, finally offering helpful advice from someone who had been in the White House trenches two years longer than I.

"Roger that, Commander," I said, as I smiled back at him. This was the only conversation I would have with him; his two-year tour of duty was soon up. But what he said would stay with me for the rest of my days at the White House.

2.

The black stretch limousine made its way slowly up the South Lawn driveway to the sound of an anxious drumroll in the distance. American and Russian flags mounted on the front sides of the armored vehicle flapped sluggishly in the sticky breeze. Young servicemen from the United States Army, Navy, Air Force, and Coast Guard lined the White House driveway, standing at attention and holding poles carrying the individual flags of the fifty states. The president's Marine Corps Band in full military regalia was planted on the South Lawn, but the only sound emanating from that celebrated assembly of musicians was the solo trilling of the snare drum.

I stood under the sparse shade of the magnolia outside the window of Dr. Lee's office, facing the South Lawn. I was observing the state arrival of Russian president Boris Yeltsin. It was June and the air was stifling. Mary Ann Chandler, the Navy corpsman, and Gary Dunham, the Air Force physician assistant, were assigned by Dr. Lee to help me cover the state arrival that morning. Both had been in the White House Medical Unit two years longer than I and were very experienced with the contingencies of such events, according to Dr. Lee. In fact, both Gary and Mary Ann were involved in my orientation process. They were vital to teaching me the White House ropes. We stood together, staying out of camera view. Our respective black medical bags were perched at our feet, resembling obedient pets at the heels of their masters. We were all wired, which meant we had our earpieces in place, listening intently to the Secret Service radio frequency. I was still trying to adjust to having the earpiece in my right ear canal almost all day. I wondered if I would ultimately lose some hearing as a result, and if my ability to detect faint cardiac murmurs with the stethoscope would be lost forever as a result of my service to my country.

I looked over at President Bush, who stood with Mrs. Bush under the green awning that faced the driveway. The president looked tired and was slightly pale as he stood dressed in his designer suit in the morning sun and Washington humidity. He must be perspiring under that suit, I imagined, as I stood perspiring in my pantsuit. The two-pound Secret Service radio was clipped to my belt, the antenna annoyingly poking my back ribs. *At least he doesn't have to wear a radio,* I thought. But I wondered if Secret Service had asked the president to wear his Kevlar vest for this outdoor event.

A crowd of more than two hundred was assembled on the South Lawn. These individuals were not just participants in a historic event. They were all potential patients for me. In addition to the president and first lady, the Russian president and his wife, my patient population today included Vice President and Mrs. Dan Quayle, ten members of Congress, the American and Russian ambassadors, the Joint Chiefs of Staff, invited guests, and the White House press corps as well as the whole Russian entourage and delegation.

The limo stopped at the entrance of the Diplomatic Reception Room in front of President and Mrs. Bush. An Army officer in full dress uniform marched smartly to the rear passenger's door as the drum-roll continued. The guard placed his white-gloved hand on the car door, preparing to open it. There was a hesitation. The military guard couldn't open the door. I held my breath as the drum droned on while the crowd on the South Lawn watched and the cameras of all the major news networks videotaped. I guessed that the Army officer had forgotten about the special latch on the door handle, a detail I had just learned in my first week of orientation training with the Secret Service. The drumroll continued for an uncomfortable few seconds longer, until a faintly audible sigh of relief came from the crowd as the guard found the latch and opened the door. The drumbeat stopped on the cue.

Boris Yeltsin emerged from the vehicle first, a shock of thick silver hair atop a bearlike skull with a beaming smile under a bulbous nose. He was round, with a protuberant abdomen that was girded by a dignified, dark business suit. His first appearance triggered my initial clinical impression that the man enjoyed his vodka. Mrs. Yeltsin, diminutive in comparison to her larger-than-life husband, was assisted from the limo by the Army officer.

President and Mrs. Bush greeted President and Mrs. Yeltsin with polite smiles and handshakes. The Russian and American interpreters took their places beside the presidents and began simultaneous translation, whispering to each leader while the other leader spoke. The presidents were then led to a stage that had been set on the South Lawn, where the ceremony was to begin, commencing with the playing of the national anthems of Russia and the United States.

I surveyed the crowd on the South Lawn. Most of the people were middle-aged and elderly. My patients were no longer the young, active-duty sailors of my earlier years as a ship's doctor. The population that I faced now was more consistent with my internal medicine geriatrics practice I had just left in San Diego. But instead of having the luxury of treating these patients in the privacy and security of a major teaching hospital, I would be attending to them as a first responder in the field. After stabilizing my patients, I would evacuate them to the nearest medical facility. This was a familiar practice for me, having studied triage and battlefield medicine at the military medical school. As a ship's doctor, I faced many situations in which my corpsmen and I would perform first-aid on a patient and then prepare the person for evacuation to an aircraft carrier at sea or medical center on land. This is why military doctors were best suited for the job of White House doctors, I thought. Military medicine demands that its doctors treat patients in the field with limited resources, stabilize them, and then evacuate them to definitive care facilities. White House medicine was like practicing battlefield medicine. This time my battlefield was the White House lawn, my soldiers were dignitaries and VIPs and heads of state, and my assistants were a hospital corpsman and physician assistant.

The Marine Corps Band then played "Ruffles and Flourishes" followed by "Hail to the Chief." I would hear this refrain hundreds of times in my nine years taking care of the commander in chief. And every time I would hear "Ruffles and Flourishes," my memory would bring me back to November 1963. My father was stationed at the Navy Yard in Washington, D.C. His cousin Marciano Mariano was a Navy steward assigned to the White House. Marciano was one of President Kennedy's valets and had told us many stories about the president. I will always remember waking up on a cold November morning, not having to go to school because of the president's funeral. I wandered into the living room hoping to watch cartoons. The networks were all televising the president's state funeral. My mother sat in front of the television, weeping as the president's casket was being brought into the Capitol Rotunda. "He was so young," my mother lamented. I wanted to comfort my mother, and went over to put my arms around her. She was inconsolable. The television showed the late president's two small children. I felt sorry for them; they had to be sad in front of so many people that day.

Then the sound of a cannon blast shattered my memories of John Kennedy's funeral procession. "A twenty-one-gun salute," whispered the husky voice over the Secret Service radio, as though the agent knew that I had been startled by the sound. Standing beside me, Gary covered his ears while a handful of people in the crowd jumped with the first sound of the cannon fire. Each blast from the cannon, being fired off of the Ellipse half a block away, brought forth a reverberation that shook the air. The sound was almost too painful to bear. And with each boom, I prayed that the only time I would ever hear such gunfire would be at these ceremonies, and never in a situation in which my patient would be harmed.

My rapid pulse slowed slightly after the twenty-one-gun salute had concluded. I glanced at the program for the ceremony. Admiring the fine white stationery with the presidential seal embossed on the cover, I ran my fingers across the engraved royal blue cursive print that outlined the sequence of events. But what wasn't on the schedule were the people who started to pass out one by one: what I would later name as ceremonial "casualties."

A man's deep voice came over the Secret Service channel, faintly audible over the Marine Corps Band's rendition of the Russian

national anthem. "Man down, driveway near the guard post." I turned
and looked past the guard post along the driveway in front of the Oval
Office. One of the sailors who had stood at attention had passed out.
Gary had spotted the man and glanced back at me as he started to walk
briskly in the sailor's direction. Mary Ann and I followed Gary, without saying a word, walking quickly and trying to stay out of camera
view. As the American national anthem played, and everyone on the
South Lawn stood still, the three of us moved swiftly to the side of the
fallen flag holder. The sailor, dressed in his crisp, white Cracker Jack
uniform, was sitting on the asphalt driveway and sweating profusely
when we arrived at his side. Gary took the pole from the man's grip,
preventing the flag from touching the ground. Mary Ann and I loos-
ened his collar.

"Are you okay?" I asked the young sailor, who looked like he was
all of eighteen years old.

"I think I locked my knees, ma'am," he confessed, looking down
at his feet. "Master Chief told me not to do that . . . I guess I forgot."

"We need to cool you off and give you something to drink," I told
him as I felt his pulse, which was rapid and faint. Mary Ann pulled out
a blood pressure cuff from her medical bag and took the sailor's blood
pressure. A UD officer came over and handed me a bottle of water.
The sailor took a few sips; we next moved him into the air-conditioned
guard post a few feet from where he lay on the driveway.

Then over our radios came that husky voice again. "Doc, there may
be another one down by the putting green." Beside the president's putting green on the South Lawn, several hundred feet from the crowd,
was an elderly, obese gentleman walking slowly toward a bench. I
glanced down at Mary Ann, who was tending to the sailor; I then
looked to Gary, who nodded at me as he grabbed his medical bag and
headed in the man's direction. With the physician assistant and corpsman each taking care of a ceremonial casualty, I was the only medical
staff left to respond to a medical emergency involving the president.

My eyes darted back to the president and first lady standing on the
stage, hands over their hearts, as the American national anthem con-

cluded. I instinctively moved closer to the area behind the stage, to the route the Secret Service would bring the president should he become ill or injured. No one had told me this is where I was to stand, except maybe my military training. You are taught to anticipate and plan for contingencies. *But stay out of the kill zone,* I told myself. The "kill zone" was the term I had heard used by Secret Service in describing the space around the president where an innocent bystander could be killed by a stray bullet or bomb. The kill zone was where James Brady stood when he was struck by a bullet meant for President Ronald Reagan. It was important for medical personnel to stay clear of it. I looked at where the president stood and analyzed where his agents were positioned. *You can't treat the president if you're dead*, I reminded myself.

Two more calls for assistance came over the radio. An elderly woman dressed in her Sunday finery was slumped in a chair, fanning herself with the souvenir program. Mary Ann had finished treating the sailor, who was now sitting in the guard shack, finishing off his third bottle of cold water. As the call for assistance came through, Mary Ann moved toward the elderly woman, who sat six rows from the stage. Gary had evaluated the obese gentleman on the bench beside the putting green. Because the man had complained of some nausea and mild chest discomfort, Gary radioed in his condition, recommending that we send him to the George Washington Hospital emergency room. I agreed. The man had refused treatment, telling Gary he wanted to watch the event and that he would see his private doctor later. I told Gary to stay with the man and try to convince him that he needed urgent care. The man had refused oxygen as well as nitroglycerin. He did accept cold bottled water and a cool cloth to wipe his face.

As we treated our ceremonial casualties, the state arrival continued as scripted with both presidents inspecting the troops on the South Lawn, followed by speeches by the two leaders. Gary, Mary Ann, and I stayed out of camera shot and moved smoothly and swiftly without drawing any unnecessary attention. At the same time, we kept apprised of the president's location on the South Lawn in case we had to rush to his side.

Fortunately, we did not need to render care to the president. He survived the state arrival and escorted President Yeltsin and his entourage into the White House through the Diplomatic Reception Room. I then proceeded to Dr. Lee's office through the Palm Room, in the opposite direction of the entourage. Gary had checked on the elderly man, who was doing well despite our initial concern over his condition. His wife had promised to take him to his doctor that morning. Mary Ann waited on the South Lawn until all the guests had departed. Once they had left the event, Mary Ann returned to the clinic in the Old Executive Office Building. In this outpatient setting, the other White House Medical Unit staff was seeing their routine run of patients while the state arrival was in progress.

I arrived at Dr. Lee's office, perspiring from the morning's activities. Dr. Lee was sitting at his desk, doing paperwork. He glanced up at me as I stood in the doorway.

"Well, how did it go?" he asked, looking over his reading glasses.

"The president did fine. We had four people with heat-related distress, but they did okay. Overall, it was an uneventful event."

Dr. Lee smirked. "Uneventful event?" he repeated after me, almost mockingly. "That's your job, Doctor. To make sure that every event goes without a medical incident." He looked down at his papers and resumed reading.

"I'll do my best, Dr. Lee," I promised. "I'll do my best." I turned away, feeling chastised and then annoyed by Burt's dismissive tone. I knew that I shouldn't expect any praise from this man. He would not be like my previous commanding officers and mentors who openly encouraged and supported me. But despite Burt's response, I was exhilarated by the morning's tour of duty on the South Lawn. I was no longer stuck in a clinic seeing a patient every fifteen minutes or spending an hour on a complicated geriatrics patient with a grocery list of medications, trying to tune them up. Unlike many of my colleagues, I was happy to practice medicine outside the safety net of a major teaching hospital. I felt more alive treating patients in the field, be it the

White House South Lawn or on the streets of a foreign capital. These were now my trenches.

It brought back fond memories of being a ship's doctor on the high seas, taking care of the crew while on deployment, where the nearest hospital was a seven-day sail away. The predictable routine of clinic and hospital rounds in San Diego had stifled me. In my first few weeks at the White House, I got a taste of the unpredictable, unexpected, and the unusual in this medical venue. The excitement of practicing medicine in a high-stakes setting at the White House ignited within me the desire for more action. If that morning's tour was what it meant to be a White House doctor, then I was looking forward to the adventure that lay ahead. This doctor was good to go.

3.

While I was becoming familiar with my new life and duties at the White House, Richard and our sons, Andrew and Jason, were adjusting to life in Alexandria, Virginia. They liked the townhouse we had found three miles from the boys' school. The basement afforded Richard a convenient home office where he would prepare lessons for his night-school classes at George Washington University Law Center, teaching legal research and writing. He prided himself on writing precisely and would often be frustrated with students who failed to demonstrate rudimentary writing skills. Richard was also approached by a law firm in town that needed a part-time attorney to handle special projects. And when he wasn't teaching or practicing law, he was raising our sons.

Andrew and Jason made friends with the children in the neighborhood. They enjoyed the change of seasons, which they didn't experience in perennially sunny San Diego, and loved their first snow days off from school that winter.

During my first year at the White House, I would have occasional weekdays off following travel and used that time to create some sem-

Left: Holding my sons Jason, age one (on the left), and Andrew, age three, in San Diego before moving to D. C. (FAMILY PHOTO) *Right: My sons enjoyed meeting Socks, the presidential cat, in my White House Office in 1995.* (FAMILY PHOTO)

blance of a home for my family. I did that one night by offering to prepare a healthy, home-cooked meal.

"Dinner's ready," I proudly announced from the kitchen after I had set the plates on the table. Richard came up from his basement office cave, while Andrew and Jason ran in from the backyard, rushing to the sink to wash their hands.

I made the boys' favorite dish of spaghetti and meatballs. Rather than use the traditional meat sauce that I had used in the past, I tried a healthy, no-salt sauce that the upscale grocery store had on sale.

The four of us sat at the table. I glanced over at Richard, who looked serene and pleased to have me home for at least a day. I felt like I owed Richard a lot for agreeing to stay home with the boys while I went off to work. By cooking dinner once in a while, I felt that I was at least doing my small part to maintain some form of normalcy in our family life. But I wondered, *What was normalcy in the life of a military woman and White House physician?*

I smiled at my two little boys, realizing that dinner with them was such a special treat for me, one I would never again take for granted. After we had said grace, the boys dug into their meal.

After biting into the pasta, Jason let out a painful howl. I thought he had bitten his tongue or that the sauce was too hot. I reached out to him as he spat out the healthy, no-salt spaghetti I had prepared. "This is awful!" my three-year-old screamed. "This is the worst meal of my entire life!" Although I had not taken culinary lessons from my father, who had cooked for the admirals and their demanding spouses, making spaghetti for a three-year-old should have been a no-brainer. But not in my family's case.

Richard watched me as I went over to hug Jason and wipe the remnants of the worst spaghetti of his life out of his mouth. "Sorry, dear," he commiserated. "I guess the boys liked the old spaghetti sauce you used to cook in San Diego." I thought I caught a mischievous glint in his eyes.

I felt like a failure. I wanted to please my family by doing one of the basics of motherhood, which was feeding them. And I couldn't even do that to their satisfaction. At that moment, I wanted desperately to escape and run back to work where I felt needed and appreciated. At that moment, I regretted accepting the job at the White House. I knew that my life would never be the same again because of it. I didn't expect that to apply to my family's life as well.

FIVE

One of the Guys

1.

D oc, do you know what the plan is if the president gets shot?"
The question was posed to me by a raven-haired, muscle-bound, mustached Secret Service agent appropriately dressed in black. He sat in the rear of the unmarked, armored, smoked-glass Suburban while I sat between two similarly brawny and brave agents from the president's detail. This was the start of my week of orientation training with the Secret Service. We were at Kennebunkport, Maine, where President Bush and his family were on vacation in the summer of 1992.

The week prior to our arrival in Maine, I had met Rich Miller, the special agent in charge of President Bush's detail. Tall, lanky, and laconic, Rich looked like the model for a Secret Service recruiting ad. "The doctor is part of the secure package," Rich informed me during his presentation in the Secret Service Command Post.

"Secure package? What does that mean?" I asked, sounding and feeling insecure.

"The secure package is the small group of essential personnel who need to be with the president at all times. This includes the doctor, the military aide, and the Secret Service detail." Rich spoke without emotion, as though he had lectured on this topic hundreds of times.

"It's important that you learn about your role in the secure package. The best way would be for you to work with the agents on the detail." With this recommendation from the president's lead agent and with Dr. Lee's blessing, I was dispatched to Kennebunkport to receive training from the president's Secret Service agents.

On a balmy Tuesday night, President Bush was having dinner in a private restaurant in town. Two agents were inside with him while the rest of his Secret Service detail sat in unmarked vehicles outside the restaurant. The duty military aide was stationed in the Control Van, while the duty nurse was assigned to the Support Vehicle. And I got to sit in the Secret Service vehicle, called Half Back, with the rest of the agents from the shift. "Lucky you," the duty nurse hissed through her perfectly pearly teeth as the agents directed me toward the vehicle.

Lucky me. As I entered Half Back, I sniffed the air and detected a hint of Brut aftershave mixed with a tinge of sweat. With six hunky men in the vehicle, the atmosphere reeked of testosterone. I was surrounded by all the president's men, ranging from ages thirty-two to forty-five, all strikingly handsome. They looked as though they had auditioned for the role of the president's protector, and won.

"So, Doc, tell me what we plan to do." The deep voice from the back of the Suburban goaded me as the other agents turned in their seats to stare at me. I leaned forward, trying to capture the agent's eyes in the rearview mirror. I caught a glimpse of his cool, hazel eyes but couldn't see the rest of his face. And I couldn't tell from those eyes whether this was a serious question or he was just teasing me. The agent appeared to be an expert at hiding emotion; I assumed he must have been good in undercover work.

"Well, first you get him out of danger, and then you bring him to a safe place where the medical personnel can . . ." I recited the protocol learned from Al Roberts during my week of training with him before he left for his next assignment at Bethesda Naval Hospital.

"Nah, you've got it all wrong, Doc." The agent interrupted me as his buddies began to snicker.

My cheeks started to flush despite attempts to hide my embarrassment. Once again I was reliving a familiar scene. Ten years before arriving at the White House, I was a ship's doctor. When I reported to the destroyer tender USS *Prairie* in 1982, I was the only doctor onboard the ship and had a crew of 600 men and 150 women. As usual, I was outnumbered, always in the minority, if not the only person of color. I spent my first six months onboard the ship proving to officers and sailors that I had the right stuff to be a ship's doctor on deployment. Now I was being tested by a more demanding crew, the president's Secret Service detail. They were checking to see if I had what it took to be in the secure package.

"All right, what did I miss?" I asked the inquisitor in the rear of the vehicle. "I am new to the job and still learning."

"Okay, Doc," he whispered as his buddies began to chuckle. "Here's the secret plan: If the president gets shot, the first thing we do is eliminate Dr. Lee. Then we go get one of the other doctors to take care of the president." The men now laughed heartily.

This didn't shock me. I had heard rumors on the White House compound questioning Burt's ability to handle an emergency. Were the agents testing my loyalty to my boss? Either way, he was still my superior officer, as we say in the Navy.

"Okay, we now have a triage situation," I responded, blank-faced.

"Triage?" asked my inquisitor tentatively, surprised by my rebuttal.

"Well, if the president gets shot and you incapacitate Dr. Lee, then there'll be at least three people down. The president gets my full attention, and I'll have to assign my nurse to one of the others."

The agent was now totally baffled. "Other patients? Dr. Lee and . . ."

"The agent with the scalpel in his foot."

There was a pause, the other agents were unsure of how to respond, until the lead agent started chuckling, and then they joined in. "And who gets priority, Doc?"

"Why, the agent of course. I do have to protect my own ass."

This drew more hardy laughter. "Doc, you can think on your feet and stand toe-to-toe. It'll come in handy." He now flashed a mischievous smile. "But, just remember, tomorrow we test your sea legs." The laughter had been reduced to snickers, and I realized I'd live to regret my cheeky, one-of-the-guys response.

2.

Sailboats danced merrily along the Kennebunk River as I drove to the dock where I was to report for boat exercises. It was a lovely August morning in Maine; the humidity was tolerable and the sky was clear. The weather was perfect for "underway exercises," as we called them in the Navy.

Today's training with the Secret Service would focus on a water rescue. President Bush was an avid boater who loved to dash across the waves in his trim and speedy cigarette boat, offshore of the family estate at Walker's Point. So the scenario for today's exercise would be to simulate a boat accident in which we would rescue the president from the water, and I would administer first-aid.

"Welcome aboard, Commander!" The agent in a dark wet suit and ball cap greeted me on the dock, as I hurried down the pier lined on both sides with an array of boats. "I heard you're Navy," he said, eyeing my polo shirt, beige slacks, and canvas loafers. He probably thought I was dressed more for a leisurely yacht ride than a water search-and-rescue mission. He was right.

"Oh, this outfit?" I responded, glancing down at my civilian attire. "The nurses told me to dress casually for today's exercise." The agent smirked, probably in collusion with the White House nurses, who no doubt had a good laugh in anticipation of this moment.

"Well, I don't know if they told you," he cautioned me, "but you could get pretty wet today." His warning, although intended to be well-meaning, came across as a challenge, almost a dare.

"I'm not afraid of water," I said dismissively. I declined his extended hand and stepped gingerly from the pier onto an orange-colored powerboat moored to the dock. "I spent two years onboard a destroyer tender, and nine months of it deployed in the Indian Ocean," I added, defending my seaworthiness. It was bad enough being the new doc trainee at the White House, let alone having my naval experience questioned.

"So, I guess you've got your sea legs," he shot back at me with a hint of sarcasm as he jumped easily into the boat and untied the line. "Well, skipper, let's get underway," he shouted to the other agent in a wet suit, who was revving up the boat's engine.

As we launched from the pier, I sat down on the sideboard that wrapped around the stern of the boat, and held on tightly as we sped away heading toward the choppy waves off the coast. Our craft was forty feet long and had a flat bottom. In the center lay a Stokes stretcher, wooden Miller board, first-aid kit, and an oxygen tank. Placed inside the metal stretcher was a dummy president, or rather a manikin substitute for the president in today's exercises.

As I examined the metal stretcher and Miller board, which would be used to strap and transport a trauma patient, I recalled my days on the *Prairie*. My corpsmen and I trained the ship's crew in how to handle casualties in the event of an accident at sea. We would routinely conduct rescue exercises such as man-overboard drills. But this time the supposed victim would not be a hapless sailor but instead the motorboat-loving commander in chief. The other big difference was that I was no longer the ship's doctor with fifteen seasoned corpsmen under my command to assist me. I was the junior White House physician accompanied by two Secret Service agents I sensed had been sent to test my worthiness.

As we made our way toward the Atlantic, four other Secret Service boats, all black and sleek, followed after us. Each boat was manned with two to three agents, as well as a team of Navy divers and SEALs. I had eyed these men on the pier as I walked up to my boat this morning. Most of the divers were bare-chested and heavily tattooed. They looked tough, cavalier, and intentionally intimidating. I wondered how well these men and I would work together during this exercise. We made an odd-looking team: me looking like a naive Catholic schoolgirl, and them at the height of macho swagger.

Our little orange boat sped up as the agent powered down the engine. Soon we were racing along the water going more than 80 knots with the other boats in hot pursuit. Jets of dark blue, cold Atlantic Ocean sprayed from the sides and stern of our boat. The scene looked like something out of the TV series *Miami Vice*. As I sat on the sideboard, feet firmly planted on the wet deck, one hand clutched a metal handle and the other my life jacket.

The sticky wind tossed my hair as the chilly ocean spat into my face. I felt more alive than ever as I trembled from the cold and sheer excitement of it all. I was also overwhelmed with a flood of memories of being deployed at sea and engaged in adrenaline-drenched rescue exercises such as today's. I was even more excited knowing that these exercises involved a mission of the highest caliber: taking care of the first patient.

Our rescue craft then reached a designated site offshore where the agent killed the engine. Four of the black Secret Service boats formed a perimeter around our boat. The senior agent in my boat barked into his radio: "Commence exercise." With that signal, the other agent tossed the manikin into the ocean. The test dummy splashed as it hit the water and in a few seconds floated to the top, with its blank expression looking up at us. Had this been the president, I can't imagine the angst we would have all been experiencing at that moment. But military training teaches one to transform angst into action. Immediately the divers from two of the boats jumped into the water and swam toward the manikin with the Stokes stretcher. Once they reached the dummy victim, they surrounded the decoy president and then lifted him carefully into the wire stretcher. They then swam holding the stretcher up to the side of my boat, where the two agents lifted the stretcher into our rescue craft. I stood to the side watching the agents bring me the waterlogged victim, my heart pounding from the anticipation of receiving "incoming wounded."

"Here's your patient, Doc," the senior agent reminded me. "Do your thing."

My thing was to first assess the victim for airway, breathing, circulation, and disability, the basic A-B-C-D of trauma evaluation. I went into my autopilot mode, thankful for the numerous advanced trauma and cardiac life-support drills in which I had participated over the years on the high seas.

I looked into the manikin's face. Expressionless and with no resemblance to anything human. Yet the adrenaline surged in my veins at that moment as I substituted the blank dummy's face with that of my blue-eyed, smiling, and full-of-life first patient. The agents stood behind me observing as I enumerated aloud the steps I would take to assess my victim.

The senior agent folded his arms across his chest, nodding his head as I zipped through the assessment. I easily immobilized the victim's neck with a hard collar, simulated listening to the chest and heart with my stethoscope, and checked the pupils in the eyes of my decoy president with a penlight. All routine protocol for me, yet the setting was far from typical. I heard murmurs of approval from the agents and the divers who watched me move briskly around my patient.

"At this point," I spoke, as I planned the treatment plan aloud, "I would evacuate this patient to the nearest Level 1 trauma facility. In this case I would call for a helo . . ."

Almost like magic, as soon as I uttered the word "helo," I could hear in the distance the familiar *thump thump thump* of a chopper. I gazed out to the horizon where I spied an orange and white Coast Guard rescue helicopter making its way to our boat.

"You got your wish, Doc," the senior agent said. "Five minutes out . . . prepare to lift."

As I knelt beside the manikin in the stretcher, I watched the chopper grow larger as it drew closer. I recalled with wonder how many helicopter missions I had been on during my life: from my early medevac to the neonatal care unit at age three days, to the chopper blades at Balboa Naval Hospital, and then to my Marine One excursions from the South Lawn. And now I could add the chilly-water rescue off Kennebunkport. All these were not simply transportation to a hospital but represented some form of a personal rescue for me. My first helicopter ride was a rescue from death at an early age. The second was a symbolic rescue from a job that had grown dull and no longer challenging. Marine One provided a temporary rescue from routine clinic work at the White House. And today's exercise at sea rescued me from the plight of being constantly underestimated. By doing well what I was trained to do, I earned the approval and admiration of the agents who initially discounted my ability and talent.

Finally the orange and white bird began to hover over our little boat; the chopper blades whirling briskly whipped up the water around us. The crew aboard the chopper dropped a cable over the side into our boat. The heavy metal clasp of the cable made a loud clunk on the deck of our boat as it hit a few feet from us, dissipating the electrical charge generated from the helicopter above. The divers and agents quickly sprang into action, attaching lines to the side of the metal stretcher that bore the victim. The lines were drawn up and attached to the cable from the Coast Guard chopper. I stood back in awe watching the smooth, orchestrated movement of the men in black wet suits. The lead agent then gave a thumbs-up sign, and the chopper slowly lifted the Stokes stretcher from the deck of our boat into the air. As I watched the ascent of the stretcher, one of the agents pulled me aside and in a loud voice, but barely audible over the roar of the rotors, said, "As you can tell, this is probably the most dangerous part of the exercise."

I nodded, looking intently at him and yearning to learn more.

"Last year we performed this exercise with a volunteer agent. We strapped him in, secured the cable to the stretcher. As the cable lifted the stretcher into the air toward the chopper, the cable snapped."

Secret Service training prepared Medical Unit staff to handle real-life emergencies. Navy nurse Vince Starks (in sunglasses) and I respond, along with the president's Secret Service detail, to a fallen motorcycle policeman during Clinton's visit to New Mexico in February 1999. (WHITE HOUSE PHOTO)

I shook my head, anticipating the tragic outcome.

"The stretcher fell into the sea. The agent lived, but was hospitalized with a broken jaw and multiple fractures. It's been a slow recovery for him."

I understood and respected the danger associated with these exercises. "Hopefully that will never happen again," I commiserated.

"Not on my watch," the agent spoke forcefully.

"I hope we never have to do these exercises in real time with the POTUS," I said aloud, not expecting a response from the agent.

By now, the stretcher was safely in the chopper. The agent gave another thumbs-up and the away sign. As he turned to head over to the opposite side of the boat, he commented, "Well, if we have to do the real thing, then we want you to be the doc at the scene."

I held close my pride, trying not to look overly eager for this morsel of praise from the stoic agent.

"Thank you," I offered. "I couldn't do the job without you guys."

He turned back and smiled. As he did so, he glanced up again at the chopper, which was preparing to move out, and said, "Now you're going to regret not wearing a wet suit."

Before I could respond, the chopper blades whirled faster, whipping up the cold ocean around us. The water poured into our boat as I held on to the side. The salty, cold brine drenched me completely. I gritted my teeth and wiped the stinging salt from my eyes. I tried to hold my breath. More water poured in as the chopper began to fly away from us. I was further enveloped. I could hear the agents laughing as we were all drenched.

I started off this morning intimidated, trying to prove my stuff, trying to look calm and collected. I ended the day totally soaked in backwash, shivering. I was grateful the exercise went well and that I had proven myself to the agents. I was also a little more humble now, acknowledging that I didn't know everything, and that I had to rely on the White House team to help me do my job. Today's search-and-rescue exercise had been my baptism into the White House brotherhood, cleansed by the waters off Kennebunkport.

As the helicopter departed, the whirlpool of water around our boat died down. In its wake was one near-drowned junior White House physician. The agents powered up the engine of our boat and we headed back to shore. As we raced toward land, they turned to look back at me, hiding their smiles like mischievous schoolboys who had just pulled a prank on the teacher's pet. Black hair dripping, clothes soaked, mushy shoes, eyes red from the salty brine, I must've looked like a dead sea rat.

I met their eyes, wiping the salt from mine. My expression was stern. One agent chided me, "Oh no, you're not going to cry, are you? The nurses do that every time in these exercises."

Another agent taunted me, as I shook my head. "No, it's not that. She's mad at us. Another doctor got really angry when we did this last time."

I shook my head again and then broke out in a smile and teased, "Well, you boys sure know how to get a girl all wet!"

This remark shocked and relieved them. Laughter erupted in our boat. The senior agent admitted, "Gee, Doc, what a great sense of humor." He stuck his thumb up. "After today, you're one of us."

Back at the Nonantum Hotel that afternoon, I took another shower, this time in warm clean water. I felt refreshed and reborn as I rinsed off the salty brine. I had passed the test of the Secret Service by demonstrating my medical skills. But most important of all, I earned their trust and respect. After a month at the White House trying to learn the ropes, I finally felt I was beginning to make progress.

As I toweled off my hair in the mirror, I heard a sound in the hall-way that was both familiar and disturbing to me. It was a wail, a cry. I moved toward my door to investigate. The wail grew louder. I couldn't mistake that sound: it was the cry of a child.

I opened the door and toward me rushed a reddish-haired, sobbing little boy, about five years old. He clutched my legs as I instinctively put my arms around him. My heart ached, thinking of my two little sons in Virginia.

"Where's my mommy? I want my mommy." The little boy sobbed and then began to hiccup.

I squatted down beside him. "I'll help you find her. What's your name?" He told me.

I instructed him to wait in the hallway while I called the front desk and asked where his family was staying. I learned that the family was in a room on the floor beneath mine. The little boy most likely had gotten off on the wrong floor from the elevator. I walked him to the elevator and we took it down to the next floor. As we got off, he saw his mother and quickly ran to her. I was relieved to see the boy safely reunited with his mother. She thanked me for helping her son. Seeing the little boy and his mother together tugged at my heart. I suddenly felt homesick for my two little boys, whom I hadn't seen in a week, since I arrived in Kennebunkport.

I returned to my room and as soon as I had shut the door, I broke down in tears. It had been a long, difficult day and the evening's finale had finally brought it all up for me. The morning started with my test by the Secret Service and had ended in my triumph. Yet as I wept alone in my hotel room that dark August night in New England, I realized it was a Pyrrhic victory. I had tried to prove to the most macho of the president's protectors that I had the balls to play with the boys. But in the end, I realized I wasn't one of the boys. It took the sound of a child's cry to remind me that I was a woman and a mother. And what made that particularly painful and the tears more bitter was the realization that I was a mother who was missing in action. *Missing in action.* I was simply not there for my sons. My job in the military kept me away from my children. I was not there for their illnesses and injuries, not there to comfort them in the night when they awoke calling my name, and not there to wipe away their tears. Instead, I would be there for the illnesses and injuries of the first family and the children of that family. As I sat on my bed and wept, I realized that my greatest achievements as a physician and career naval officer would become my most painful failure as a wife and mother.

SIX

The New Face of the White House

1.

When George Bush lost his reelection bid in November 1992 to Bill Clinton, I was home in Alexandria watching the returns, eager to see who would be my first patient come January 1993. Dr. Burt Lee had accompanied President Bush to Houston on election day, and he was there when the president conceded. As the junior physician, I was relegated to covering the clinic and White House tours on the days leading up to the election. Dr. Lee and his staff of nurses had been with the first family for several years. While I had been at the White House less than a year, I still felt sad for the Bush family. They were honorable people and very gracious. I then switched the channel to hear Bill Clinton's victory speech. He was definitely charismatic and telegenic. As the camera panned over the crowd of Clinton supporters, I was struck by the mix of Hispanic, Asian, and African-American faces in the crowd. Perhaps I would fit in better with this new administration.

When George and Barbara Bush returned to the White House the day after the election, they were greeted by a welcome home party on the South Lawn, which was decorated with balloons and flags. There was a band playing and office personnel from the Old Executive Office Building were ushered out to welcome them back. It resembled a pep rally for a losing football team. Many of the people gathered on that cold, cloudy day realized that they would lose their jobs in January, so the welcome was a little strained. I stood on the lawn and watched President Bush and the first lady walk from the limousine to the Truman Balcony. He thanked everybody who had campaigned for him. Despite the fanfare, music, and cheers, the mood was mournful. Afterward George Bush put his arm around Barbara and waved to the crowd. Tears filled his eyes.

Over the next few weeks, the medical unit wondered about how they would be received by the new president and his family. We had heard rumors that the president-elect did not like the military, and that he would replace the entire military White House Medical Unit with

Before George Bush left office in January 1993, he invited me for a ride in the back of the presidential limousine. (WHITE HOUSE PHOTO)

civilian health care providers from Arkansas. The doctors and nurses were in a panic over the prospect of losing their jobs at the White House and being reassigned to other military stations. Even worse was losing a president and first family that had loved the medical unit and favored the doctors and nurses over most of the White House military staff. It did not look hopeful for us.

Rumors continued to swirl about the White House compound, more each day as we drew closer to Bill Clinton's inauguration. Anger over the outcome of the election flared up in the medical clinic, often with open partisan criticism of the incoming administration. Several of the nurses refused to remain at the White House to treat the new president and requested reassignment before the inauguration. Having been a career naval medical officer, I never got to pick my patients; they were always assigned to me. In this case, the American people had designated Bill Clinton as the first patient. Patients were patients whether they were Republicans, Democrats, or members of the press. However, some of my colleagues in the medical unit did not share my view.

On the final full day of the Bush administration, January 19, 1993, Colonel Larry Mohr assembled the medical staff in the Old Executive Office Building. This was our final meeting before the new president was to arrive. Larry was the senior military physician at the White House, responsible for the administrative functioning of the unit. Larry had called us together to give the latest scoop on the incoming administration. He sat at the head of the table in a room with tall ceilings and a dusty, worn blue rug. There was no substance to his scoop. He then introduced his replacement, Army Colonel Bob Ramsey, who sat quietly as Larry ran the meeting. Bob looked just as bored as the rest of us. Larry announced that he would brief the new president and first family about the services of the medical unit. If he was unavailable, then Bob Ramsey would assume the duty. I suggested that Larry give us talking points on what to tell the first family about the medical unit in case any of us ran into the new president or his family. Larry disagreed; he felt it was his or Bob Ramsey's job to brief the new president and his family.

The meeting was interrupted by an urgent phone call from the doctor's office in the residence. Dr. Lee's secretary, Debbie Sudduth, was calling, informing us that the doctor was tending to Barbara Bush, who had fallen, lacerated her arm, and might require stitches. He wanted to know if any of us were comfortable with suturing.

I raised my hand. "I've done a lot of suturing, usually with drunken sailors, so I guess the first lady should be easy to do."

Larry released me from the meeting, which was a tremendous relief. Army PA Tom Millikin volunteered to come along since he was specially trained in orthopedics. When we arrived at the doctor's office, Barbara Bush was seated on the exam table dressed in black. Then I saw red blood from the laceration on her forearm; she had fallen on a wet floor in the residence and struck the side of a table.

"I'm sorry, Doctor, to bother you with this," she apologized.

"I'm sorry, too, Mrs. Bush. It's not what you needed on your last day in the White House." I smiled and touched her shoulder.

Mary Ann Chandler, the Navy corpsman chief, had also joined me. I asked for the surgical pack to be opened and placed on a tray beside the table. I invited Mrs. Bush to sit back in the exam chair. Slipping on my sterile gloves, I examined her wound. It was deep but fortunately did not touch any tendons or muscles. It would require sutures. I informed my patient of what was needed, and she consented.

After applying a local anesthetic and cleaning the wound, I placed several sutures. Burt Lee then entered with President Bush and his photographer, Dave Valdez. I finished suturing and then asked Tom to place the dressing. Dave took photographs of the event. In the photographs, Burt dominates the picture, holding up Mrs. Bush's hand. I looked away, wishing to disappear from the scene. Burt then told the president, "Tom did a great job taking care of the wound." Tom looked at me, but I shook my head. Helping my patient was more important for me than taking the credit.

I wanted to say goodbye to President and Mrs. Bush on their last day with us, but by the time we had finished, there were too many people in the room for me to bid them a private farewell. I quietly slipped away from the office where my patient was surrounded by nurses, medics, and Burt Lee.

It was already 5:30 P.M. I went to the OEOB clinic to collect my coat and briefcase. I had not driven to the compound that day, since parking was impossible due to the inauguration preparations. Instead, I had taken the Metro.

As I exited the OEOB facing 17th Street, I walked along a street filled with people who had arrived in town for the next day's inauguration. The wind was cold and bitter. My heart felt the same way. It was cold because I was going to miss my old first patients and had to toughen up for the new ones, who may not even want us there. It was bitter because I felt unappreciated by both Burt and Larry for the work I'd done in the White House Medical Unit.

As I walked to the signal light at 17th Street and Pennsylvania Avenue, I heard a police siren. I stopped at the corner and noticed that a motorcade was passing. I knew it wasn't President Bush's, since he and his family were to remain on the compound that final evening. The phalanx of vehicles was coming from Blair House across the street from the White House. As I paused to watch the vehicles

pass, I saw a lead police car, a black Secret Service Suburban, followed by an unmarked limousine without flags or the presidential seal. Inside the vehicle, behind a

After President Bush left office in 1993, I was reunited with my first First Patient at the Volunteer Summit in Philadelphia in April 1997. White House nurse Michelle Adams is on the left.
(WHITE HOUSE PHOTO)

tinted bulletproof glass window, the blurry image of a woman with blond shoulder-length hair looked in my direction. I then did something I've never done. I waved. Hillary Rodham Clinton waved back to me from the passing limousine.

2.

When Bill, Hillary, and Chelsea Clinton moved into the White House on January 20, 1993, they did not know they had inherited a village of military doctors, nurses, physician assistants, and medics assigned to take care of them. The first family also did not know that most of the natives in this village were restless and Republican, nor did they know that at least one of them was anxious to serve the new president as she had done the last one.

"Why don't they ask about us?" protested one of the medical unit nurses on the third day after the Clinton inauguration. This young Navy lieutenant and I sat in Burt Lee's old office, the doctor's office, on the ground floor. It was our first day of duty to cover the new president, and we were in the dark as to what he wanted to do that day. "The colonel has been trying to brief the president on the medical unit," she added, "and so far no one has called to ask about us."

"I have a feeling the medical unit orientation isn't at the top of their list," I snapped, irritated when I detected a whiff of whine in her voice. "Let's do our job, and when they want to hear about the medical unit, they'll let us know."

"Well, it's not done that way," the nurse protested.

"Never, ever say that again," I reprimanded the junior officer. "This new administration doesn't want to hear 'we've always done it this way.' Remember that we used to take care of the other guy, the former president. Well, Clinton's people don't want to hear about how Bush did it. I'm certain they want to do things their way."

This day was already off to a bad start. I had just scolded the duty nurse, and now we sat in uncomfortable silence. We missed the Bush family, were in fear of losing our jobs with the new Clinton administration, and had no idea what the president wanted to do today. I had arrived at 6:00 A.M. to a White House compound that was now invaded by Democrats. I smiled quietly to myself as I strolled onto the compound and was greeted warmly by several new White House staffers who were young, enthusiastic, and many of them people of color. They probably thought I was one of them.

"Doc, you look like one of them," observed the senior White House PA in the waning days of the Bush administration, of the Democrats who would be taking over the White House. Good, I thought, I'd like to be one of them in fact.

Anything that hinted of the previous administration was generally suspect. If you were a holdover, the new president's people would wonder where your loyalties lay. In the case of the military, we were supposed to be devoid of politics, serving the president regardless of our political affiliation. But with each new administration, the White House starts anew and sometimes this extended to the military staff as well.

The nurse and I sat quietly in the office, listening to the Secret Service radio traffic to see what the president had planned that day. Our answer came over the radio, "Eagle wants to run on the Mall . . ." We knew the routine. The Secret Service vehicles would be parked warming up on the driveway of the South Lawn, including an ambulance, support and press vehicles, and the van that would carry me, the duty nurse, and our medical gear. The plan was to trail the president on his run. But now we had been waiting four hours with no word from the new upstairs resident. Even the Filipino valets were out of the loop, since they were trying to be invisible yet accessible to a new White House family that didn't know who they were or what they did.

The past three days had been very stressful, disorienting, and confusing for the medical unit. One day the cars parked on West Executive Boulevard all had Bush-Quayle bumper stickers, and the following day the cars had Clinton-Gore plastered on them. The large Bush portraits and event photos decorating the West Wing had been taken down by the Usher's Office as per protocol. These were replaced with photos of the new president and vice president that hung on stark walls; the remaining space would be filled with large prints from the Clinton inauguration.

"Eagle, ground floor, going to the cars . . ." the voice announced on the radio. The nurse and I jumped, grabbed our bags and defibrillator, and stepped into the hallway. Bill Clinton had just gotten off the elevator wearing jogging pants. This was the first time I had seen him this close. He was tall, fair-skinned, and youthful, with a head of wavy dark hair. He looked tired and preoccupied, as though running wasn't what he wanted to do this cold January morning. A slender boyish-looking staffer stood beside him and walked with him as they headed toward the cars on the South Lawn.

Typical of the White House tempo is this indeterminate wait followed by a frenetic rush to the cars. After four hours, we were now hustling to our van. In a matter of seconds, the motorcade took off for the Mall across from the White House compound. There, the president stepped out of the limo and started to jog with his Secret Service detail to his flank and rear. The nurse and I sat in the van, watching him. He waved to people on the Mall, who were surprised to see him out jogging. He enjoyed meeting people, I observed. This is a man who loves being out with the people. My education about Bill Clinton had begun.

The president finished his jog in thirty minutes and then stretched against a bench on the Mall, while his Secret Service detail surrounded him, cautiously eyeing the pedestrian traffic. One of the valets ran over to the president and handed him a towel and bottled water. This surprised the young president, who warmly greeted the valet, asking his name, touching his shoulder. The nurse and I sat in the van watching him. "He has no idea we're here in the van," she lamented.

"Hey, remember what the military office says—be invisible. We're the invisible nurse and doctor," I reassured her, squeezing her arm. She smiled back halfheartedly.

Bill Clinton discusses his allergies after a run on the beach in Coronado, California, in June 1996. (WHITE HOUSE PHOTO)

I didn't see Bill Clinton until later that day. Instead, I was busy in the doctor's office seeing a few patients, including a member of the first lady's family. Her father had been visiting for the inauguration and became ill. Hugh Rodham Sr. was a delightful curmudgeon of a man with a long list of medications. After blood tests, I discovered that he needed a little fine-tuning with one of his medications and adjusted the dose. He was going to be all right, but he asked that I brief his daughter about his condition.

His daughter? The first lady of the United States, Hillary Rodham Clinton.

Except for the split-second wave to her in a limo on the day before the inauguration, I had had no contact with the first lady. In fact, none of the medical staff had any direct contact with her or the president since their arrival at the White House. The medical unit's two Army colonels had argued over who would brief the president. The Navy captain in charge of the White House Military Office had now declared that he would do the briefing. But in the end, none of the "big boys" got to brief them. Instead, the job went to the junior White House doctor—the quiet, underestimated "little lady" who had White House duty that day.

The phone rang in the doctor's office, and the duty nurse answered it. Her face turned pale as she put the call on hold. "Doc, I think it is the first lady calling."

"What do you mean, you think? What did she say?" I prodded, standing over the phone, counting the number of blinks on the hold light.

"She said, 'Hello. This is Hillary Clinton. May I speak to the doctor?'"

I picked up the phone, took a deep breath, and spoke cheerfully, "This is Dr. Mariano; may I help you?"

The voice was calm, smooth, and reassuring. "Hello Doctor, this is Hillary Clinton. I understand you saw my father today."

"Yes, ma'am," I answered, realizing that her father most likely mentioned the exam in the doctor's office. "He asked that I brief you on his condition."

"Oh, of course. Can you come upstairs and see me?" she asked politely, as though I could refuse.

"Yes, ma'am, I'm on my way."

The nurse looked at me. "You're going upstairs?"

"I guess I am. There's only one problem."

"What's that?" she asked eagerly, wanting to help.

"How do I get up there?"

I had never been to the second floor during President Bush's term. Usually Burt Lee and the nurses were allowed upstairs to attend to the president and first family. This was my first time, and fortunately it was rather simple. I just walked over to the elevator across the hall and hit the button for the second floor. The elevator automatically stopped on the first or State Floor, and an usher got onboard and took me up to the second floor of the residence, the inner sanctum for the first family. Although my job was to take care of the president, I had learned from my predecessors an old White House doctor's secret: you can't take care of the president without the blessing of the first lady. Nothing happens at the White House without the approval of the lady of the house. This meeting was also significant because it would be the first time that anyone from the medical unit was to speak privately with the first family. This was a chance for us to start off on a positive note with our new patients.

I stepped onto the second-floor landing and gazed around. I had entered another world, of polished wooden floors with plush, brilliant carpets, oil paintings with gold-plated frames, delicate antique furniture, breathtaking floral centerpieces, and sparkling chandeliers. I felt a rush of nostalgia. I was eight years old again, looking past my father's kitchen door into the admiral's quarters, sneaking a glimpse of his private rooms. This time, however, it was the private quarters of the president of the United States. But I didn't feel now what I had feared when I was eight years old: that someone would tell me to leave, that I didn't belong here.

I looked down the hallway to the west and saw her for the first time. She was without makeup, wearing large-framed glasses with thick lenses. Her hair was straight, shoulder-length with blond highlights but not coiffed, strands limp and undisciplined. Hillary Rodham Clinton didn't see me when I stepped into the room. I found her admiring a painting on the wall of the family living room. She looked drained, and as she gazed at the picture on the wall, her expression seemed to ask "was it all worth it?"

"Mrs. Clinton?" My voice was soft, trying to be polite and invisible but also realizing that my face time, as we called it at the White House, was about to begin.

"Oh, hello, Doctor," she greeted me, assuming correctly that I was the doctor, not the nurse. She walked toward me and extended her hand. Good handshake, firm but not masculine. Her smile was cheerful and her eyes, though tired, were bright blue and clear.

"It's good to meet you, Mrs. Clinton," I began. "I'm Dr. Connie Mariano, one of the White House doctors."

Hillary Clinton took my arm and pointed to the sofa under the arched window facing west. We sat down on the sofa, and I gave her a report on her father's condition and the adjustment to his medication. She thanked me and asked that I follow up with his hometown physician. And then in a manner that betrayed her barrister training, Hillary Clinton began her polite deposition of me.

"How many doctors are there?"

"Currently four doctors: two Army—including one who's retiring in a few months—one Air Force, and one Navy, and that's me."

"You're military?" she asked, looking at my dark-blue pantsuit, white blouse, and Secret Service lapel pin.

"Yes, ma'am. When we have duty, we wear civilian clothes to blend in with the president's entourage."

"You have duty today? What does that entail?"

I spent twenty minutes giving the briefing that the Army colonels and director of the military office thought they would be giving the president. Instead, I presented the information to the first lady, who with a nod of her head, or a periodic "uh huh," reassured me that my presentation was to her satisfaction. As I spoke to her, I felt comfortable but not casual in her presence. Even though she was dressed in a pink jogging suit and wore no makeup, sitting on the sofa in her living room, she carried herself in a dignified manner, though she was neither cold nor stuffy. To me, at that moment, she appeared unflappable; I didn't think anything could rattle her steady nature.

And then she laughed. I don't know what I said that was so funny, but I'll never forget the sound. It was a wondrous belly laugh, a self-deprecating guffaw that I found refreshing and endearing.

President Clinton walked into the room at that moment. He still had on his jogging pants from the morning run, a ball cap on his head, and a slight swagger in his walk. I stood up promptly when he entered.

Hillary glanced up at him and said, "Bill, meet Dr. Connie Mariano, our new doctor here at the White House." The president came over and shook my hand.

"Well, what do you think, Doc? Am I going to make it the next four years?" he half jokingly asked me, his eyes twinkling but tired.

"Well, Mr. President, after seeing you jog this morning, if you cut back on the fast foods, from what I hear, you might make it for eight years." The president and first lady exchanged looks and laughed. You could see the bond between them in that look, a silent dialogue developed over years of assessing people and their intent. Couples are known to read each other, but this look spoke volumes. Afterward, Bill Clinton said his good-byes and sauntered down the hallway with a little extra strut—he liked people, and this exchange had energized him.

And they did stay for eight years, and I was there with them the entire time, through the triumphs and the tragedies. My eight years with the Clintons may never have happened but for that first fateful meeting with Hillary Clinton as a result of treating her father. When we talked, she was actually interviewing me, checking me out, and deciding if I was the right person to take care of her and her family. I think the clincher for both of them was my reply to her husband. I could almost hear her say to Bill, "Any doctor who can keep up with you is good to go."

SEVEN

Change Is Our Friend

1.

"Hey you!" The voice was female, harsh, and commanding.
Worst of all, it sounded as though it were directed at me.

I cringed. Even though I was a mature professional and a seasoned
military officer, the tone of maternal disapproval always reduced me
to a cowering, guilty child. I slowly turned in the direction of the
speaker, hoping I wasn't being accosted in this manner, and again
heard the grating tone, "You! The president needs some water now."

It was the first month of Bill Clinton's presidency. He was giving
a speech at a hotel in downtown D.C., one of many in-town events
during his first month in office. This was my second "movement" in
which I accompanied him as the duty physician. From the first day the
new president arrived, business on the eighteen-acre White House
compound was far from customary. I learned early on that Bill Clinton was predictably unpredictable. From his frequent off-the-record
events in the evenings, when he and the first lady would visit friends
in town or dine at local restaurants, to following his own time

schedule, the new president kept the Secret Service, the White House Military Office, and the White House Medical Unit in a state of ready alert.

The first year in a presidential administration is always the most difficult. The transition, far from being a honeymoon between the new president's staff and the nonpolitical personnel at the White House, is more like a rocky marriage between two ill-matched partners staying together for the good of the children. For holdovers from the previous administration, it can be particularly painful, like welcoming a conquering army. When Clinton arrived at the White House, the medical unit had to shed its affection for their previous first patient and court favor with the new president and his staff. It seemed an impossible task because none of us had any political currency, few were Democrats, and no one had a connection to the Clinton campaign. It seemed that the medical unit was doomed from the start.

"You! I'm talking to you!" The woman's strident voice grew louder as I came around to face a middle-aged, heavyset African-American. She was perspiring profusely and glaring at me through the steamed-up lenses of her glasses. I had noticed her once before, at a previous in-town event during the second week of the new presidency. She had been the staff lead for that event and had spent most of her time scurrying about getting papers for the president and lining up guests for a photo opportunity.

My nurse and I were standing outside the president's holding room in the hotel while Clinton chatted with the greeters in the hallway. The man was in his element, surrounded by adoring fans who hung on his every word, and he was talking nonstop. All was calm, uneventful, and smooth as silk until this woman staffer descended upon me with her shrill demand for water.

I glanced over at the president, who was laughing, and I didn't detect any hoarseness in his voice. He didn't look like he needed a glass of water, just a long breath. Then I stared back at the woman staffer with an expression that said, "This isn't a presidential medical emergency." Before I launched into the first argument between a

member of the White House Military Office and the new administration's staff, the president's valet, Lito Bautista, came to the rescue.

Lito had been waiting in the president's holding room, heard the
ruckus in the hallway, and rushed out carrying a bottle of cold water.
He quietly handed it to the staffer, who grabbed it, turned without
thanking him, and stormed off toward the allegedly thirsty president.

"Thank you, Master Chief," I uttered in disbelief. "Have I done
something wrong here? This is my first month with the new president, and I don't want to ruin things by getting off on the wrong foot
with a staffer but . . ."

"Ma'am." He patted me on the arm reassuringly and spoke in a
gentle, soothing Filipino accent that reminded me of my father.
"Don't worry. This isn't the first time I've seen this kind of thing."

"Why did she pick on me?" I asked naively.

Master Chief Lito Bautista, a veteran of four previous presidential
administrations, pointed to the teal-colored Secret Service pin on my
jacket lapel. I touched the pin and then realized that this incident was
the result of mistaken identity. All the members of the White House
Military Office, from the drivers and the valets, to the White House
doctors, wore the pin that signified we were military and would
be allowed close access to the president. The staffer, who was new to
the White House, must have figured that since all the valets wore the
special lapel pin and since I happened to be of Filipino descent, I
must've been one and thus responsible for providing water to the
president.

I thought of my father, who had joined the United States Navy in
the 1940s when Filipinos and African Americans were automatically
assigned to the steward or mess specialist rating. My father would
have been irate if he knew that his daughter, a physician and United
States naval commander, had been mistaken at the White House for
a steward because of her heritage. And being called out not by a
white man but by an African American woman would add to the
affront. I would not have expected this from a "sister" of color. I was

certain if the stereotype were placed on her, she would have cried foul. But instead of making a scene, I bit my tongue and swallowed my pride.

We watched as the woman staffer charged up to the president with the bottled water. He waved her off, and continued with his charming soliloquy. She withdrew to the side, shook her head, twisted off the cap, and proceeded to drink the water herself.

Lito added with amusement, "See, ma'am. POTUS didn't need the water now. That woman is all pucked up . . ."

I laughed out loud, knowing fully well from my roots that native Filipinos pronounce the letter "F" as "P."

This is going to be a long, painful transition, I thought to myself. The president and his staffers were gradually learning about the business of the presidency and how to conduct the day-to-day affairs of the office. They were still unsure about the holdovers from the last administration, who greeted them somewhat suspiciously on inauguration day. Meanwhile, we in the medical unit and military office were learning to work with the Clinton staffers. They expected a show of allegiance from us to demonstrate that we would serve a president for whom many of us had not voted but would now work side by side with to push his agenda. This would become a delicate dance in which both partners struggled to avoid stepping on each other's toes. But first we had to make sure we weren't stepping on our own toes.

2.

The transition to the Clinton administration was a painful period, particularly for the physician to former President Bush.

"Burt, is that you?" I asked, answering the phone in the treatment room of the doctor's office.

"Shh . . ." came a male voice on the other end of the line. "I don't want anyone to know I'm calling."

When President Bush left the White House, his political staff had departed with him. That is, all but one: his doctor. Burt had moved his belongings out of the office on the ground floor of the residence, but he had yet to remove himself from the White House Medical Unit. As a political appointee, he no longer had an office or a job when his first patient left. But Burt refused to leave. Instead, he stayed at home and called in daily to ask the nurses how the new president was treating them and how the medical unit as a whole was adjusting. Seemingly it sounded like a concerned paternal gesture, but I came to believe that the phone calls were actually more like covert surveillance on the enemy.

"Burt, I know it's you," I said, growing impatient. "I know you're calling to get information."

"Connie, why did you give the president the allergy shot? I refused to and I got canned . . ."

Burt was referring to the first involvement by the White House Medical Unit with the new president's medical care. Bill Clinton had received allergy shots on a routine basis from his allergist, Dr. Kelsey Caplinger, in Little Rock. When Clinton arrived at the White House, a courier had delivered a package from Caplinger's office with the serum for the president's routine allergy shots. Burt refused to allow the Medical Unit to administer it even though he was not technically responsible for any aspect of the new president's care. I had verified with Dr. Caplinger the authenticity of the serum and had spoken to his internist, Susan Santa Cruz, about Clinton's medical history. I had then administered the allergy shot to the president without any untoward effects. The only side effect was that the military office discovered that Burt had not left and was getting involved with the new president's personal health issues.

"Burt, you were asked to leave; you were President Bush's doctor and have no reason to be here." I tried to reason with my former boss, who was becoming somewhat of an adversary. "You weren't fired by the president or his staff. The White House Military Office had your access pulled. If anything, *they* fired you."

"Damn military," Burt growled.

I felt bad; I owed my job to him. He interviewed me and picked me on the spot for this once-in-a-lifetime opportunity. And he supported me more than the Army colonels who were left in charge of the medical unit. With the change of administration, Burt had to leave but couldn't seem to do it. The proximity to power can be as intoxicating as power itself. And now Burt Lee was banished from his beloved presidential palace. I remained at the White House with the other members of the medical unit, many of whom were also picked by him. And now he was no longer in the loop, no longer one of the team. It must have been painful for him. It was painful for me to turn my back on my old boss, but that's how it's done in the military. A change of command, a change of allegiance.

"Well, I'm not going to be quiet about this," his tone growing defiant. "The press needs to know about this . . ."

"About what, Burt?" My apprehension was growing at the mere mention of the press. Larry Mohr, the medical unit's senior military physician, had lectured me during my orientation to the White House, "No news is good news." This meant to stay out of the White House press coverage. I had a feeling that a bad-news storm was brewing on the horizon.

"Read it in tomorrow's *Post,* Connie," Burt said bitterly and then hung up.

An exposé by the former president's doctor in the *Washington Post* or *Washington Times* would not endear the medical unit to the new president and his staff. And an article alleging that Bush's doctor got fired by Bill Clinton could be disastrous. I feared that with bad and inaccurate press coverage about Burt being asked to permanently vacate the premises, the president would get fed up with the lot of us and we'd all get canned. Something had to be done. It was time for damage control or, at a minimum, a preemptive strike.

I picked up the phone and paged Larry Mohr. "Larry, Burt is going to the press saying the allergy-shot incident got him fired." My message was succinct and urgent.

Larry, usually the proper gentleman, uttered an expletive under his breath. "We need to do something now, before the president and his staff think we're disloyal to him."

I started to think out loud. "What if we go to the president's press secretary, Dee Dee Myers, and tell her what Burt's planning? At least she won't be caught off guard in the press briefings."

"Good idea," Larry said slowly. "Meet you in the press secretary's office in five minutes."

Great runner's legs. That was my clinical assessment of Dee Dee Myers as I was ushered into her cramped office in the West Wing. In the early months of the administration, Dee Dee had experienced a baptism by fire as the first woman press secretary. But the scuttlebutt at the White House was that she was fair and easy to work with. Her schedule that day was filled with meetings with the president and briefings with the voracious press. But after my urgent call to Larry, we were added to her schedule without any problem. Entering her office with Larry Mohr, I didn't want to intrude on her busy schedule but felt that she needed to know of potential bad press from Burt Lee.

A tall, fit blonde with a pleasant demeanor, Dee Dee was all business as Larry and I sat down to talk with her. "Now, you're doctors here at the White House?" she asked uncertainly.

"Yes, Dee Dee," Larry Mohr spoke hesitantly. Since Larry was the senior officer, I let him do the talking. "We are responsible for the health of President Clinton, his family, and staff."

Dee Dee looked confused; she had never seen either of us before and was trying to figure out how we fit into the life of the new president.

"The military assigns doctors from the Army, Navy, and Air Force to take care of the president and first family," I explained.

Dee Dee lit up when she heard Navy. "Oh, my dad was a Navy pilot. I'm a Navy brat." She smiled and turned her gaze to me.

"That's wonderful." I was relieved that we had something in common. "I'm the Navy physician and Colonel Mohr is from the Army," I explained as she nodded her head in understanding.

Larry cleared his throat and continued. "Dee Dee, we're here because we've heard rumors that the former physician to President Bush is going to go to the press with negative accusations about President Clinton."

Dee Dee looked confused. "What does President Bush's doctor have to do with the president?" Good question, I said to myself.

"Dr. Lee, a civilian doctor, lingered on at the White House a little longer than he should have. When the president's allergy serum arrived from Little Rock, he refused to give him the shot," I reported hesitantly.

"Dr. Lee shouldn't have been involved in the care of the new president and was asked to leave," Larry explained further.

"Who asked him?" she asked.

"The White House Military Office," I reported, wondering too late if we should have first gone to the new director of the military office. Are we jumping the chain of command? The thought raced through my mind as I sat with Larry in the press secretary's office reporting on our former boss. Should we be handling this on our own? A sick feeling settled in the pit of my stomach as I reminded myself that I was still on active duty and had an obligation to report to my superiors. Maybe Larry and I would be the next doctors fired.

"Burt is going to the press saying that the president fired him," Larry added, getting to the point.

"Well, that's the first I've heard of it," Dee Dee solemnly said.

"We wanted to give you a heads-up before the story broke in tomorrow's *Post* or *Times*," I continued. "Burt is reacting poorly to losing his job."

"I get it." Dee Dee nodded. "Thanks for the heads-up. This is a big help. You guys are great."

You guys are great? You guys are traitors, I felt. We're turning in our old boss who gave us our jobs here. And while we're doing so, we've jumped the chain of command and not informed the military office.

Larry and I shook Dee Dee's hand and walked out of her office in the West Wing, heading back to the doctor's office in the residence. As we slowly marched along the Colonnade, I shared my fear with Larry. "I just realized we didn't include the mil office in on this . . . Is that going to be a problem?"

"I'll handle it," Larry spoke, taking charge.

One of the things I learned at the White House is that when bad press about the administration is on the front page, it doesn't stay very long. Sooner or later bad press about something else inevitably replaces it. Burt did go to the local newspapers and his accusations about being relieved by Clinton were picked up by the national media. However, the story was soon bumped off the front page by other bad news. In addition, Dee Dee faced the press that afternoon armed with the information we had given her and was not caught off guard when reporters asked her about the allergy-shot incident. Since our preemptive meeting with Dee Dee, a friendship arose between her and the medical unit staff. She would sit with our nurse or medic in the staff van, and began to see the human face of the medical unit. Whenever I was on the road with the president and Dee Dee, she was always friendly and appreciative. In the end, Burt's apparent attempts to subvert the new president actually helped facilitate the medical unit's acceptance by the administration. Since we came forth to protect the president from bad and inaccurate press, we were considered on the side of the administration. But what got us through the early transition from President Bush to President Clinton was a sense of humor and *Semper Gumby*.

3.

Semper Gumby. This was the two-word mantra that helped me through the transition from the Bush to the Clinton administration. It was a funny saying concocted by my medical school classmates at the Uniformed Services University School of Medicine. *Semper* was Latin for always, as in the Marine Corps motto, *Semper Fidelis*: Always

Faithful. But *Gumby*? Remember that green rubber toy figure from our childhood? You can bend Gumby but you cannot break him. That struck a deep cord within me. I had been Gumby all my life: constantly moving, always changing schools and friends, adapting to new environments, forever flexible. I survived as a Navy brat by being malleable. So, for the presidential transition, the survival phrase became *Semper Gumby*. Always flexible. You can bend me but you cannot break me.

Before the Clintons arrived, I knew I would like my new patients from their press coverage. They had an easygoing manner with flashes of humor and genuine concern for working-class Americans. The challenge was for them to like us in the medical unit and be convinced that we could be trusted with their day-to-day care. How do you get the new president and his family to trust the former president's medical team? First, prove to them and their staff that you have a purpose that will serve them. And second, do it in the most pleasant, memorable, and unobtrusive way. How did I know this? Who showed me how it's done? I learned from the world's experts in the field of presidential transitions: the housekeeping staff.

I observed the skill with which the White House butlers, housekeepers, cooks, valets, and ushers easily earned the trust of the new president and first family. They were proficient in *Semper Gumby*. There was rarely any mention of the previous inhabitants of the house, or any comparison drawn and made to them or among themselves. Although we were not politically appointed, our loyalties and allegiance were now with the new occupants. *Change is our friend* was the catchphrase uttered by candidate Bill Clinton throughout his campaign. It was likewise repeated within the medical unit, or at least by me, as we all sought to embrace the change of this transition. It would greatly affect our daily working environment in the immediate future and in the years to come. For me, change would indeed become my friend, but it would later return as my foe.

Change would first be my work ally. I identified with the new president and his staff as they sought to create change and look at problems from a different perspective. I welcomed the challenge of trying to prove myself to them and, more important, finding ways the medical unit could better serve the president, vice president, and their families. From the day I arrived at the White House, I often questioned existing procedures or, more often, the absence of procedures and standards. Many of them I learned in my orientation had been passed down from generations of White House physicians. But were they efficient and did they apply to the existing president and the threat to his life in this era? The Army colonels in charge were wary of my "what if we did this?" ideas. They would usually respond with "We've always done it this way." I wasn't satisfied with this answer, nor was I complacent with protocol driven by tradition. But I couldn't change procedures without the power and time in which to do it. I was not the senior physician, and my two-year tour was almost over. To use a political analogy, I was a lame doc.

"Connie, it's not a matter of *if* the president gets killed," Rich Miller, Bush's senior agent said bluntly, his blue eyes cold but honest. "It's a matter of *when* . . . " I had cornered Rich on one of President Bush's final flights on Air Force One. In the privacy of the Secret Service compartment, I sat down with Rich, who had been an agent for several presidents. I respected his experience. He had worked closely with the medical unit for many years, so he knew my predecessors as well as how the medical unit operated. I asked him a simple question: "How can the White House Medical Unit do its job better?"

His words, not *if* the president gets killed but *when*, haunted me. The specter of assassination hung over all of us. The death of a president in office was the unspoken and undeniable fear of every White House physician. For any doctor to lose a patient was tragic, but to lose the first patient meant a devastating and very public failure. And for a military physician, to lose the commander in chief meant dishonor from failure to carry out their mission. My pulse quickened as Rich shared privately with me his concerns about how the medical unit operated. His thoughts were similar to mine.

These sobering comments from the president's senior agent brought home the realization that the medical unit had to work closer than ever with the Secret Service. We had to parallel their actions and movements on the road, and become more tactical and scientific in our protocols and procedures. We had to embrace state-of-the art technology and drill on a routine basis with them. We needed to evolve into the medical counterpart of the Secret Service and provide what I have termed Protective Medical Support.

But my hands were tied. Larry Mohr had been in the medical unit for six years and was preparing to retire. His successor was Army Colonel Bob Ramsey, a hematologist-oncologist from Letterman Army Hospital. Ramsey was doomed from the start of his tour in the White House Medical Unit. First, he was more conservative than what the administration was seeking. He came across as quiet, almost standoffish, and not very friendly. From the time he arrived, he failed to earn the approval of the "Holy Trinity"—the Secret Service, the military office, and most important, the president. Ramsey had been labeled by the military aides as awkward and out of place. And worst of all, he had failed to establish rapport with the first patient.

The final kiss of death for Bob Ramsey's assignment involved the president's blood type. Bob participated on an overseas trip with the White House advance team, where he represented the medical unit. His job was to designate and brief hospitals that would be used in the event of a presidential emergency during our foreign trip. As part of his pre-advance mission, Bob was to meet with hospital officials and assess the medical capability of the facility. He was authorized to share need-to-know information with the attending hospitals, such as the president's age, height, weight, and blood type. Unfortunately, for unknown reasons, he relayed the incorrect blood type to the hospitals involved. This was subsequently discovered and reported by the medical advance medic, who followed in Bob's wake. The military office quickly learned of this snafu.

"Doc, I'm going to transfer Colonel Ramsey," John Gaughan, the director of the White House Military Office, confided to me as we stood outside the Arkansas church where Bill Clinton was attending his mother's funeral.

This had not been a good week. The president's beloved mother, Virginia Kelley, had died in her sleep, and we had flown to Arkansas to bury her in a tearful ceremony. The medical unit and I loved Virginia Kelley. She was colorful, irreverent, warm, witty, and full of life. Because of her prior profession as a nurse anesthetist, we had made her an honorary White House nurse. And now after seeing her son become president and barely finishing his first year in office, she had passed away.

I tried to concentrate on what John Gaughan was telling me. At this point I almost didn't care, outside of my affection for Bill and Hillary Clinton. My tour of duty was almost over and I had already received a new assignment in San Diego. I would be leaving half-heartedly. There were so many improvements that could have been instituted to make the White House Medical Unit better. As a subordinate, I never got a chance to implement any of these changes. I felt as though I had personally failed the president. And now, Bob Ramsey would leave his position as director of the medical unit, and another colonel would no doubt be assigned to take his place.

"Who's the lucky full bird replacing him?" I said somewhat bitterly as John and I stood leaning against the side of the church.

"No." John shook his head. "The president wants you to be his doctor and to run the medical unit. It's yours, if you want to stay on."

His announcement hit me with a mixture of joy, fear, and trepidation. I had secretly wished to lead the unit but knew it was impossible. I was only a Navy commander and the director billet was reserved for captains or colonels. And while I was the first woman assigned as a White House military doctor, to head up the medical unit would be unprecedented. Talk about flouting presidential tradition.

I stared back at John in disbelief. He nodded his head with a smile on his face. I found my voice and finally blurted out, "But . . . but the Navy just issued my new orders. I'm to report back to San Diego to be director of the medical clinic at the Marine Corps Recruit Depot."

John winked at me as his smile broadened. "No, ma'am, those orders will be rescinded. The commander in chief just issued your new orders. You stay on as his physician and director of the White House Medical Unit."

Even though I was in civvies, I stood back and saluted, "Aye, aye, sir. I serve at the pleasure of the president." Grinning, I picked up my medical bag and headed back into the church to check on my patients. The thought crossed my mind that I should check with my husband, since this affected him and my family as well. But we were a military family and my two-year assignment had now been extended to four, by no less than the president himself. Who could argue with that?

"The damn mil office!" I cursed freely to my new administrator, Lieutenant Bill McGee. I had been director of the medical unit for six months. Colonel Ramsey had been quickly reassigned to the Pentagon. The colonel's departure and my promotion to director were greeted with relief by most members of the medical unit, if not all.

"What is it, Commander?" Bill asked me calmly, glancing up from his computer at the desk outside my office.

As the new director and the president's physician, I had moved into Burt Lee's old office on the ground floor of the White House. The past six months had flown by so quickly. The only constant had been change. But it was change for the better, I told myself. One of my first acts as director was to institute an arrangement with the Secret Service for the medical unit to provide twenty-four-hour on-site medical care to the president. This agreement was lauded by the Secret Service, who for years had been trying to institute this change.

It had been met with resistance by my predecessors, who didn't want to assign someone to overnight duty at the White House. Some members of the medical unit, past and present, didn't want this duty. I explained that it was an issue of security and urgent medical response for the first patient. If the president had a heart attack in the middle of the night at the White House, it didn't make medical sense for the Secret Service to have to throw him into an ambulance and head to the hospital. We were already assigned as his medical team to resuscitate and stabilize him in such an emergency. Seconds counted and having an on-site medical provider who knew his history and could treat him immediately would be lifesaving.

It was ironic that if the president were out of town, or out of the country, he would have a bevy of physicians, nurses, and medics near him at all times. But when he spent the night at the White House, everyone in the medical unit went home, leaving the president in the hands of Secret Service agents with only basic first-aid training. I felt as though the medical unit was deserting the first patient. Heart attacks don't just happen out of town. The president or members of his family could also slip or fall in their home, as Barbara Bush had on her last day there. I would have trouble explaining to Congress that, while his doctors were at home asleep, the president died at the White House. As a result of the change, there was a medical unit representative at the White House 24/7. I was the first medical person to stand overnight duty under the new plan. It is in effect to this day.

The Secret Service became my powerful ally and supportive of my effort to re-create the medical unit in the image of the Secret Service. Most of our resistance came from the military aides of the White House Military Office. The issue involved power and proximity to the president. The military aides felt responsible for the emergency-action role of the military and felt that the medical unit fell under their command. I chafed at that perception for two reasons: as the president's physician, I outranked the military aides and did not take orders from them. Second, the medical unit had a special, personal mission to take care of the president and first family and to respect their privacy. Any medical information regarding the president's health was on a need-to-know basis, and it was shared with the military aides only if pertinent to tactical operations.

In the final analysis, my conflicts (and those of my predecessors) with the military office were not due to chain of command and mission-related issues. The friction arose from a clash of egos: face time with the president and the sense of importance that it bestowed. A trivial incident such as an elevator ride would be a battleground if the military aide was not manifested on the elevator with the president. When there was not adequate space on an elevator, the military aide might be bumped from the elevator ride with the president while the doctor and Secret Service agent always accompanied the president.

I became very protective of the medical unit and its mission. I sought to create the world's benchmark of executive medical care through global, comprehensive on-site and electronically linked-up medical care for the president and his family. I worked long hours reviewing, upgrading, or creating protocols for this state-of-the-art medical unit. Anyone who interfered drew my anger.

"Goddamn mil aides," I blasphemed to Bill McGee, who stood up as I stormed into his office. "They're trying to bump the duty nurse from Air Force One and manifest her on the support plane, while they stick the mil aide in the med compartment. That violates patient confidentiality. I told the military office that if they take the nurse off Air Force One, I'll have no one to help me in case of an emergency. Is the mil aide going to assist with a cardiac arrest code?"

Bill's face turned crimson as he innocently stood in the path of my wrath. "No, ma'am, I can't imagine it."

"I told them that if they take the nurse off, they'll be depriving the President of the United States care standard for even South American dictators," I ranted in Lieutenant McGee's office on the ground floor of the White House. It had been slightly more than two years since I had stood up to the intimidating Burt Lee when he refused to leave his position at the White House. And now here I was ranting and raving against Burt's old nemesis, the military office.

I stopped short in midcurse when I realized who I sounded like. "My God, Bill," I spoke softly now. "I used to complain about Burt's foul language, his tantrums over the military office. Now look at me. I'm becoming Burt."

Bill shook his head. "I don't think so, ma'am." Bill had known me since my first week at the White House, when I was the junior Navy physician who would call on him at Bethesda, where he served as deputy director of the presidential suite. Bill had been the go-to medical service officer who provided the medical unit with funds, medications, and services from the Navy. While instituting twenty-four-hour medical coverage for the president was my first act as director, my second was to hire Bill McGee as the White House Medical Unit's first administrator and my right-hand man.

"Doctor, although you may sound like Burt Lee at times, you're more hands-on, more of a trench fighter."

I listened to Bill quietly. He was right in that regard, but was that enough?

"Well, that's how I got this job, by standing up to him. Burt knew from his own experience you had to be tough to work in his job and defend your mission daily. But to lead this unit?" Bill saw the distinction and nodded his head. "Well, maybe I should have given Burt Lee a little more credit."

I turned around and walked slowly back into my office, gazing out the window facing the South Lawn. I thought of how much I had changed from the time I first stepped into this office, wide-eyed and ready to serve. This job took more than being a good doctor, and I drew on resources I didn't know I had in me. I had embraced the arrival of a new president and helped with this transition while others resisted. In doing this I had followed the example of the housekeeping staff, being a servant to a higher calling. And now I was being called upon to lead the charge. It would indeed take *Semper Gumby,* Always Flexible. But as I sat down at the desk that had been Burt Lee's, as well as the previous presidential physicians, I recognized that it would take more. I had become tougher, more outspoken, and more confident in my leadership. As I complained about the mil aides, I realized that I had to take my ego out of the equation. I had to be strong but humble, I had to become my father and my uncles while at the same time transcending my roots. I had the roots. Now I needed to test my wings.

EIGHT

The Presidential Road Show

1.

The sun was setting in the land of the rising sun as our motorcade departed the garage of the Hotel Okura in Tokyo. I stared out the tinted window of the armored limousine and then leaned back onto the padded rear seat. I was dressed in a long, black-velvet evening dress with my radio latched to my belt, hidden under my jacket. My garb may have looked glamorous but with my medical bag and defibrillator case, I was more like an elegant bag lady. That was the duty attire for the black-tie event this evening.

As the duty physician, I rode in the spare or backup limo. It was commonly known in Secret Service jargon as the decoy limo. When I first learned of this moniker, I shuddered at the thought of serving as assassin bait. But after a year as White House physician and in recent months as the new president's primary physician, I nonchalantly regarded my seat in the decoy vehicle as business as usual. I accepted this risk as part of the inherent nature of my job. As a military officer, the White House assignment was the equivalent of a war zone, except the uniforms (business suits) and transportation (limousines, Air Force One, Marine One) were certainly luxurious compared to what my counterparts encountered in traditional military deployments.

As the motorcade made its way through the cramped streets of Tokyo, hundreds of Japanese with small American and Japanese flags in their hands waved at the parade of black, shiny stretch limousines. Schoolchildren waved, jumped up and down, some covering their smiling mouths, as they pointed to the American procession. This had been a week of multinational motorcades in Tokyo as the city was invaded by six foreign leaders and their entourage of staff and reporters.

I had first arrived in Tokyo three months earlier as part of the White House pre-advance team. For every foreign trip, the White House assigns a team of advance staff to survey the city in preparation for the president's visit. As the medical representative to this team, my mission was to assess the medical facilities in the city, designate a hospital to be used in the event of a presidential emergency, and meet with the host physicians involved in providing medical care at the summit. In addition, I toured with the team the sites the president would visit. I looked closely at environmental health risks at each site that might pose a danger to my patient, such as those causing heat exhaustion, or shortness of breath from poor air quality, endemic illnesses, and potential "loss of dignity" hazards such as falling or tripping.

"What are you looking for?" the American embassy nurse practitioner asked me, her blue eyes curious at the manner in which I examined every site the president would visit.

"I'm putting myself in my patient's place and taking his steps at each event site. While my Secret Service comrades look out for bullets and bombs, I look for bugs and bad environmental conditions that pose a danger." She nodded her head in understanding. "I just want to make sure the president doesn't become ill or get hurt during this visit."

"We want the same thing as well," she said with a smile, and then added, "Although we have grown to like your team and can't wait to have the new president visit, we're really looking forward to your departure from our lovely city."

"I can well imagine," I said in commiseration. After months of major preparation for the president's visit, the embassy staff was pretty frazzled and no doubt secretly looked forward to Air Force One's wheels going up on the final day of the summit.

When I wasn't examining hospitals and event sites, I was taking care of members of the White House staff at the hotel. I learned during my first pre-advance trip that this work never ended; many hours of trip preparation were interspersed with patient care. After a long day of meeting with hospital officials and scouring potential event sites, I would return to the hotel to find a note taped to my door that a WHCA (White House Communications Agency) staffer or advance team member was ill with traveler's diarrhea, bronchitis, or back pain.

For my pre-advance trip, I had packed a medical bag containing stethoscope, blood pressure cuff, and an assortment of antibiotics and analgesics, but no narcotics. If a patient was too sick for me to treat at the hotel, I would refer him or her to the local American military hospital or seek the assistance of the embassy nurse or physician to locate civilian care. After one week on my pre-advance trip, I returned to Washington to report my findings and recommendations to the medical unit.

In the months following my trip to Tokyo, I assumed the position of President Clinton's senior physician and director of the White House Medical Unit. As the senior physician, I was now going to accompany the president to this G-7 economic summit in July 1993. It was advantageous that I had also conducted the pre-advance trip and knew the contingency plans very well. I now assigned a White House nurse as the medical unit advance-team member, and she flew to Tokyo two weeks before our arrival to make final preparations.

As I sat in the spare limo, I waved back to the Japanese children. They must have thought I was Japanese. Many of the physicians at the designated Keio University Hospital had made that mistake and began to address me in their native language. I would smile, bow my

head, and utter a polite *"Wakarimasen,"* which meant "I don't understand." They would look confused, and to add to their perplexity, the
blond American embassy nurse would explain in flawless Japanese
that I was in fact the American president's Filipino doctor.

The week in Tokyo had been filled with summit activities, bilateral meetings, and photo-op sessions. President and Mrs. Clinton had
received a warm reception. This was the president's first foreign trip,
and it was important for him to make the right impression at this international summit. I, too, was aware of my role, although somewhat
minor, as a representative of America during my visit to Tokyo. I was
cautious to avoid stepping into any cultural potholes that might of-
fend our hosts.

But on this starry, muggy night in Tokyo, all the laborious preparations and work to start off on the right foot were about to be de-
railed by "Clinton time."

The prime minister of Japan seethed politely through clenched teeth
as our motorcade rolled up the cobblestone courtyard of the Imperial
Palace. Bill Clinton had arrived. And he was seven minutes late for
dinner with the emperor of Japan.

As I sat in the back seat of the spare limo, I could see the prime minister's expression. Beside me sat the president's aide, Andrew Friendly.
He was young, dashing, enthusiastic, and now anxious knowing that
his charge, the leader of the free world, was running late. Andrew had
repeatedly reminded the president earlier at the Hotel Okura, "It's
time to get going, Mr. President." But phone calls and short-fused
meetings with senior staff kept devouring the president's preparation
time. We then found ourselves rushing Bill Clinton into the elevator
for departure as the minutes ticked away.

It was show time and our performance on the international stage
was off to a bumpy start. Timeliness is next to cleanliness to the Japanese. In fact, the prime minister, who stood in the courtyard waiting
for the American delegation, had been sitting beside President George

H. W. Bush during his gastrointestinal upset at a state dinner a year earlier. Now the new American president would commit an even more shocking gaffe than his predecessor, who had thrown up in the prime minister's lap, and that was being late for dinner with the emperor.

"Eagle and Evergreen: arrive Imperial Palace," whispered the voice in my radio earpiece, almost sheepishly, as though the Secret Service knew the Japanese would be displeased with our tardiness. The president's limo, Stagecoach, pulled up to the front of the reception hall as the prime minister stepped forward to greet Bill and Hillary Clinton. The president looked handsome in his tuxedo and Hillary radiant in her evening gown. On the hotel elevator ride down to the vehicles that evening, the president had eyed his Secret Service agents, who were all donned in black-tie suits. "Don't we look sharp," he remarked. I stood in the back of the elevator trying to be invisible when the president spoke. Dressed to kill, I thought to myself, knowing the agents were wearing ballistic vests and were armed.

The prime minister bowed crisply and shook hands with the president and first lady. And then, sensing the tension, Bill Clinton worked his magic. He charmed the angst right out of the prime minister. I couldn't hear what he said that brought a wry smile to the man's lips, but whatever Clinton told him, it worked wonders. The prime minister now ushered them into the grand hallway to join the other summit leaders and their spouses.

Andrew and I jumped out of the spare limo and followed the lead agent into the Imperial Palace. The staff lead for the summit dinner at the palace was Steve Bachar. With his movie star good looks, Steve was calm and in control despite our initial arrival faux pas. He watched as the president and first lady, and one Secret Service agent of Asian descent, were led into the Grand Ballroom, where the other leaders were waiting. The massive doors to the room were then shut and agents were posted in front of it.

"This way, Doc." Steve pointed to a room to the side of the entrance. This was the hold room for the staff of the G-7 leaders, a place for us to wait and be ready to assist if needed. But most important, it meant one thing: food. All the White House staffers knew this for a fact, especially on foreign trips where they were usually overworked and underfed. In the medical unit, I had developed a ranking system for the type of holds we would encounter. A Level 1 hold, like a Level 1 trauma center, was top-of-the-line, best of the best, "doesn't get any better than this." For a hold to earn a Mariano Level 1, it had to offer hot food and cold refreshment. The ultimate hold would be a Level 1 with a television to monitor the event and your leader. As we entered the small antechamber in the Imperial Palace, I was anticipating a Level 1 hold. The promise of one of the finest meals in Tokyo made me salivate. The Navy military aide on duty was thinking the same thing as we stepped into the room and he wistfully said, "We'll probably get some pretty good sushi tonight."

Steve led us to one of seven tables bearing the flag of each nation represented at the summit. I looked down the length of the room and spotted the Russian flag at the end, on a table occupied by three heavyset men who appeared weary and bored. Our American contingent of Steve, Andrew, the military aide, the WHCA officer, and I, sat down at our table. I glanced at each delegation and was struck by how homogeneous they appeared: mostly male and predominantly either Caucasian or Asian. On the other hand, the American delegation had an African American male WHCA officer, and me, representing both Asians and women. We stuck out because of our ethnic mix, which made me proud to be an American.

Our rectangular table had an American flag posted on a small stand at the end with a simple white tablecloth draped over it. On the table were three items: a Waterford crystal case that contained cigarettes, a silver platter laden with bananas, and a stainless steel bucket with five bottles of Kirin beer on ice. I glanced at my companions, who by now were all eagerly anticipating our meal. We left the cigarettes and bananas untouched, trying not to spoil our lungs or our appetites. And since we were all on duty, we couldn't drink the beer.

But during our three hours in the Imperial Palace hold room, no food was offered or served to us—not even a grain of rice. There were just the cigarettes, beer, and bananas. And halfway through the evening, the platters of bananas were removed from all the tables by palace servants dressed in black suits. The other delegates had no compunction about helping themselves to the cigarettes and beer. So my comrades and I at the American table sat in the smoke-filled, banana-less room starving, tired, and jet-lagged.

"Eagle and Evergreen, moving to the cars," announced the Secret Service agent, which brought elation to our table. We were leaving the palace and going back to the hotel. "Room service, here we come!" the military aide joked as we scampered out and over to the motorcade, steps ahead of the president and first lady.

The ride back to the hotel seemed to take longer than planned. As I rode up the elevator with President Clinton and the first lady, the president glanced over and asked me in a hoarse voice, "Well, Doctor, did you have a nice time at the palace?"

The Navy mil aide standing beside me looked away. "Yes, sir, a most memorable evening," I remarked diplomatically. I knew that my job that night was not to have dinner or even have a good time; my job was to take care of my patients.

Hearing the president's voice made me refocus on my purpose. "Sir, I notice you're a bit hoarse this evening. Is everything okay?" The first lady glanced at me and nodded her head quietly.

"Oh, I'm just tired, Doc. Just need some sleep and to rest my tired vocal cords," he said wearily as he and the first lady stepped out of the elevator. "Good night everybody . . ."

I watched as the agents escorted the president and first lady to their suite. Then the announcement arrived over our radios: "Eagle and Evergreen: in for the night."

I stopped at the room beside the presidential suite where the valets were staying. The door was open and I could see Lito Bautista ironing one of the president's shirts. Joe Fama was packing some bags and Fred Sanchez was pouring coffee. The three men looked up as I trudged in and placed my heavy medical bags on one of the chairs.

"Doc," Joe greeted me. "You look hungry."

These valets are amazing mind readers, I thought. Before I could open my mouth, Joe led me over to the kitchenette where he took hot water, poured it into a cup of Ramen noodles, and handed it to me with a silver spoon.

I sat down at the tiny table near the stove as Fred brought me a glass of Coca-Cola with ice. I inhaled the hot noodles, burning the roof of my mouth as I hurriedly swallowed to satiate my hunger. The valets smiled as they watched me.

As I recall that night in Tokyo, I remember the grandeur of the Imperial Palace and the pomp and circumstance of the G-7 summit. But the memory that lingers on is how for me, a simple bowl of noodles was the finest meal served in Tokyo that night.

2.

It was not often that I got to attend a gala event with the president where I wasn't schlepping my bags around and waiting in the wings. My first time as a guest at a White House event was my most memorable and most eventful.

We were standing under the grand, twinkling chandeliers in the State Dining Room. It was 1992, the week before Christmas, and all through the White House, two hundred or more of George and Barbara Bush's close friends filled the mansion to celebrate the Bushes' final holiday party before leaving office.

Looking and feeling chic in my red satin blouse and black silk skirt, I was also free this evening from the burden of the bulky Secret Service radio on my hip, or bulging out from under my evening attire. I stood in line with a small platter in hand, ready to fill it up with roast beef, crudités, and the White House chef's famous large, succulent cocktail shrimp.

"I think he's choking on the shrimp," the man whispered to me as I put down my platter. I had been working my way around the buffet table, and out of the corner of my eye I had spotted a short and stout, red-faced middle-aged man, reminiscent of a younger Santa Claus, clutching his throat. He was trying to be as discreet as he could while choking to death in the middle of revelers in the State Dining Room of the White House. Guests stood shoulder to shoulder in line, eyeing each other's designer suits and glittery holiday dresses. Everyone in the room felt special to have received the coveted invitation to the president's holiday party. This was a time to appear cool, calm, and glamorous. If anybody else noticed the choking man, they were ignoring him and his impending social gaffe.

"Can you speak?" I reflexively asked the man, stepping in line beside him. He was trying to cough and didn't look up at me, staring down at the red and gold carpet the whole time. All I could hear from him was a high-pitched wheeze. That ominous sound made my pulse accelerate.

"Can you speak?" I asked again, preparing myself to respond to this emergency.

He shook his head and continued to grab his throat. I instinctively shifted into rescue mode, albeit elegantly in my holiday attire. And mindful of my environment, I moved smoothly to the back of the choking man, reached around to the front of his abdomen, and placed my two fists between his breastbone and belly button. And then almost to the beat of the symphony score being played by the Marine Corps Band in the background, I delivered three smooth thrusts into the man's abdomen. The room was filled with laughter and pleasant chatter, but all I could hear was the sound of my own breath as I counted "one, two, three" with the thrusts.

On the third thrust, the man leaned forward, his hands on the table. I started to perspire and adjusted my stance, anticipating that he was going unconscious and slumping forward. My next move would be to gently lower him to the floor. Then I would need to straddle him and deliver more forceful abdominal thrusts. I did envision the awkwardness of that routine emergency maneuver in the midst of the Bushes' Christmas gala. And while I was not dressed this evening to straddle a choking man, I wasn't going to allow him to die because it was socially inconvenient.

Fortunately, he leaned forward and coughed up a juicy piece of shrimp. His partner, who had remained silent and still throughout this emergency, handed him a napkin. My victim wiped his mouth, still not making eye contact with me.

"Are you okay now?" I asked, wiping the sweat from my forehead. The man nodded, still looking down at the carpet.

"Hey, Doc," a woman's voice rang out from the din of the crowd. "Do you need some help?" It was Senior Chief Mary Ann Chandler, the senior corpsman in the medical unit. Mary Ann was on duty that night along with Gary Dunham, the Air Force physician assistant. The duty physician for the event was downstairs in the Diplomatic Reception Room shadowing the president during the holiday photo ops.

Gary soon arrived at our side. He looked over at the man and said, "I'll help clean him up in the men's room." Gary accompanied the man and his partner out of the dining room. I watched them as they walked away, noting that no one else in the room seemed to notice the emergency.

I stared at Mary Ann. "Where've you been?" I asked. "I could've used you a few minutes ago."

"We were waiting in line to get to the serving table. I saw you with that man and wondered what was going on. It never occurred to me that there was a problem," she said.

"You saw me? Didn't you realize the guy was choking and I was performing the Heimlich maneuver on him?" I quizzed her, shaking my head.

"Actually we didn't, Doc. You looked so calm that I thought he was just a friend of yours and you were giving him a big hug."

I took her comment as a compliment. I had performed my first

Heimlich maneuver since medical school, and some would say I actually saved the man's life. But I never found out his name. He never returned to thank me, although throughout the evening, as I would wander into the different rooms on the State Floor, he and his partner were often just a few feet away.

Before the evening ended, I returned to the State Dining Room for coffee. As I poured cream into my cup, I glanced over toward the buffet table. The man and his partner had returned to get a second helping. As they passed the shrimp platter, I overheard his friend say to him, "Are you sure you don't want any more shrimp?" I shook my head in disbelief.

At that point, six months into my White House tour of duty, I attributed the choking man's oversight in thanking me to poor manners. But I would soon come to realize that this job is best performed anonymously. In fact, history doesn't record the name of the first physician to treat a president, or a first-family member, in the White House. John and Abigail Adams were the first occupants of the nearly completed White House in 1800. During their tenure, medical folklore has it that an anonymous physician had been called to the White House one evening to treat one of the Adamses' children. No one knows how that physician was compensated, if at all, for his services.

In many ways, the job of White House physician is a silent service, best provided quietly without a fanfare. Later, when I learned of this bit of history, I recalled my choking victim in the State Dining Room that Christmas. I never knew the man's name, and I'm certain he never knew mine, since in the urgency of the situation, I neglected to introduce myself. I am grateful both he and I survived our close encounter of that holiday season unscathed. Even today, I often wonder when I walk through a buffet line whether that incident gives him pause whenever reaching for oversized shrimp. Other such incidents among the political elite would show me how the fear of embarrassment can be so strong that a person might be willing to die of choking to avoid calling attention to him- or herself. And that thought alone is enough to take my breath away.

3.

During my eight years as President Clinton's physician, I accompanied him on 132 presidential trips overseas. On each mission I was faced with the ongoing challenge of keeping all my patients healthy. I was also keenly aware that as the American president's physician, I represented the United States of America. I kept this in mind as I toured these countries, especially in the Third World. In countries where the medical care was substandard by Western norms, the eager physicians and hospital staff who greeted our pre-advance team were proud of their "finest" of facilities. After touring an operating room where rice was being boiled and the trauma bay reeked of human excrement, our foreign counterparts would urge the White House Medical Unit to designate their hospital for the visit of the American first patient. To graciously decline their offer and seek appropriate alternate medical care elsewhere required astute contingency planning. But most important, it demanded tact and cultural sensitivity. During times that called for diplomacy, I relied upon my upbringing as a Navy brat who had lived overseas.

I grew up on military bases in the Philippines and Taiwan. In my early teens, I recall sitting with my mother and siblings on a bus loaded with American military dependents, coursing through the narrow streets of Taipei. As the bus made its way to the countryside, I looked out the grimy window at the muddy rice paddies where Taiwanese farmers tilled the soil. The fields reminded me of my homeland in the Philippines. I felt fortunate to be sitting comfortably on the American bus. This was one of many times in my life that I felt blessed to be on the other side of the window looking out.

This feeling was even more acute during President Clinton's visit to the Philippines in 1994. As our motorcade proceeded through the streets of Manila, I sat in the spare limousine looking out through bulletproof glass at the Filipinos in the streets. Any of them, from the tiny bare-bottomed street urchin to the wizened, toothless beggar, could easily have been relatives of mine, or even me in another life. But the grace of God had placed me on this side of the looking glass. And I was determined not to waste this opportunity.

My thoughts returned to that bus ride in Taiwan. As we drove past the rice paddies outside Taipei, one loudmouthed American teenage boy pointed to the Taiwanese farmers and remarked, "Look at those stupid foreigners!" I turned and glared at the pale-skinned, freckle-faced, pudgy teen. The fool didn't appreciate that he was the foreigner in this country. His rude remark epitomized the Ugly American stereotype. It was an image that I pledged to avoid in my journeys as the president's physician. But despite that promise, a sense of duty turned me into an Ugly American one hot, muggy summer day in Morocco.

The air was thick and steamy in Rabat in July 1999 when Air Force One touched down on the tarmac. Leaders from around the world gathered in this ancient North African capital to pay homage to King Hassan II, who had ruled Morocco for thirty-eight years. The sudden death of the king precluded the typical medical pre-advance screening of the city. Instead, we deployed our best advance-team member, Air Force medic Master Sergeant Jim McLeod. He pronounced his Scottish name "Mac Cloud." We called him "Mac" but nicknamed him the "Black Cloud," because whenever he had the duty bad things seemed to happen. Mac had developed the reputation for being cool and calm under the most difficult of conditions, for which he was at his best. Whenever there was a cardiac arrest or major trauma in a hospital or emergency room, Mac would be in the eye of the storm. I knew of his reputation when I picked him to be the senior medic at the White House. He always handled adversity with steely-eyed resolve, razor-sharp clinical acumen, and lightning-fast emergency

skills. While the Black Cloud seemed to be a magnet for medical ca-
tastrophes, the outcome typically was miraculous.

I assigned Mac to set up the medical coverage for the king's funeral in Rabat. Twelve hours before I boarded Air Force One for
Morocco, Mac called me on my secure line at home to give the
medical advance report.

"Ma'am, weather in Rabat for the funeral is Ghana hot and Manila
muggy," he drawled nonchalantly.

"Sounds like we'll need to use an extra-strength antiperspirant for
this trip," I suggested facetiously as I jotted down my notes.

He responded with a dare. "Doc, you'll never see me sweat." But
on this trip, the Black Cloud ultimately did sweat; we all did.

Thousands of Moroccan mourners lined the serpentine streets as
our motorcade arrived at the Royal Palace. President and Mrs. Clinton, along with former President George H. W. Bush and former
Secretaries of State James Baker and Warren Christopher, exited
their limousines surrounded by a heavy cover of Secret Service protection. I stood outside the palace gate beside the president's limousine. The palace was crowded with world leaders, and security was
very tight. This was the best place to position myself. If the president
were to be attacked, he would be brought back to the safety of his
armored vehicle and I would be waiting for him there.

The noonday sun was beating down upon my uncovered head and
dark pantsuit. Even the strongest antiperspirant could not save me
from soaking my suit that day. I began to stare off into space and
then nod off, the jet lag kicking in. I had not slept well on the eight-
hour flight from Andrews. This was going to be a trying overseas
excursion for me, being sleep-deprived, jet-lagged, hungry, and
sweaty. I thought of my medical training that mandated physicians
not work longer than an eighteen-hour shift to avoid injury to patients. I chuckled when I calculated that I had been on duty for close
to fifty hours. I knew this job was dangerous, but I never expected
my fatigue to be the source of danger for my patients. From the way
I felt, if bullets were to fly in Morocco, I would need to rely upon

the Secret Service, my Black Cloud medic, and my own reserve of adrenaline to take care of the president.

My radio now crackled with the announcement, "Eagle, exiting the palace." This signaled the drivers of the motorcade to start their engines for the ride to the mausoleum. My hand was on the door of the spare limousine when a whispered second announcement, this time from the special agent in charge, broke the momentum, "Eagle says he wants to walk in the procession."

"What?" I asked aloud and looked toward the president and his phalanx of agents leaving the palace. Mac was trailing the group, and I signaled him to remain Velcroed to the president while I stayed with the limousine.

"I got it, Doc," Mac mouthed to me, acknowledging my nod.

I watched the assembly of male world leaders and their respective bodyguards spill into the narrow streets of Rabat to trail the casket of the late king. Hundreds of thousands of Moroccans wailed and chanted as the procession of leaders followed the royal cortege. The late king's coffin lay atop an army truck on a rich green cloth embroidered with verses from the Koran. The truck rolled slowly along the streets with bicycle-rack barricades on each side to keep the screaming crowds from surging onto the streets.

The only vehicle trailing the procession was the president's limousine, with me in the back seat. The sight of the large, unruly, shrieking crowds that lunged toward the passing leaders took my breath away. This was a tragedy waiting to happen. Our president was surrounded by foreign leaders, with only a handful of his own agents encircling him, walking in the open streets of a foreign Muslim city with wild, uncontrollable crowds. More than one million people had descended on Rabat for the funeral. The president could be attacked from the crush of the crowds, from a bomb on the streets, or from a rooftop assassin. As the leaders marched behind the casket, I thought of one thing: this was a death march more than a funeral march.

The fervor of the crowd made my pulse quicken. I stared at the president's agents, and for the first time in my seven years at the White House, the men I had always regarded as unflappable looked terrified. Their movements, normally smooth and confident, were quick and ready to react as they glued themselves to the president. Even getting close to him was difficult, with the other world leaders crowding around.

Meanwhile, the two former secretaries of state appeared pale in their dark business suits in the boiling sun. I could see the back of Mac's head as he walked beside Secretary Baker, who was trailing behind former President George Bush. One bomb and we would lose our president, a former president, two former secretaries of state, as well as Israeli and Arab world leaders. This was the march from hell, and all I could do was watch helplessly from the president's vehicle. Although I was in an armored limousine, I never felt more vulnerable, sitting in a large black target that bore the seal of the American presidency.

Hysterical mourners surged against police lines. In the heart of the procession, President Clinton marched beside the new king, King Mohammed VI, who was dressed in flowing white robes with a red fez atop his head. The young king moved slowly beside the American president, both undisturbed by the fervor of the crowds. The procession ended at the mausoleum, where the president and the male delegation proceeded into the holy space. Meanwhile, Mrs. Clinton and the other wives were ushered to a separate site. In focusing completely upon the safety of the president, I had become oblivious to my other patient, the first lady. Fortunately, she was covered by the duty White House nurse, who stayed close to her and the female delegation.

The burial site for the late king lay within the mausoleum. I knew from the advance-trip briefing that the mausoleum was no place for a woman, especially one wearing a black pantsuit who had neglected to bring the requisite head scarf for any female entering this sacred place. If I had dared to follow my patient into the mausoleum, I envisioned an outcry by the mourners inside that an Asian-American infidel had invaded their holy site. Such negative attention would not help our image in the Muslim world.

So instead of following the president into the mausoleum, I sent my Black Cloud male medic and sat worrying in the air-conditioned limousine. Muslim funeral prayers were chanted in the mausoleum while I quietly prayed in the limousine for this funeral to end and for us to be on our way back to the airport.

After a few minutes of silence, the radio crackled with the lead agent's whispered, tense voice, "Has anyone seen Doc Connie?"

My heart stopped. "This is Doc, I copy direct."

"Doc, Eagle needs you in here."

"En route," I said, clicking my radio receiver. My feet moved faster than my mind, as I tried to envision what "Eagle needs you" really meant. I bolted out of the limousine, lugging a medical bag that seemed heavier than ever. As I stepped into the thick Moroccan air, my black pantsuit immediately became soaked with sweat. Touching the top of my head, I had a pang of guilt but knew that I was prepared to barge into this holy sanctuary uncovered.

I had to become the Ugly American now. All the niceties of cultural sensitivity were abandoned. Diplomacy was ditched. I was now on a mission to get to my patient. *The mission comes first* was the credo drilled into me repeatedly at my military medical school and on active duty.

A beefy site agent met me at the large door leading into the mausoleum. "Eagle needs you inside," he spoke quickly as I followed him into the mosque. As the agent opened the heavy door, I was immediately overcome by the smell of body odor: a musky, nauseating stench. All I could see in front of me were wall-to-wall Moroccan men. The agent grabbed my hand and pulled me through this crowd. Mourners stood chanting and immobile in front of me blocking my way. I moved past and through them in the only way I could: shoving and pushing, I rammed them with my medical bag, jabbing them with my elbows along the way. It was futile to issue polite "excuse me's," since they couldn't hear me above the loud wailing and wouldn't understand me anyway.

Each step of the way, each body that came into my path, I had to shove, ram, or jab. I didn't care whom I offended along the way. The first patient needed me. I kept envisioning the scenario I would encounter when I got to his side. Was he calling for me with chest pains after the long procession? Was he light-headed from dehydration and jet lag? Was his back bothering him? What was so urgent that the president needed his doctor right away and couldn't wait until he returned to the safety and privacy of his limo?

The smell got worse the farther in I ventured, and overwhelmed me. I tried not to vomit. Get me to my patient. The agent pulled me through the last grouping and delivered me to the president, who was in a corner of the mausoleum a few feet away from the burial site. His lead agent came up beside me.

"Doc, I was worried. The president looked a little pale for a while so I handed him some bottled water." The agent's face was solemn but relieved that I had arrived.

I examined the president, who had tiny beads of sweat on his forehead, his wet face devoid of color against the contrast of his black suit. Reaching for his hand, my fingers went to his radial pulse, which was rapid but strong.

"Hey, Doc," the president murmured in between sips of water. "I'm a lot better now. The heat just got to me."

I nodded my head in understanding and turned to his lead agent. "He looks okay now." Then looking closely into the president's eyes, I asked him seriously, "Sir, any chest pain or light-headedness?"

The president shook his head. I was relieved. "We're good to go," I reported to his agent.

"Ready, sir?" the agent asked, as he looked at the president. Bill Clinton nodded, finishing his bottle of water.

"Eagle moving . . . toward the cars . . ."

I latched on to one of the agent's coattails as we worked our way back through the crowd. Once again, wall-to-wall wailing, obstinate bodies stood in our path. I clung to the agents who surrounded the president, and pushed and shoved whoever got in my way. I didn't want to get separated from the detail and left behind in this sea of male mourners.

When we finally extricated ourselves and exited the mausoleum, the cars were waiting, engines revving. As I headed for my vehicle, Mac quickly ran up to me. "POTUS looked pretty pale in there, but I couldn't even get close to him," he quickly reported. Mac, the Black Cloud, was drenched in sweat.

"He's going to be okay," I reassured him as I opened the door of the spare limo. Mac turned back with a thumbs-up as he headed toward the Support Van.

"Let's go home," I announced to the limo driver as I collapsed into the rear seat.

NINE

Life in the Kill Zone

1.

G un!" the lead agent yelled into his sleeve mike right before shots rang out from the second-floor window of the dilapidated, abandoned building across the street from our motorcade.

The president was working the rope line, and as soon as the agent uttered the dreaded warning, the shift agents engulfed the president with their bodies, forming a protective shield that rapidly moved toward the armored limousine.

I was posted on the opposite side of the limo while the president was at the rope line. As soon as I heard the agent's alarming announcement, I reflexively jumped into the limousine, perched on the edge of the rear seat behind the driver, my medical bag at my feet. Within seconds, the agents shoved the president onto the back seat, his head landing in my lap. His face was pale and he was breathing rapidly.

With a squeal of tires, the massive vehicle rocketed forward, away from the scene of the attack. The lead agent had leaped into the right front seat, barely making the rapid departure.

"Is he okay, Doc?" he asked breathlessly, staring at me in the rear-view mirror.

"I'm doing my medical assessment, give me a second," I muttered impatiently, my attention focused on the victim, who appeared to be dying in my lap.

When it comes to treating a casualty in the field, medical personnel are taught to follow the basic A-B-C-Ds of an initial assessment: *Airway, Breathing, Circulation, Disability.* All the advanced trauma and cardiac life-support certification courses I had taken in my medical career were to culminate in the back seat of a moving limousine.

I was looking down at my patient, who was a victim of a sudden attack. He was groaning and trying to utter a few words, incoherently. The man's airway was not occluded. He was breathing but his breaths were rapid and shallow. I put two fingers on the carotid artery in his neck and found that the pulse was rapid. His eyes were open, with dilated but reactive pupils. I grabbed the stethoscope from my medical bag, and as I lifted his shirt to listen more closely to his lungs, spots of red blood oozed from a small puncture wound in his left chest.

"Chest wound!" I shouted. "It looks like a bullet fragment, could even be a sliver of glass, but we have to get to the Level I trauma center immediately." The blood dripped onto my white blouse. *Damn! Another blouse ruined,* I thought.

"As per the doc, POTUS has chest wound. The Secure Package en route to Level 1 trauma center now," the agent announced calmly into his sleeve mike.

The limousine then turned a sharp corner, and I swung to the left of the limo, my stethoscope still tethered to the president's chest wall, trying to listen for breath sounds.

Then a thought came to mind that I could not overlook. Looking up from my victim, I told the lead agent, "Alert the military aide. Even a slight wound may require surgery and anesthesia. It could be Twenty-fifth Amendment time."

"Roger that," said the agent, with a satisfied look on his face, as he reported it on the Secret Service closed frequency.

"All posts. Secure from exercise."

The limousine in which we rode was a training vehicle, retired from the field five years ago. The "president," who lay bleeding in my arms, was an agent assigned in today's exercise to be POTUS. He had been dressed in frighteningly accurate moulage to simulate a wound to the left chest. A big hole in the president's chest would have made my response easier in noting an obvious life-threatening gunshot wound. But what about something more benign, do you still treat it as an emergency and consider invoking the twenty-fifth?

We had just concluded another Attack on the Principal—AOP—exercise at the Secret Service training compound in Beltsville, Maryland. Since I became director, I had mandated that every member of the medical unit participate in an AOP with the Secret Service shift agents once a month. All agents were required to participate in these exercises that simulate real-life scenarios. I felt it was important that the medical unit train with the Secret Service on a routine basis to familiarize ourselves with the protective detail's protocol, but even more important, to keep our trauma skills current. Not only was it vital that the medical unit practice state-of-the-art field medicine when it came to treating the first patient, but because our patient was the leader of the free world and a nation with a nuclear arsenal, we had to keep in mind succession of the office of the presidency. Every AOP exercise tested the White House physician's ability to assess and treat trauma in the field. But just as important was assessing the White House physician's ability to determine whether the president was medically incapacitated and, if so, would the Twenty-fifth Amendment need to be instituted.

When President John Kennedy was assassinated in 1963, the on-duty White House physician was Admiral George Burkley, who was riding in the rear of the motorcade. Admiral Burkley arrived at the Parkland Hospital emergency room in Dallas after the fallen president had been wheeled into surgery. As a result of the Kennedy assassination, the White House Medical Unit began to work closely with the Secret Service, including participating in AOP drills. But through subsequent administrations and different leaders of the medical unit, and despite attempts on the lives of both presidents Ford and Reagan, the practice of training with the president's protective detail fell by the wayside.

The words of SAIC Rich Miller, special agent to President George H. W. Bush, haunted me when I took the reins of the medical unit in 1994: it is not a matter of *if* the president is attacked but *when*. My job was to prepare the medical unit to effectively respond to the worst-case scenario. To do so would mean working side by side with the Secret Service, knowing their protective moves, knowing how agents assess threats in the field, knowing how agents think.

The injuries that the medical unit and I were called upon to assess and stabilize in the field were similar to those we would have seen in battlefield conditions. What was different from a war zone were the types of vehicles in which we traveled (armored limos, Marine and Air Force One), uniforms (business suits instead of camouflage), and triage. In the military, medical personnel in the field are taught to treat multiple casualties in order of severity of injury and the likelihood of patient survival. The casualties least likely to be saved are set aside. The wounded with the greatest chance of being saved are given first priority. For the White House physician, the commander in chief is at the top of the triage list. Period. The agents and medical team exist to ensure the president's survivability. But what if you have multiple casualties at a scene?

The new White House nurse fidgeted in her seat waiting for the next test question. She sat at a dark wooden table in the medical unit's administrative office on the top floor of the Old Executive Office Building across the street from the White House. Seated around her were the medical unit's nurses, medics, physician assistants, and physicians firing off the questions. She handled each scenario with nervous energy and a touch of cockiness in each excellent retort she provided. She was acing the oral boards. Every member of the medical unit had to pass an oral board that included a tabletop exercise in which they had to think on their feet about what they would do given a particular scenario. So far, the nurse, who had been a decorated ICU nurse with impressive credentials, had been answering every question successfully. And then the final scenario.

The senior nurse read the script while all eyes focused on the new nurse.

"A gun goes off in the crowd near the stage where the president, first lady, and members of the first family are seated. The president is hit in the right shoulder. He is breathing, conscious, but in pain. What would you do?"

"Rush to the president's side," the new nurse fired off rapidly.

"Bang! You're dead." The senior medic pointed a finger at the nurse's head, suppressing a wicked grin. "Look out, but you've got a gunman at the scene, and the area is not secure yet."

The nurse opened her mouth to respond, but stopped when the senior physician on the board spoke, "We are taught in the medical unit the old adage: you can't treat the president if you're dead. Safety first. Wait till the scene is secure."

"Okay." The new nurse nodded.

The senior nurse continued and smiled quietly, since she knew her novice nurse was going to step into that scenario quagmire. "The scene has been secured, the gunman has been subdued. The president has been removed from the stage by his shift agents, and the White House physician is with him in Stagecoach making their way to the hospital."

The nurse nodded her head, wiping some perspiration from her hairline, hoping the testing would end soon.

"But there are multiple casualties. The first lady is down with a laceration to her forehead. Members of the first family are also injured.

The president's elderly uncle has been struck in the chest and is in shock. As you move toward the first lady to assess her, she waves you off telling you to take care of the first uncle. What would you do?"

"Go to the first uncle?" the nurse responded with a question.

"But the first lady has been injured; she's bleeding from her head . . ." The senior nurse emphasized the word "bleeding."

"Well, then I'd go to the first lady . . ." The new nurse searched the faces of the board members looking for a hint of affirmation.

"But remember, the first uncle has been hit in the chest and is in shock," the senior physician assistant reminded her.

"Well, then I'd go to him first." The new nurse tried again, her frustration and confusion mounting.

"And why?" the senior physician inquired.

"Well, because . . . because . . . he's seriously injured . . . most likely his breathing is compromised by trauma to his lungs or heart . . ." The new nurse defended her response, growing more anxious as the group looked at her with a blank expression.

"Is there any other reason you would go to this person first?" the senior nurse asked.

"No, I don't think so," the nurse responded. She looked at the board members who began to shake their heads. "Okay, I guess I'm missing something here."

"Hint: remember you're assigned to the White House." The senior medic taunted her.

The nurse blinked her eyes rapidly, trying to think of the answer.

The senior physician rescued her. "Okay, there is another answer, but it's the politically savvy answer."

The senior physician assistant chimed in, "So here it is: you go to the victim because . . ."

And the whole board responded, "Because the first lady told you to!"

2.

The Secret Service calls it the "kill zone." To be in the presence of the president is to stand in the kill zone and to sense the rarefied, exciting, and potentially deadly experience of being in close proximity to an assassin's most prized prey.

For nine years, I lived and worked in the kill zone as part of my everyday job. During this time, there were numerous threats on the life of President Clinton. When I first arrived at the White House, hearing from the Secret Service that someone "unstable" or evil would want to hurt the president would cause me to take offense. Why would anyone want to hurt my patient? My naïveté quickly faded with each threat made and each alert issued to his staff. I accepted that my patient's fate was to live a life of danger during his term of office. My fate, in turn, was to be ready to take care of him if he were wounded or injured. At the same time, I knew that my own safety was at constant risk.

Not everyone who has spent time in the kill zone has escaped unscathed. In 1981, President Reagan's press secretary, James Brady, became a victim of the first of John Hinckley's bullets. I thought of Brady in March 1997 when President Clinton was at Bethesda Naval Hospital recovering from surgery on a torn quadriceps tendon.

"Doc Connie, we've got a problem." The shift agent leader had approached me the afternoon before the president was to be discharged from the hospital. "None of our vehicles will accommodate the president in a wheelchair."

"Don't you have anything in the Secret Service garage left over from the Roosevelt era?" I quipped sarcastically to the agent, who was surprised by my offhanded remark. I had been glued to the president's side for three straight days since he tore his hamstring walking down the steps of golfer Greg Norman's home in Jupiter, Florida. I was tired, unbathed, and weary-eyed, wearing my thick nerdish glasses. All civility abandoned, I was on the edge of near-exhaustion and my sense of humor was strained. I caught myself and shook my head. "Sorry, let me start again. You're telling me we're going to have a problem driving the president from Bethesda back to the White House?" I spoke softly.

"Yes, ma'am," the agent responded, all business. "Can we carry him into the limousine?"

"No way," I said, quashing that suggestion as I recalled the president's indignity at being physically carried by his agents from the limousine to Air Force One in Florida. "He leaves Bethesda in a wheelchair, and when we arrive on the South Portico, he stops to chat with the press while seated in his wheelchair."

The Navy military aide was standing nearby and heard our conversation. "Can we borrow a van from someone who uses a wheelchair?" he suggested. "Isn't there a congressman who lost both legs in Vietnam and uses a wheelchair?"

The agent perked up. "Hey, good suggestion." He thought for a moment. "Even better, how about James Brady? He must have a specially equipped van."

So the afternoon before President Clinton was to be discharged from Bethesda, the Secret Service contacted James Brady, who graciously loaned us his van. I thought of the kill-zone connection, sitting in the rear of Brady's spacious but unarmored vehicle while President Clinton sat upright in his wheelchair beside me. Clinton, who had been the object of numerous threats, survived his time in the zone. His only connection to an attempted presidential assassination was hitching a ride back to the White House in James Brady's van. That was fine with me. It was as close to the specter of assassination that I was willing to get.

Physicians are trained to do battle with injury and death. But most physicians don't expect to be at risk. As military physicians we accept our duty to practice medicine in harm's way. White House physicians believe that our patient's life and safety come before our own.

This maudlin realization is usually handled with dark humor in the medical unit. The antidote to what we called "ego proximity attacks" at the White House is to realize that if Air Force One were ever to go down, the headlines would scream "President and Others Perish." And we all knew that we would be the soon forgotten "others." It provided little comfort to us or our loved ones but it kept our egos in check.

3.

Wearing a flak jacket, helmet, and headphones, I sat on the plastic bench of the Air Force C-17 designated as Air Force One because the president was onboard. President Clinton was flying from Sofia, Bulgaria, to Skopje, Macedonia. We were on the tail end of a ten-day trip that started in Istanbul, Turkey. After Turkey we traveled to Greece and stayed for the night, but we kept close to the hotel because the streets were filled with protesters setting cars and garbage containers on fire.

When Air Force One lifted from the tarmac in Athens en route to Italy, the chief flight attendant stepped into the medical compartment where I sat with my nurse.

"May we help you?" asked Lieutenant Vince Starks, my senior nurse, anticipating that the chief needed some Motrin or had a personal medical question.

The chief appeared slightly distraught and looked carefully at the medical bags on the floor. "No, sir. Just checking the bags."

"Checking?" I asked. "For what?"

The chief, satisfied after surveying our compartment, looked at me and winked. "For something that shouldn't be here."

"You mean something ticking?" Vince asked.

"Uh, yes, sorta," the chief said evasively, and hurried out of the compartment.

I later learned from the Secret Service that as Air Force One was rolling down the runway, a voice came over the radio and announced that a bomb was on the plane and would go off in fifteen minutes. The pilots made two smart moves: 1) they summoned Secret Service to the cockpit to listen to a recording of the threat, and 2) they set their timer for fifteen minutes. Fortunately, no bomb went off and we made our way to Italy, Bulgaria, Macedonia, and Kosovo.

Our trip to Macedonia on the C-17 was considered another dangerous mission. Many of the sites we visited there granted military personnel "imminent danger" pay for setting foot in such hazardous areas. We touched down in Macedonia and boarded helicopters for Kosovo, where the president was engaged in bilateral meetings. There were signs posted around the military base where we landed, cautioning personnel about the land mines in the area.

The senior physician assistant, Craig Ashby, met our helicopters at the landing zone. Because the security for the trip to Kosovo had been listed as high, I also brought my deputy, Dr. Richard Tubb, on this trip. He flew on Nighthawk Two, the backup helicopter. Even though the trip was rated as dangerous by the Secret Service, I felt confident at our end because I had the most senior and experienced members of the medical unit with me. On the flight home, I

Sitting beside Secretary of State Madeleine Albright on the C-17 flight from Kosovo to Italy in November 1999. Albright is holding up the book she is reading, Guns, Germs, and Steel. (UNKNOWN)

realized that bringing all the best and the brightest together on a hazardous mission was not the smartest thing to do. There needed to be survivability in the medical unit in case the president and medical unit senior members were lost.

The visit to Kosovo was a quick stop, and we soon boarded the helicopters to take us back to the C-17, which would then fly us to the tarmac in Macedonia. There, Air Force One was waiting to fly us to Washington. This mission had so many "moving parts": helicopters, armored cars, C-17 aircraft, and the mother ship, the 747 Air Force One. I felt like a combination robot and lemming, following my patient to each site, getting into a car, helicopter, and plane. Each step was automatic to me; carrying my bags, taking my position just out of the kill zone but close enough to observe my patient and respond to him in case he was injured or wounded.

I was grateful this dangerous mission to Kosovo had been completed without incident. My reward was to ride back to Air Force One with my team on the C-17. As the behemoth aircraft climbed to altitude, I gazed at my tired, half-asleep medical-unit team, who sat across from me on the uncomfortable aircraft benches. I looked at Dr. Tubb, his blond, signature cowlick standing upright from the back of his head, giving a boyish appearance to a man who was a full-bird colonel. Leaning back in the seat beside him was Craig Ashby, the medical unit's senior physician assistant. Always serious and with a Clark Kent–like mien, Craig rarely smiled, but I now detected a wisp of a grin. Beside Craig sat the charismatic senior nurse Vince Starks, who welcomed every dangerous mission as an adventure. But the sustained excitement of this long trip had worn Vince out and he closed his eyes and started to snore.

As I stared at the three men, I suddenly realized I had made a potentially serious mistake. I had brought my most senior personnel. If the aircraft were to crash and the president and others were to perish, the vice president, under the Twenty-fifth Amendment, would assume the powers of the presidency. But who would run the White House Medical Unit and take care of the new president?

I signaled for the communications officer to hand me a secure phone. The operator connected me to Lieutenant Commander Barbara Idone, the medical unit administrator who was posted at our administrative offices at the Old Executive Office Building.

Barb's voice was crisp and cheerful when she answered the phone.

"Commander Idone, please copy the following succession plan . . ." I spoke slowly and clearly over the static of the phone.

She picked up on the gravity of my tone. I gave Barb the specific names for the senior physician who would run the medical unit, the senior nurse, and the senior physician assistant who would replace those on the C-17 if we were to become history. Barb repeated each name after I announced it. I envisioned her sitting on the edge of her seat, writing the names onto a yellow pad.

"Do you copy, Commander?" I asked.

"Unfortunately, I do, ma'am," she responded, her voice cracking. "Anything else I can do?"

"If we are forced to institute this succession plan, remember to reserve a spot for me across the river at Arlington," I reminded her, surprising myself with my lack of emotion when it came to details about my remains. "My personal requests for burial are in the office safe, including services, pallbearers, music, and so forth."

"Yes, ma'am," Barb responded, holding back tears.

"And Barb?"

"Ma'am?

"If my remains should be found adequate for being dressed, remember that my preferred uniform is service dress blues . . ."

"Yes, ma'am." Barb sniffed, blowing her nose.

"Service dress blues, Barb," I emphasized. And acknowledging my vanity to the bitter end, I added, "As you know, service dress blues are so much more flattering."

When I had finished my call to Barb, I hung up and sat back on the bench with an ironic smile. I knew that I was one of only a handful of first-patient physicians around the world who had to worry about such a plan on their drive home from the office. Except unlike most physicians, my office was at 1600 Pennsylvania Avenue and my ride home was on a big, baby blue 747 that bore the presidential bull's-eye seal.

TEN

The King and I

1.

It *must be good to be king*, I thought as I boarded the sleek, mahogany-adorned yacht of the royal family of Spain. It was a balmy Sunday afternoon in July 1997 and President Clinton, Hillary, and Chelsea had been invited by King Juan Carlos I and Queen Sofia to sail on the *Fortuna* off the coast of Palma de Mallorca. The president was on his way to Madrid to participate in the NATO summit, and he was to use the first leg of this trip to spend private, casual time with the king and queen. How do you let your hair down with a monarch? I had pondered this question when the president's daily schedule was announced at the advance-team meeting the previous night.

The only White House staff allowed onboard with the president and his royal hosts were one Secret Service agent, the on-duty Navy military aide, the White House photographer, and me. The rest of the White House staff was relegated to smaller boats that kept their distance from the royal yacht as it bobbed up and down on the sea off the coast of Mallorca.

I trailed behind the agent, mil aide, and photographer as we stepped across the bow onto the boat. I felt almost unworthy to board this stately vessel. It wasn't "my place" to be sailing with the monarchs of Spain, who were historically connected to my Philippine heritage, as the islands had been a Spanish colony for centuries. The Philippines had been named for Crown Prince Philip II, and now I was to set sail on the Mediterranean with descendants of the namesake of my family's homeland. My Filipino peasant ancestors would be rejoicing in their graves.

Although I had been comfortable taking care of American presidents for five years, this was my first encounter with royalty. With servant blood coursing through my workingwoman's veins, I felt inferior and out of place. I was a Navy ship's doctor who felt at home riding big, gray, diesel-fueled ships and not glamorous yachts. I had been the daughter of a Navy steward growing up, and the mantra of "you're not good enough" still plagued me, especially when it came to dealing with the high and the mighty. I now battled that curse with the sword of purpose: I needed to be near my patients in case they became ill or injured.

"Doc, I bet this ship is a lot nicer than the ones you're used to riding," joked the Navy military aide as we made our way to the bridge of the yacht.

"I'll tell you after I get a look at their sick bay," I quipped, following him up a spiral staircase that led to the wheelhouse.

We were greeted by a striking, swarthy Spaniard who introduced himself as the yacht's captain, the lucky navy man whose job was to sail the king's yacht. The captain gave us a brief tour of the compartment, which proudly displayed the finest nautical gear. The Navy military aide, who had been a ship driver in his previous command, was envious of the captain's fabulous vessel. The White House photographer tried to snap some photographs of the compartment, but the captain asked him to refrain for security purposes. During this exchange, the Secret Service agent and I leaned back against the bulkhead and gazed out the porthole at the azure sea around us.

The *Fortuna* set sail under the thrust of a powerful inboard engine, humming confidently over the waves. I admired the shoreline of Palma de Mallorca, the largest of the Spanish islands, and was awed by the white-sand beaches that hugged the coastline. The military aide handed me a pair of binoculars and nudged me, pointing to the beach. I peered through the "big eyes" and saw fleshy, pale forms frolicking through the white sand. A nude beach. But those that pranced free of clothing and care did not have the toned, tan, and youthful bodies you would expect to be proudly on display. Instead the nude beach was populated by droves of grandmas, grandpas, and portly Uncle Josés—all overweight and victims of gravity's sag.

"Hey, Doc, when you become admiral, does the Navy give you a boat like this?" Ralph Alswang, the White House photographer, kidded me. Ralph was loved around the White House for his irreverent sense of humor. Whenever he was the duty photographer, we could always anticipate laughter and a good prank. White House staffers who dared to fall asleep on the job would awaken to the loud click of a camera, and look up to find a grinning Ralph capturing the moment on film. The photograph would later be resurrected at the staffers' birthday or farewell party, with a clever comment signed by the president or first lady. When Ralph was the duty photographer, there was never a dull moment.

We could periodically hear laughter rising from the cabin down below where the king and queen entertained the Clintons. We wanted to give the royals their space by staying as far away as possible but close enough to respond to their call. The captain's cabin was a safe place to hide away.

Thirty minutes after we had set sail, we heard the voices from the family cabin grow louder. I turned in that direction to find Bill and Hillary Clinton at the top of the stairs. Behind them were the king and queen of Spain.

The atmosphere in the cabin switched instantly from relaxed

observation to formal decorum. I could almost hear the Navy military aide whisper under his breath, "Attention on deck," as everybody in the compartment stood up.

"Hello, everybody," President Clinton greeted us with a relaxed grin. I smiled back at my patient, glad to see he was in good spirits and enjoying his visit. Beside him stood Queen Sofia, who had been the last to enter the compartment. She was petite with delicate facial features; her soft, auburn hair was set in a pageboy framing her lovely face. In her hands the queen held a silver platter of hors d'oeuvres. She walked toward me and held out the platter. For a moment I thought she wanted me to take it from her and serve the others. Then I caught myself and realized that the queen was being a gracious hostess offering crudités to me. I declined the offer with a soft "No thank you, ma'am," and lowered my eyes, bowing my head. *I am not worthy, Your Majesty, to partake of the royal pupus*, spoke my inner servant voice. But my feisty Yankee spirit prodded me to help myself to the munchies spread around the cabin. If I was good enough to be a White House physician, I was at least good enough to help myself to a smoked salmon on toast points from the royal platter.

However, I watched enviously as Ralph and the Navy military aide helped themselves to the queen's hors d'oeuvres. The Secret Service agent stood in the corner away from us, a silent sentinel who didn't participate in this social gathering with the monarchs and his protectees. I wanted to also disappear into the corner alongside him and become invisible. Mingling with nobility just wasn't in my blood. I was on duty and that meant work and not play or socializing with my patients and their friends.

King Juan Carlos stood beside Bill Clinton. The king was strikingly handsome, with wavy dark hair and strands of silver. Even in his polo shirt and casual slacks, he carried himself with an air of nobility. The captain gave a brief tour of the compartment to the leaders and their spouses. I watched the group as they surveyed the equipment in the cabin, and I slowly made my way to the corner, close to the Secret Service agent.

Bill Clinton saw me try to scoot away from the group and drawled slyly to his host, "Your Majesty, I'd like you to meet my doctor." I froze in position and smiled sheepishly. The two men walked toward me.

The king eyed me up and down and asked Clinton in disbelief, "This young, lovely woman is your doctor?"

"Yes, Your Majesty." Clinton smiled proudly. I felt exposed, no longer able to hide.

The king stepped forward with his hand extended. Before I could reach out to him, the king of Spain dropped to his knees, appearing to pass out in front of me. I automatically reached forward and grabbed his elbow with one hand, while checking his pulse with the other. He now looked up and started to laugh.

Juan Carlos had feigned a faint to see what I would do. My instinctive reaction amused and impressed him. The royal flirt, I thought. The Navy military aide, Ralph, and the yacht captain all laughed. The queen and first lady shook their heads. The king stood and made a slight bow. "So quick and so lovely."

I felt my cheeks burn in embarrassment. I had tried to disappear but instead called the worst kind of attention to myself. Was the king really trying to flirt with me? At such events I tried to appear professional and all business, with my black hair cut in a conservative bob and in my navy blue generic pantsuit. I chided myself that perhaps I didn't convey a business-enough appearance.

"It's an honor to meet you, Your Majesty," I said, and trying to recover, I added, "You have a strong pulse."

The king and president both laughed. Their wives grinned at my comeback, and the four of them disappeared to the family cabin below deck.

"Hey, smooth moves there, Doc," Ralph teased me after the leaders had left the cabin.

"Thanks, Ralph," I responded, tired of being teased. "Only move I'm going to make now is to the head."

The captain overheard my remark and led me down a passageway to a commode. The toilet was different from any toilet I had ever

Traveling with the president meant meeting former presidents and other celebrities. President Clinton introduces me to former president Gerald Ford in Vail, Colorado, after a golf game in August 1993.
(VAIL VALLEY PORTRAITS, INC.)

encountered, even onboard Navy ships. The commode was connected to a series of convoluted pipes in the bulkhead and had various switches. As the captain gave instructions on how to use the toilet, my mind drifted back to the king's performance, and I didn't pay attention to the captain. *How complicated could a toilet be?* I told myself sitting down on the seat. When it was time to flush, I looked for the handle, but there was none attached to the body of the toilet. I looked at the switches and pipes on the bulkhead beside the commode. I turned the first switch but rather than making the toilet flush, it made the water in the bowl rise. I flipped the switch in the opposite direction, but the water kept rising.

The higher the water rose, the more I began to panic. I reached for the second switch and turned it; a hissing sound came from the toilet. I tried the third switch and it did nothing. The higher the water rose in the toilet, the more anxious I became. I had tried to be discreet and invisible during this whole outing. Instead I had the king flirting with me and now I was about to flood his royal yacht because I didn't know how to flush the toilet. Do I yell out: "Help! Flooding in the compartment, abandon ship!"? I tried to remember my shipboard experience on USS *Prairie*, but those toilets were simple flush-handle models. The water reached the top of the toilet seat and began to run over the brim, down onto the deck. Fortunately, there was a drain in the floor. As the water began to cover the floor, I heard a knock on the door.

I had the honor of meeting His Holiness Pope John Paul II four times during my White House assignment. Here, President Clinton introduces me to the pontiff in October of 1995. (WHITE HOUSE PHOTO)

"Hey, Doc, are you done in there?" asked Ralph. I knew I would never live down this moment with him, but I didn't care. I didn't want to flood the compartment.

I opened the door quickly. "Ralph, I've got a problem here . . ." I confessed as he looked in at the overflowing toilet.

"You sure do, Doc," Ralph said. "Let me get the captain."

I didn't stay for the arrival of the captain. Perhaps I should have remained at the scene of the crime, but I just couldn't handle any more attention that afternoon on the yacht. Apparently the captain was able to stop the flooding. To Ralph's credit, he never took a photograph of the flooding toilet nor of my embarrassed face that day on the king's yacht. But he didn't have to record it. We both remembered it, and for weeks after the event, I would avoid using the bathroom anytime Ralph was present. And I would also avoid fainting, flirtatious kings on future trips abroad.

2.

It was December in Washington, D.C., and the winter chill didn't bother me because I would be traveling that day to the warmth of South Florida with the president and first lady. The United States was hosting the first Summit of the Americas on December 9–11, 1994, in Miami. The Clinton administration had made elaborate preparations for this summit, which would bring together all thirty-four heads of state from North and South America. It was going to be a grand event, one of the biggest in Clinton's first term.

As we boarded Air Force One on December 8, I was still flying high from my own event, having been promoted to the rank of captain the day before we left. The president had conducted my promotion ceremony in the Oval Office on December 7, Pearl Harbor Day. As the president's physician, I was given an early promotion based on the act of Congress from 1927 giving the senior White House physician the automatic rank of captain or colonel. I became one of the youngest captains in the Navy, an honor that was especially poignant for my father, who had retired as a Navy master chief steward.

As I departed for Florida with the president and first lady, I felt that this was going to be a good trip. That was often determined by the staff who accompanied me. I was bringing with me Air Force Captain Wendy Van Dyke, the duty Air Force One nurse. Originally from St. Vincent and the Grenadines, Wendy was exotic in appearance with her olive skin. Her raven black wavy hair was braided into a tight bun per military regulations. But her Caribbean appearance was misleading; she was truly American in spirit with her feisty do-or-die nature. Wendy, like senior medic Mac McLeod, also attracted disaster. I knew with her onboard that I could expect lots of patients; she was a magnet for the sick and injured. But besides her nursing skills, Wendy also had a riotous sense of humor that would have me laughing no matter how tired we got on foreign trips.

In the Oval Office, President Clinton assists me in donning my Navy captain uniform, bearing the four gold stripes on the sleeve. My sons and my parents observe. (WHITE HOUSE PHOTO)

The summit in Miami was destined to be memorable because I had also assigned Major Ed Luminati as the medical unit advance person. Ed was an Air Force physician assistant who, with his silver hair and mature bearing, always looked serious. But like Wendy, his appearance was deceptive. Although appearing stern, Ed had a heart of gold and a silver tongue. The medical unit would refer to him by his last name, Luminati, or his nickname "The Loomer."

This often led to name confusion with the president's special agent in charge, Lew Merletti. Lew had been a Special Forces medic in Vietnam, and then a superstar in the Secret Service who would ultimately become its director after his assignment as Clinton's lead agent. Lew was a trained killer with a lethal sense of humor. Whenever he was covering the president, I always felt safe and confident at the start of the day, and afterward we often shared a laugh, even when times were tough.

Showing off my gold captain stripes in the Oval Office after my promotion ceremony as my family applauds. (WHITE HOUSE PHOTO)

So, I was going to be at the Summit of the Americas in Miami with Wendy the disaster magnet and the "two Lews": Luminati and Lew Merletti. Something strange was bound to happen.

"Captain," Major Luminati addressed me on the first day of the summit, while we sat in the staff hold room.

I was getting used to being addressed as Captain instead of Doctor or Commander. Captain sounded like a much nicer title to me.

"Yes, Major," I responded, sipping my Diet Coke as I flipped through the summit trip book, which outlined the day's events.

"I'm not complaining or whining . . ." Luminati began.

"Of course you're not," I said, pouting as I listened to his plaintive and whiny tone. "Go ahead."

"Since I travel so much with the vice president, I don't think the president even knows my name. What if he gets sick and I wind up being the first to respond? He may look up at me and ask, 'Who the heck are you?'" Luminati was really concerned, with a strained voice and pained expression.

"Well, Ed, we'll just have to introduce you to him," I responded in a maternal voice.

Wendy overheard our conversation and piped up. "Ed, why don't you let me do the honors?" she asked, building up a head of steam. "Mr. President, Mr. President, I'd like you to meet our star physician assistant: Ed . . ."

"The Loomer!" Ed interjected.

". . . Luminati." We all broke into laughter. The advance staff sitting in the hold room looked up at the three of us laughing. Then the representative from the State Department walked up to me, unsmiling.

"I hate to interrupt this," the State Department representative said, his dark glasses perched on his beaklike nose. "But did I overhear you were with the medical unit?"

"Yes, we are," I responded. "I am the director and the president's physician, Major Luminati here is the medical advance for the summit, and Captain Van Dyke is the White House nurse."

"Can we help you with something?" Wendy asked,

SCHEDULE OF THE PRESIDENT
FOR
WEDNESDAY, DECEMBER 7, 1994
FINAL

tba 07:15	MORNING RUN
NOTE:	NSC Briefings will be on paper.
8:30 am–9:15 am	COFFEE WITH DLC TRUSTEES ROOSEVELT ROOM Staff Contact: Linda Moore CLOSED PRESS
	— The President and Vice President Gore will meet and greet with guests.
9:30 am–9:45 am	MEETING OVAL OFFICE Staff Contact: Leon Panetta
9:45 am–10:00 am	PHONE CALL TO PEARL HARBOR SURVIVORS OVAL OFFICE Talking Points: Tony Lake Staff Contact: Tony Lake WHITE HOUSE PHOTO
10:00 am–11:30 am	BUDGET BRIEFING CABINET ROOM Staff Contact: Bob Rubin
11:30 am–3:30 pm	PHONE AND OFFICE TIME OVAL OFFICE
3:30 pm–3:40 pm	PROMOTION CEREMONY WITH COMMANDER ELEANOR C. MARIANO OVAL OFFICE Staff Contact: Alan Sullivan WHITE HOUSE PHOTO
3:40 pm–3:45 pm	MEETING OVAL OFFICE Staff Contact: Billy Webster
3:45 pm–4:15 pm	SPEECH PREP FOR SUMMIT OF THE AMERICAS OVAL OFFICE Staff Contact: Don Baer

A copy of the presidential schedule for December 7, 1994, showing my promotion ceremony at 3:30 P.M. in the Oval Office.

staring at the man's beady eyes. "Are you not feeling well? You don't look so good."

"I feel perfectly fine," the man sniffed. "It's not about me. It's about the president of Guatemala. Our liaison informs me their president has a very painful toe. Can you help him?"

"We can," Luminati responded promptly. "Take me to him and I'll see what I can do."

Luminati and the State Department representative disappeared from the hold. As I watched them walk out, I recalled previous summits in which the medical unit had been approached to render medical aid to a foreign leader or dignitary. This was the "silent service" part of our mission: to assist in the care of foreign leaders who would benefit the United States and the presidency.

But often these requests at summits were unusual and fodder for potential international embarrassment. During the APEC—Asia-Pacific Economic Cooperation—Summit in Vancouver in 1993, I was asked by the representative from the national security advisor's office if we carried ChapStick. The sultan of Brunei needed some. Surely, I thought, he could have brought his own. He could have easily bought the whole company for a ready supply. ChapStick was not in the medical unit inventory but the duty nurse, Lieutenant Gina Kiefer, carried her own supply and handed one to the highly paid gofer. A few minutes later, the NSC representative returned with the ChapStick and handed it back to Gina.

"No, thank you," the man said with an edge to his voice. "The sultan says it's already been used." We were all surprised and looked closely at the ChapStick; the seal was unbroken. Sometimes we can't please everybody.

And there were times we had to be cautious as to what requests we filled. During the same summit, the State Department representative came to me with a strange query.

"Doctor, do you carry any cough syrup?" she asked in a serious tone. None of the State Department folks ever smile during these summits. It appeared to be a painful experience for them.

"Yes, I do," I responded as I started to rummage through my medical bag.

"Well, it's for the Koreans. The Japanese delegates have asked that we give the Koreans the cough syrup. They say that they are coughing too much."

I stopped looking for the cough syrup. "Uh, so sorry," I said, "seems like I didn't bring any with me after all." I could imagine how insulted the South Korean delegation would feel, if I or someone from the American delegation walked up and handed them the cough syrup, unsolicited. Perhaps I had averted a major international incident.

My summit recollections from Vancouver were interrupted by Luminati, who returned to the hold thirty minutes later.

"And how is the president of Guatemala?" I asked, ever eager to provide some medical support to a summit foreign leader. I was actually trying to round up some patients for the medical unit to treat, since Wendy's disaster magnet wasn't working this time out, and we didn't have the usual line of sick-call patients at the hotel that morning.

Ed was looking through his medical bag as he spoke, "The poor man is in a lot of pain. He's having a gout attack of the big toe and can hardly walk. He's tried all the usual oral medications. I'm looking to see if we have something stronger for pain."

I reached into my medical bag and handed Luminati a Bristojet of Toradol. "How about this?"

Luminati read the label. "Toradol. Ah, yes. Like injecting someone with Motrin or Advil, but it's a lot stronger and will cut down the inflammation."

"And it isn't very sedating, so he can go on with the summit and make decisions clearheaded," I added, sounding like a drug representative.

Ed took the Bristojet from my hand and dashed out of the hold. Somewhat later, with the first day of the summit almost over, Wendy and I moved from the hold to the benches outside the conference center. As we sat watching the delegations walk past, we listened to our radio traffic. President Clinton was still in the summit conference room meeting with the other leaders. Lew Merletti was posted near the door watching POTUS with eagle-sharp eyes. Lew would turn and nod with a smile. I knew the president was in good hands.

Luminati soon reappeared. "I haven't been able to give the Guatemala president his shot yet. But his assistant said we can meet in the men's room and I can give it to him there."

"Isn't there a better place you can use?" I asked.

"Actually, not." Luminati shook his head. "No private rooms in this building. Anyway, it won't take long."

Wendy perked up at the sound of this rendezvous. "Loomer, sure you don't need an experienced nurse to assist you in the men's room?"

Luminati laughed. "You wish."

Ed went straight into the bathroom adjacent to the conference hall. In five minutes, we saw the president of Guatemala and his small entourage of three agents walk toward the men's room. The president was walking slowly, limping and grimacing with each step, and looked like a man who needed a shot of Toradol. He went inside while his three men waited outside, standing post.

As the president of Guatemala stepped into the men's room, we heard over the Secret Service frequency the voice of Lew Merletti, "All posts on Oscar. Eagle needs to use the bathroom. We're moving to the men's room."

I suddenly realized that the presidents of Guatemala and the United States were about to have a close encounter of the unexpected kind. I sat on the bench with Wendy, watching the president and his band of agents, led by Lew Merletti, strolling into the men's room. Ten minutes later, we heard boisterous laughter and Merletti's voice announced, "Eagle now moving back to conference hall."

Still smiling, Bill Clinton charged briskly out of the men's room with Merletti by his side. Moments later the president of Guatemala walked out gingerly, his three men joining him as he headed back as well.

The last man to exit the restroom was Ed Luminati. He shuffled toward me with a face as red as his tie.

"Mission accomplished, Major?" I asked, confirming that the injection of Toradol had been administered.

"Well, yes, but not without incident," Ed added, and then explained. "I was about to give the president the injection of Toradol. The man had his pants down at his knees, and was bending over the counter to receive the injection in his right gluteus, when Eagle walked in."

While Ed and I spoke, Lew Merletti walked up to us and looked at Ed, shaking his head and smiling, and letting him finish.

Lew Merletti then took it from there. "Eagle and I are walking into the men's room, and the first thing we see is two men, one with his pants down and the other with a needle. I realized that Eagle does not know Ed, and I probably didn't recognize the president of Guatemala."

"Well, not from that angle," Ed joked.

Merletti chuckled and went on. "So Eagle only sees these two men in a compromising position, stops in his tracks, grabs me by the arm and says 'Lew, I think they're doing drugs in here.'"

Lew and Luminati couldn't stop laughing.

"I told Eagle, 'Sir, this is Ed Luminati from the medical unit. And I'm sure he's just administering medication.'

"Then, when the president of Guatemala heard Clinton's voice, he pulled up his pants and walked over to shake President Clinton's hand."

Luminati and Lew Merletti now laughed so hard their eyes started to tear up. I smiled as I looked at the two laughing men. I knew the two Lews would be forever linked in White House lore to the men's room incident at the Summit of the Americas in Miami.

3.

If it was good to be king, I learned that it was better to be John
Kluge. I came to this realization one evening in Biscayne Bay as the
president and thirty-four heads of state from North and South America were driven pierside to the two-hundred-foot yacht owned by
the American billionaire. The media entrepreneur had lent his private vessel to the president and first lady so they could host a sunset
dinner cruise for the leaders and their spouses attending the summit.

"Just look at that boat!" Andrew Friendly, the president's personal
aide, exclaimed after letting out a loud whistle as our limo rolled
down the pier toward Kluge's yacht.

"It puts royal yachts to shame," I said, recalling the *Britannia* of England, on which I had sailed with the president and first lady in June
of that year. I admired not only the size of this boat, but also its polished wooden decks and shiny brass that glistened in the Florida sun.

"Stagecoach has arrived dockside," the lead agent's voice announced
over the Oscar frequency, indicating the arrival of the president's
limousine.

Another black-tie event, I thought. It had been a hectic week at
the summit in Miami. What I found more challenging than the long
hours and unpredictable requests for medical assistance was the different types of attire I had to pack for this three-day mission. Usually
one small suitcase would suffice for a five-day or less domestic presidential trip. But the activities for the Miami summit required more
than my usual two navy blue nondescript pantsuits that served as
my civilian on-duty uniform. To blend in at summit social activities,
I packed golf wear, a black-tie outfit, and business attire that was
slightly more formal than the day-to-day working pantsuit. I was surprised that I didn't need to toss in a duty bathing suit as well.

My dress for the evening's boat ride was a long, black chiffon skirt
and a silk black and gold jacket. I also carried the usual accessories:
simple gold stud earrings, Secret Service radio clinched to a belt hidden under my jacket, and my duty medical bag with the medical unit

emblem embroidered on the front flap. I was dressed to fit in with the formal setting but prepared to spring into action if I were called upon to provide care.

A moist breeze lifted my thin skirt slightly as I walked briskly across the bow, following the Marine Corps duty military aide, who wore a mess dress uniform for the evening's formal event. The two of us boarded ahead of the president and first lady. We positioned ourselves along the rail away from the quarterdeck, to watch them board, followed by the other leaders. We also wanted to stay out of the shot of the many cameras, which were positioned along the pier and beside the military honor guards posted as side boys at the arrival point.

Bill and Hillary Clinton strolled down the red carpet toward the yacht. The president looked tired, with swollen bags under his red eyes. His voice had become raspy during the week's many meetings, and several staffers approached me during the summit to ask if I could do something about his hoarseness.

"He needs one thing: voice rest," I would respond, having answered this question on numerous occasions when the president's vocal cords had become strained by overuse, allergies, or reflux. The president's staff would invariably react to my terse answer with incredulity. Surely, you can't be asking the oratory wonder Bill Clinton to not use his voice, not to speak, they would ask. It was like asking him not to breathe.

"Okay, then," I would offer. "Hot tea with lemon, Altoids, and sips of room-temperature water would help." That remedy would suffice until sleep and silence restored the presidential timbre to its customary action.

Hillary walked beside the president dressed in a chic, black, low-cut evening gown, her décolletage covered discreetly by a sheer sheath. Her shoulder-length blond hair was swept into an attractive up-do. The first lady radiated confidence and glamour. At this point in my White House assignment, I had been the president's and first family's personal physician for almost a year. I had visited them in their private quarters on numerous occasions, and on many of these house calls, they would be wearing casual wear or just pajamas. Seeing Hillary this evening dressed so elegantly made me do a double take; I had never seen her look so regal and stunning.

I glanced down at my frumpy, utilitarian garb. I was dressed for work, not to entertain or be photographed. I often fantasized about going to one of these events dressed in an elegant evening gown, and not having to shy away from the cameras. As I stayed out of the spotlight, always trying to be invisible, I could hear the familiar refrain from my childhood: "you're not good enough." Today I shrugged off this chiding voice from the past, rationalizing that I had already proven my worth: I had been promoted in the past week to the rank of captain by the president of the United States in the Oval Office. At least he thought I was good enough, I reasoned.

The staff lead on the yacht signaled to me and the military aide, pointing to a cabin belowdeck that was the staff hold. We stepped down a carpeted stairwell, catching glimpses of the living spaces and other cabins as we made our way down. Magnificent oil paintings hung on the mahogany bulkheads, elegant thick carpeting lay across the decks, while crystal and silver sparkled from serving trays that were being prepared in the galley. We only got a brief glimpse into the living quarters of the fabulously wealthy before we were ushered into the staff hold.

A handful of White House staffers sat comfortably on the plush sofas there, munching on sandwiches and watching the news on television. I didn't feel like planting myself in the hold while my patients and their guests were topside, socially engaged but also exposed. I felt the yacht gently sway as we pulled away from the pier. I wanted my face in the salty breeze, watching the sunset off the horizon, just like my days onboard ship. My sea legs energized, I scampered up the stairwell onto the deck where I found a discreet spot from where I could gaze out at Biscayne Bay. Fortunately, it was also a few feet away from the main cabin where the Clintons were entertaining the other leaders and their spouses.

The yacht sailed like silk on the bay while I listened to the sounds of laughter and music rising from the cabin. Fireworks now lit up the sky above us as the revelers watched in awe from the main cabin deck. Even in the most powerful, the sight and sound of the pyrotechnic display orchestrated for the evening's cruise evoked childlike wonder.

I glanced at my watch and noted that the cruise would be over in another hour. I needed to visit one of the restrooms on the yacht and found my way to the ladies' powder room on the main deck. As I reached to turn the knob leading to the restroom, the first lady stepped out.

"Hello, Dr. Connie," Hillary said in a cheerful voice. But despite the smile on her face, I detected a slight sadness in her eyes. "Congratulations on your promotion this week! Bill told me about it. We're so proud of you."

I was startled to run into the first lady on her territory. I silently reprimanded myself for not having done a better job staying out of the way of my patients. But it was difficult to not run into someone, even on a yacht of this size.

"Thank you, ma'am," I answered, searching her eyes for the source of sadness. "It was a great honor to have the president promoting me in the Oval Office. I'll never forget that."

She smiled and put her arm around me. As she did, one of the White House photographers suddenly appeared from nowhere and snapped our photograph. And in a flash Hillary disappeared from my side, headed back to the main cabin. I stepped into the restroom and afterward moseyed over to the main cabin. I stood outside looking in, watching Hillary move from one leader to the next, smiling, shaking hands, laughing, appearing comfortable in her role as a gracious hostess. I could see the president watching her as well; for despite their marital difficulties, which would soon become very public, they would always be a formidable political couple.

As I observed the gathering of leaders and their spouses in the main cabin, it felt as though I were watching a masquerade ball. All

Hillary Clinton congratulates me on my recent promotion to Navy captain, onboard the Kluge Yacht during the Miami Summit in December 1994. (WHITE HOUSE PHOTO)

the participants dressed and acted as they wished you to perceive them. Hillary, a dynamic and outspoken attorney by profession, was costumed as an almost demure hostess and acted her role. The leaders and their spouses, many of whom came from small, underdeveloped countries, dressed and behaved as though they represented large, powerful nations.

As I stood outside the cabin looking in, I realized that I, too, was not only an observer but a participant in one of life's charades. For as accomplished as I was as a physician, as senior and as decorated as I was as a naval officer, I was admittedly a failure as a wife and mother. With my recent promotion to captain, my tour at the White House had been extended. Whatever promises I had made to my husband and family about retiring and returning to San Diego to live a normal life had been rescinded. And while I was receiving congratulations from my fellow officers and colleagues at the White House, my husband was less than enthusiastic about my promotion and extended tour of duty.

I was reminded of that night and of these reflections years later when my marriage had been irrevocably broken. My extended time taking care of the first family was the beginning of the end of my marriage and own family's cohesion. This fate befalls many careerists, both men and women, but I now recognize the sadness I saw in Hillary's eyes that night; I've seen it in my own for years.

ELEVEN

The White House Bag Lady

1.

"I've wanted to come here all my life," Hillary Clinton confessed to the cheering crowd at the Sydney airport, who were there to greet the Clintons on their presidential visit to Australia in November 1996. I, too, had always wanted to visit the land down under. But I never expected my first trip would be accompanying the president, first lady, and an army of a hundred White House staffers, security, and traveling press. I once had a stopover in Tasmania during a Western Pacific cruise on the USS *Prairie* in 1983. That clunky gray diesel-fueled ship with wooden decks was a sharp contrast to the sleek 747 jet airliner that had whisked us across the globe to this part of the world.

A thunderous twenty-one-gun salute now honored President Clinton's arrival on the first leg of our trip to Australia. The Aussies welcomed the Clintons with open arms and an upbeat mood. Australian security was cooperative and friendly toward us and our agents. So even the Secret Service was looking forward to this nine-day presidential trip, which would culminate in the president's attendance at the eighteen-nation Asia-Pacific Economic Cooperation Summit in Manila. The hospitals here were excellent, the country was English-speaking, and our hosts were sunny and cordial. This had all the hall-marks of a pleasant trip. And in addition to the usual meet-and-greets, speeches, and official events, there was also vacation time on the sched-ule for the president and first family. But for the medical-unit staff on this overseas mission, I made it clear: "When the president plays, we work."

Jet lag was a way of life for me. I adjusted by timing my meals and sleep periods to the destination's time zone. On overseas trips, the Air Force One crew was savvy to feeding the passengers meals adjusted to our final destination. It sometimes felt awkward to be awakened from a long sleep to eat dinner, or find your stomach growling while trying to fall asleep on a long night flight. I avoided taking sleeping pills be-cause I needed to be ready at all times to respond to an emergency. I didn't want to be in a state of Ambien-induced slumber if my services were required.

On our third day in Australia, my jet lag hit with full force. I was dozing off in the middle of the day, hiding my yawns while I stood beside the spare limo watching the president work a crowd. They were going wild over Bill Clinton in Australia. As usual, he was charming crowds everywhere he went. Through sleepy eyes I watched the president shaking hands in the crowd. He never seemed to get tired. In fact, just watching him work made me tired. He would plunge into a crowd, surrounded by agents, and the more hands that Clinton touched, the more enlivened he became. It was as though he were re-ceiving a transfusion of energy from the crowd. The adulation of the people is a politician's lifeblood.

Meanwhile, as the day wore on, so did my energy wear out. When the president and first lady finally boarded the Sikorsky chopper to Port Douglas in Cairns, my physical stamina was at an all-time low. The helicopters we flew were smaller than the rotund grasshopper-appearing choppers that usually shuttled us from the South Lawn.

The helo for this leg of the trip only accommodated eight passengers, seated like sardines in the back, except for the president and first lady, who sat in executive swivel chairs facing each other.

To exit this helicopter, the other passengers would have to squeeze past these fixed chairs to get to the cabin door. This was no easy task since we had to avoid crossing in front of the cameras as they were filming the president departing the aircraft. So we had to board before the president and leave after him. All this required timing, smooth maneuvering, and, as I would painfully learn later, an extra pair of hands. This was especially true if you happened to be the medical bag lady of the White House.

The helicopter hummed soothingly as we made our way to Port Douglas. I was nudged against the duty military aide on a bench across from President Clinton, who was taking a power nap. I couldn't see Hillary, whose seat had its back facing us. I covered my mouth, hiding my yawn, and wished that I could also take a power nap. Bill Clinton was blessed with the ability to "log off" at will on these short flights. When he awakened, his eyes would pop open and beam bright. He would then announce, with a smile and a stretch of his arms, "Show time!"

"You working overtime, Doc?" the mil aide asked, noticing my eyes at half-mast.

Smart-ass, I thought. He's not suffering from jet lag. This mil aide got to sleep in Sydney while his alternate carried the football and followed the president around on his tour.

"I'm always working overtime, Major," I shot back, my patience short. Then I remembered that my relief was at the site. "Fortunately, I've got Dr. Eschbach at the landing zone. Once there, I'm handing off the medical bags and, most important, the president to him."

I gestured to the bulky black-canvas bags crammed at my feet and beside the bench where we sat. I surveyed the gear around the compartment: my leather briefcase, personal backpack, duty medical bag, defibrillator, and the two insulated boxes with the units of blood for the president and first lady. When we lifted from Sydney, the advance-team physician's assistant had helped me get the bags into the chopper before the president and first lady boarded. Once we landed in Port Douglas, I would need to grab the bags and make my way quickly to the motorcade.

"That's a lot to carry, Doc," the mil aide remarked skeptically, counting the bags around us. He eyed my small frame and slender, tanned arms. "You got any help on the ground?"

"Eschbach and our medic Gary Hoertz should be at the LZ," I reassured him. "Don't worry. I'm used to being the bag lady."

The White House bag lady. I considered this title with ironic humor. My physician friends regarded my position as glamorous: take care of the president, travel around the world, attend fabulous social activities, and witness historic events. They didn't realize that I spent most of my time schlepping medical gear, jumping in and out of cars, helicopters, and planes, while half asleep, tired, and grumpy. I lugged around a bevy of bags that carried medicines, first-aid gear, blood, and electricity— just in case the first patient needed them. Despite this onus, I was proud to be the president's doctor.

The helicopter began to descend to our arrival in Port Douglas. Dr. Jeff Eschbach

My hands were always full carrying bags; here I'm accompanying President Clinton between sessions at the G-8 Summit in Birmingham, England, in 1998. (WHITE HOUSE PHOTO)

would be waiting for me at the landing zone. Board-certified in family practice, Jeff was the other Navy physician in the medical unit. With his baby face and crew cut, he resembled the television series character Doogie Howser. Some of the staff called him "Baby Doc," while the agents referred to him as "Doogie." As I glanced out the window, I could see the sun setting over the tropical terrain. Below us lay an open grassy-field landing zone the size of a football field. To the side was a dirt road where the motorcade had been assembled.

Jeff Eschbach had arrived in Port Douglas a week earlier with Master Sergeant Gary Hoertz, who at the time of the trip was the senior medic at the White House. Unlike his successor, Jim "Black Cloud" McLeod, Gary had a "white cloud." Blond with rosy, cherubic cheeks and a good-hearted nature, Gary was easy to work with. However, his fair skin made him prone to sunburn. I had cautioned him before our trip to lather up with a sunscreen or we'd be calling him the "pink cloud."

One by one the other Sikorsky choppers ahead of us landed. The duty nurse was on Nighthawk Two. I now looked past the mil aide out the window of the chopper. I strained my eyes searching for the nurse exiting Nighthawk Two on the ground. She would be heading to the Support Van taking her back to the hotel; Gary and Dr. Eschbach would meet me beside my chopper.

Marine One touched down in the open field, and it wobbled side to side on the uneven ground. I held on to the bench, and when the rotors stopped, unbuckled my seat belt. In seconds, the Marine One guard exited the opposite door and went to the hatch facing the president and first lady. With crisp precision, the marine opened the hatch. Moist, sticky air broke the comfortable chill of our air-conditioned cabin. I could hear the buzzing of cicadas in the field, competing with murmurs from the press and the clicks of their cameras as the president and first lady got off the helicopter.

The other senior staff followed them out the hatch. I scooted out off the bench and started collecting my bags. The mil aide grabbed the black football, and as he exited the helicopter turned and glanced back at me, "Need any help, Doc?"

"I got it, Major," I reassured him, as I started grabbing the bags one by one. Beads of sweat started to form on my forehead. As I pulled the bags together and started to lift them by the handles, I realized the sum total was too heavy for me to carry. I turned toward the open hatch but could not move forward. The bags were too bulky to slip past the narrow space between the swivel chairs.

I looked outside the helicopter, but there was no Dr. Eschbach or Gary Hoertz in sight. I yanked the bags one by one past the chairs and plopped them down onto the muddy ground. As I did, I heard screams from the open field. I turned and saw several of Hillary's women staffers making their way from the chopper through the tall grass to the motorcade. As they walked along, frogs leapt in front of them. Startled, the women screamed out in alarm. I then recalled the advance briefing about this site. Twenty-seven of the world's deadliest snakes could be found in this region. I wondered if any of them were lurking in the tall grass. The humidity clinging to my skin and the sounds of the wild showed just how far we were from the concrete jungle of D.C. How I longed for a cold shower. But at that moment what I needed more than anything was an extra pair of hands.

As I stared at the motorcade, the ominous words came through my radio earpiece: "Signal depart." This meant the motorcade was leaving. And without me! I pulled up the bags to run for it, but couldn't even lift them. I was simply too tired and too weak to proceed. Where was my medical staff? Where were my guys? I looked at the passing vehicles and saw a hand waving from the spare limo where I should've been seated. I assumed it was Dr. Eschbach. I was relieved that he was with the president in the motorcade and would accompany him to the overnight site. As the cars whisked past me, two other sets of hands waved frantically from the Support Van. I assumed those belonged to Gary and the duty nurse. At least they had made the motorcade, each with medical bags. The backup medical gear was in the ambulance at the tail end of the procession.

I now looked down at the colony of bags assembled at my feet. I was in the land down under and feeling more down and under than I had in a long time. I had missed the motorcade, which was considered a faux pas in the medical unit and a source of ridicule among the mil aides. At this point, I didn't care. I was tired, jet-lagged, hungry, and homesick for my family back in Virginia. I was in a place I always longed to visit, yet I was miserable, stuck in this open field, and surrounded by leaping frogs and poisonous reptiles no doubt coursing through the tall grass toward me.

Although I had missed the motorcade, this was not a life-or-death matter. The president was in good hands. What was more painful was that I felt defeated and humbled. I should have asked for the mil aide's help, but asking for help was an admission that I actually needed someone. In my stubbornness to be self-sufficient, I had always set too high a standard in my quest to be superwoman. Standing beside the empty chopper in this open field, I didn't look or feel like superwoman at all. I looked more like a stranded Filipino bag lady.

And then I heard a familiar, welcome voice. "Hey, Doc, need a hand?" Master Chief Joe Fama grinned as he strolled up to me. He had stayed behind at the landing zone to gather the rest of the president's and first lady's bags.

Once again, the president's valets, my guardian angels, had come to my rescue. We loaded the bags onto the van and had a good laugh on our night drive to town.

2.

Bill Clinton loved his Uncle Buddy. He so adored his uncle that he granted the man the highest honor any sitting president could bestow: he named the first pup after him. The chocolate Labrador, who comforted the president during the most painful times of his presidency, was named Buddy six months after Henry Oren "Buddy" Grisham passed away at age ninety-two.

On a sweltering Arkansas day in June 1997, Bill and Hillary Clinton joined family and friends in the president's birthplace of Hope to pay their last respects to Uncle Buddy. The president never met his biological father, William Blythe, who died in a car accident before he was born. In many ways, Uncle Buddy was a father figure to him, whom he had revered since boyhood.

I accompanied the president on all his trips to Arkansas. I always enjoyed visiting the state because the towns there reminded me of my parents' hometown of Santa Rita in the province of Pampanga in the Philippines. The simplicity and unpretentious nature of the townspeople in Arkansas was similar to rural Pampanga. In these small communities, everyone knew your family. And when you brought a friend to visit, the townsfolk would welcome the stranger with warm hospitality. In Arkansas I was welcomed by the Friends of Bill with the same kind of hospitality. "Are you Bill's doctor?" asked one of his many friends. I nodded my head and smiled. "Thank you for taking such good care of him. We sure do love him."

I was housed, fed, driven, and repeatedly hugged by the devout and fiercely loyal Friends of Bill on these special trips back home. But feeling at home in southern Arkansas, just north of Louisiana, took time. During my first visits there, I carried the burden of my memories of traveling through the segregated South during the 1960s.

As a career Navy enlisted man, my father was transferred to Washington, D.C., in 1961. At the time, we were stationed in Hawaii, and our family took a transpacific boat ride on the USS *Sultan* to San Francisco where we picked up our car. My father then drove our family to Washington. The cross-country trek took seven days, and half the trip was made through the Southern states.

This was a difficult journey for my family. I was six years old and knew that we were different from the typical American family. Unlike Hawaii, which was a melting pot of Filipinos, Chinese, and Japanese, we stood out by color and culture in mainland America. As we drove through the Deep South, we realized that there were no brown people in the cities we visited. There were either blacks or whites, and the two races didn't mix. Public bathrooms and even water fountains were clearly marked "colored" or "white." So my family wondered: where did Filipinos fit into this scheme? With our brownish-yellow skin, we thought we would be considered by whites as a shade above black. But blacks had been in America longer than Filipinos, so they would consider us lower on the totem pole. No matter where we would venture in America, people would perceive us as foreign and alien.

As night fell during our trip across the South, we would be in search of a motel room. My father would first drive around the neighborhood looking for blacks. If there were any in the area, this would be a good sign that the motel would accept us. Once we found the right location, my father would check out the adjoining restaurant, and if there were blacks in the dining room, it would be further confirmation that this was the motel for us. My dad would register and get a small room without an air-conditioner for the five of us. We would not eat in the restaurant. With the family's "don't leave home without it" rice cooker, my mother would boil rice and cook hard-boiled eggs on a one-burner portable hot plate. With her black skillet, Mom would also fry a chicken and the leftovers would sustain us for several days on the road.

Recalling the sensitive racial tensions of the 1960s, when I visited Arkansas for the first time with Bill Clinton early in his presidency, I anticipated a less-than-friendly welcome. What I received instead was kindness from the president's friends and acceptance from the local Arkansans. On that trip, the Army duty nurse was a striking African American. I saw a reserve in her as well, which people of color assume when they are unsure of their reception in a potentially unfriendly environment. The nurse and I were both pleasantly relieved when we were greeted like everyone else in the president's entourage.

Returning to Hope on this occasion was a sentimental, melancholy journey for the president. As our motorcade made its way from

Little Rock to Hope for Uncle Buddy's funeral service, the president needed to use the restroom during the two-hour ride. The only facility along the route was a dilapidated gas station. The attendant jumped up from his chair in surprise as our line of black limousines sidled into the station. The president went straight for the men's room. As he reached for the doorknob, he encountered a wad of rolled-up toilet tissue. This was the rural Arkansas that Bill Clinton knew and loved, and he wasn't fazed in the least.

I followed close behind, heading toward the women's restroom located next to it. A bulky shift agent stood post outside the men's room. Seeing me, he pointed to the toilet-paper knob on the men's room door.

"It doesn't get any better than this," he wryly commented to me.

"We're not in D.C. anymore, Toto," I remarked, as I quickly went into the ladies' room and then exited before the president. I didn't want to get left behind here.

At the crowded little chapel in Hope, the president spoke eloquently about the life of a simple man. He cherished his Uncle Buddy as a friend and mentor. Standing at the pulpit in a dark mourning suit, Bill Clinton eulogized his uncle as "a man without wealth or power and without position or any pretense, but who . . . was smart and wise, and profoundly good." *What a wonderful way to be remembered,* I thought, as I listened from the back of the chapel, fighting back tears. Great men, even presidents, would die for such a eulogy. I had never met his Uncle Buddy but felt as though I had after hearing so many touching stories about the man from the president. His eulogy was heartfelt and beautifully spoken. The chapel was nearly still as the mourners clung to every word the president spoke. The only movement in the room came from a handful of finely dressed Arkansan ladies who were fanning themselves vigorously with their memorial programs.

The day was filled with remembrances and reunions with old friends and family for Bill and Hillary. The Clintons were exhausted as we got into the motorcade headed for the RON, the "remain over-night" site, a small motel in Hope. The town had no four-star hotels. I don't think it even had a Motel 6. Instead, we stayed in a place that was more like a Motel 3.

I followed the president and first lady up the stairs to the second-floor landing of the motel. As we made our way up the stairs, no elevator in sight, I noticed the back ends of air-conditioning units protruding from the windows of the rooms. These window units were humming loudly with water condensate dripping onto the concrete floor below them. The White House staff led us to the "presidential suite"—two adjoining rooms, each bearing the air-conditioning window units.

If the first couple's sleeping quarters consisted of these two adjoin-ing small rooms, I wondered what accommodations lay in store for lowly little me.

The hotel advance staffer cheerfully escorted me three doors down to my assigned room. The medical gear, including the overnight phar-macy bag and additional first-aid supplies bag, was already in the room, delivered by Glenn Powell and the White House transportation staff. I entered the small, dark room and immediately had a flashback to the motel rooms my family stayed in on our 1961 cross-country trip to Washington. All that was missing was the rice cooker and the hard-boiled eggs.

Without air conditioning, the air in the room was damp and musty. The curtains were paisley and dark. Mold clung to the rug. I don't even recall if there was a television set, but I was too tired and sleepy to even notice. I just wanted to brush my teeth, shower, and get enough sleep to survive our early morning departure and flight back.

As I went to the bathroom sink, I saw something that reminded me that the day was about remembering Uncle Buddy, not my creature comforts. Mounted on the wall next to the medicine cabinet was a flyswatter. There were no other customary amenities in the room except for that single red-plastic flyswatter: purposeful, simple, and effective. But above all, it was Arkansas humble and unpretentious.

The next morning, after five hours sleep, I went to the front desk to check out. The owner of the motel was standing at the desk chatting with Ralph Alswang, the White House photographer. Cheerful and proud that the president and first lady had slept at his motel that night, the owner was telling Ralph about his plans to renovate and upgrade his motel.

The man spoke with the familiar Arkansan twang through his missing teeth, announcing to us, "I'm thinkin' of even puttin' in those samples of shampoo and soap in the rooms." The man beamed from the thought of this contemplated upgrade. I smiled back and handed him my government credit card to pay for the night's room. The taxpayers wouldn't complain about this bill.

As I walked to the spare limo, I glanced back at the Motel 3. In my nine years at the White House, I had spent the night in many luxurious accommodations around the globe: the British yacht *Britannia,* the Akasaka Palace in Japan, hundreds of five-star hotels, and even the Queen's Bedroom at the White House. I thought of my parents' humble roots in the Philippines, and how they were always in awe of what I did and where I traveled during my White House tour of duty. But in my youth, one thing my parents always struggled with was being sure our family wasn't treated as second-class citizens or as foreigners. From finding a motel in the American South to choosing a city in which to settle in California, my parents sought out places where we would be accepted. They, and Uncle Buddy, would have liked the fact that I didn't mind spending the night at this motel where the only amenity was a humble little flyswatter. The fact that the president of the United States was fine with similar accommodations was even better.

3.

"Dr. Mariano, do you mind if we see a few patients before you go to your room?"

The request was innocent, almost pleading. But coming from Wendy Van Dyke, I was sure it meant more than a "few patients." Wendy was infamous in the medical unit as the "black cloud nurse" who was a magnet for the sick, lame, and diarrheic on our foreign trips.

I had just arrived with the president and first lady in Jakarta, Indonesia, for the Asia–Pacific Economic Cooperation Summit. It was November 1994, and while heading up the White House Medical Unit, I still accompanied the president on all his foreign travels and almost all his domestic trips at his request as his primary physician. I did not send a backup physician to Jakarta for this trip since I felt Wendy, who was an experienced emergency room nurse, would be able to handle a few colds and cases of traveler's diarrhea at the summit site in Southeast Asia.

The hotel where we stayed with the president, first lady, and White House staff was a beautiful, modern high-rise in the middle of crowded, polluted Jakarta. It was nightfall when we arrived, and fortunately the president and first lady planned to go directly to their suite for the evening. I had the same plan in mind until Wendy greeted me outside the presidential suite.

"Not a problem, Wendy," I halfheartedly responded, hoping to see only one or two patients with colds or diarrhea, to prescribe antibiotics, and then send them and me to bed.

This was not the case. Wendy had prepared, in medical unit jargon, hotel Grand Rounds for me. Or rather, in this luxurious setting, it was Grand Hotel Rounds. It took three hours for us to see the twenty patients lined up for this evening's sick call. We went from one hotel room to the next attending to White House staffers and press corps members with colds, but mostly suffering from traveler's diarrhea. Many of them were already recovering after the antibiotic treatments that Wendy had instituted under my direction after calling me the night before my arrival. But two were dehydrated and needed intravenous fluids. Wendy was adept at inserting IV lines, and once we had two liters of fluid in the patients, they felt better and didn't need to be sent to a local hospital.

What amazed me was that many of those fallen with gastroen-
teritis were reporters used to traveling to Third World countries and
fully aware of the health hazards.

"Did they all eat the same food, Wendy?" I asked after seeing another reporter with "Jakarta belly."

"You never know with the press," she said with a shrug, having
taken the initial history from all the patients before I saw them.
"Most of them ate at the hotel, but some went out on the town."

"I guess even a dirty ice cube would do it," I surmised as we
moved on to the last patient on our list.

It was almost midnight when we knocked on his door. He was
also with the White House traveling press corps, and I recognized
his name from prior trips.

"Dr. Connie's here to see you," Wendy announced as a forty-year-
old, boyish-looking man opened the door. He was wearing a hotel
robe and terry-cloth slippers, and looked pale with a weak smile on
his lips.

"You're a sight for sore eyes," said the reporter in a feeble but
cheerful tone.

"What's this about sore eyes?" I asked, taking his remark literally.
"I thought you had diarrhea."

"Nah, just an expression, Doc." The man shuffled over to a king-
size bed and sat on the edge. I grabbed a chair and sat across from
him while Wendy went through her medical bag checking the antibiotics left after the evening's house calls.

"Well, you never know with the press," I spoke half jokingly. "I
was told by my predecessor that reporters suffered from blurred vision and only saw what they wanted to see."

"Oh, Doc." The reporter shook his tousled "bed head" hairdo.
"You can trust us. We like you guys."

I had him lie back on the bed as Wendy took an ear temperature.
It was 100.6: low-grade fever. I looked in his throat, peered into his
ear canals, and gently felt the lymph nodes under his jaw and on his
neck. He complained of the same mild sore throat that most of the

press corps members had been experiencing. His throat was a little red but his tonsils were not enlarged and had no pustules; there were no swollen lymph nodes in the neck either. My throat was already sore that night from talking to twenty patients, and from the dry, cold air-conditioned air in the hotel.

Wendy handed me my stethoscope, and I leaned over to listen to his abdomen. I heard active gurgles or bowel sounds. I palpated his stomach and it was soft but not tender.

"Abdomen is not acute," I spoke technically for Wendy's sake, forgetting that my layman-reporter would not understand the terminology.

The reporter glanced down at my hands that were poised gently over his six-pack abs. "Excuse me?" he asked rather facetiously. "Did you say my abs were rather cute?"

I smiled as I put away my stethoscope. "I said your abdomen was not 'acute,' meaning you didn't need to be evaluated for surgery." I turned back to him. "And, yes, you have cute abs, clinically speaking, of course." The three of us had a chuckle.

"Sounds like you've got traveler's diarrhea, like most of your buddies. We'll leave a three-day supply of antibiotics along with some Imodium to slow things down."

"And drink plenty of liquids," Wendy added for good measure.

"Wendy is right. Lots of clear broth, Gatorade, flat soda, bottled water. You don't want to get dehydrated," I intoned. "And, avoid alcohol."

"What! No booze?" he protested. "How am I supposed to survive this summit?"

I was aware that a lot of these reporters liked to party. They had a stressful job of constant travel, long hours, and short deadlines. Many of them were overweight smokers who were fueled by adrenaline and alcohol. And I was as concerned about their health as I was the president's and other members of his entourage.

"You'll just have to abstain till you feel better," I reminded him. "All things in moderation."

Wendy handed him an envelope with the antibiotics and the Imodium. He thanked her and shook her hand.

I reached over to shake his hand to say good-bye. The reporter looked up at me with dark rings under his slightly sunken eyes. He did look ill. I was glad we were able to see him this evening, even though I was tired and didn't want to make rounds.

"Thanks, Doc," he whispered, holding my hand between his two cold hands. His jocular tone now faded to something more serious. "I do need to get back to work. Like everybody, I've got deadlines."

"Fortunately, while the summit officially starts tomorrow, it's just for show," I reassured him. "You and your press corps buddies should have another day to get up to speed. So, even if you look like the walking wounded, you'll still be able to do your job."

The reporter squeezed my hand tightly. "Dr. Connie, if there is anything we can ever do for you, don't hesitate to ask."

I smiled, patted him on the hand, and started to leave the room with Wendy. Then a thought came to my mind too tempting to resist, and I turned and looked back at him.

"Maybe there is one thing you and your press buddies can do," I answered, testing the waters.

"What is it, Doc?" The reporter sat up in his bed. "You name it."

I thought if I were to continue as the president's physician, a large part of my job would be interacting with the media when it came to reporting on the president's annual examinations and answering questions about his overall health. I must've sensed that the president was going to have a rough time, and it would take its toll in illness and injury.

I paused for a moment and then made my request. "Just one thing: never give me bad press . . . unless I really deserve it." I was smiling but dead serious.

Wendy was taken aback by my request, which probably came across more like a demand.

The reporter laughed but gave me an earnest appraising look. "You got it, Doc."

My house calls that evening in the hotel in Jakarta seemed to have paid off because during my nine years at the White House, I do not recall receiving any bad press. More likely that was due to my avoiding, unlike my predecessors, the two "killer Ds" when it comes to dealing with the press: deception and denial. I would also like to believe it was because I developed a reputation for honesty and forthrightness. But a part of me believes that my good graces with the White House press corps may have been sealed the night my "black cloud nurse" took me on evening rounds in Jakarta.

The rest of our visit in Jakarta went smoothly. The patients with traveler's diarrhea all recovered within two to three days. The air pollution bothered a lot of people, including the president, who decided unadvisedly to go for a morning run in the streets of Jakarta.

On the final day of the APEC Summit, the leaders of the Asian Pacific nations gathered at the summit site outside the city. All the leaders were dressed in traditional Indonesian garb, including President Clinton, who donned a beautiful batik shirt. He and the other leaders stood together for a group photo on the second-floor balcony of the summit conference building.

The press corps was assembled on the lawn, aiming their cameras up at them for the group photo. I stood behind the photographers, keeping my eye on the president as well as the spare limo parked a few feet behind me in the waiting motorcade. Wendy then came over with several Asian men in tow.

"This is Dr. Mariano," she announced to them.

The distinguished-looking Asian men in Western suits were Japanese, Chinese, and Malay. They each bowed slightly, took my extended hand, and muttered their names. I have always been a failure at remembering names, and was at a loss as I listened to theirs, which I could hardly pronounce. They each wore summit credentials with their photographs, and what appeared to be a name inscribed in Indonesian. But they were easily recognized as physicians by the black leather bags they carried. So if I had to address them, I could just call them by their first name, "Doctor."

"These gentlemen are the physicians of the other summit leaders," Wendy pointed out as I shook hands.

After we shook hands, we stood for a few awkward seconds smiling, and then looked up at the balcony as the group of leaders answered the call for one more photo.

One of the Asian doctors then stepped forward and asked me politely, as the others looked at me closely, "Doctor, which one of them is yours?" he asked, pointing to the leaders on the balcony. The other doctors, who could all pass as relatives of mine, examined me closely and also looked up at the balcony. I guess they couldn't figure out which Asian Pacific leader was my patient.

I laughed and answered, "The tall white guy," pointing out President Clinton in the second row of the group. They were impressed.

TWELVE

The House of Sorrow

1.

"I hope, Doctor, you will enjoy thoroughly your new life of vital service to our country in a position of transcendent responsibility only second in importance to the Presidency. . . . You will be faced with serious demanding obligations; however, you will be a most privileged person in your profession. I found the White House to be a house of joy, sorrow and tragedy. It always has been such."

This letter was addressed to a woman who served as presidential physician. But it wasn't to me. In February 4, 1961, retired Navy Admiral Joel T. Boone, former White House physician to three sitting American presidents, penned this congratulatory letter to Dr. Janet Travell. She had just been selected as physician to President Kennedy and was the first woman to serve as the president's doctor. I was to follow her as physician to another young Democratic and charismatic president thirty-two years later. The letter from Admiral Boone, while set in its own historical context, actually transcended it as a timeless statement for all who tread this path. It was written in admiration yet proved to be foreboding for Dr. Travell, who lost her patient when he was assassinated in November 1963, two years after Admiral Boone's letter.

Dr. Boone spoke with the authority of experience when saying the White House was a house of "joy, sorrow and tragedy." With every sorrow and tragedy suffered by the occupants of the White House, illness has followed, which the doctor has been summoned to treat. When the president suffers, his doctor always feels his pain.

"Doctor, I hate to call you this early." Major Rusty Shorsch's voice was gravelly and grave in tone. Rusty, the Army military aide to the president, called my White House home drop line at 5:00 A.M. on a Thursday morning in January 1994. I knew that any calls from the White House in the wee hours of the morning could mean only one thing: bad news.

I sat on the edge of the bed with the phone in one hand, rubbing the sleep from my eyes with the other. Years of being the doctor on duty trained me to respond with ready reserve when a ringing phone would rouse me from light slumber. I spoke clearly. "Good morning, Major. You've got some bad news for me?" My pulse began to speed up as I braced myself for the anticipated shock.

"First of all, the president is okay," Rusty reassured me, immediately laying to rest my worst fear. "But there's been a death in the family. Mrs. Kelley, the president's mother, died in her sleep this morning."

I groaned aloud, waking my husband, who had been sleeping soundly on the other side of the bed.

The president's mother, Virginia Kelley, had died from breast cancer. She was "mother" to the president, "Ginger" to Chelsea, and "Virginia" to me.

"Please don't call me Mrs. Kelley," she corrected me when we first met shortly after her son's inauguration in January 1993. "Call me Virginia."

It was difficult to address someone of my parents' generation by her first name. I was taught to honor my elders, and the mother of the president of the United States ranked fairly high on my respect scale. I overcame my hesitancy easily, drawn in by her casual and humble nature. The first mother would walk into a room and the people there would instantly light up as she greeted everyone with a smile and a hug. And if you were a stranger, she took it as a personal challenge to charm and befriend you. When I first met Virginia, I knew instantly where her son inherited his legendary charm. Recalling her that morning, I thought of her youthful spirit, those bright laughing eyes that resembled her son's, and her riotous, lovable laugh. And now she was gone.

"It's going to be a rough day on the eighteen acres," I surmised. "I assume the president has been told."

"Yes, ma'am," Rusty responded. "The family in Hot Springs called him early this morning."

"Has he made his way over to the Oval yet?" I asked, glancing at the clock on my nightstand.

"Not yet, Doc. Lights still on upstairs in the residence," Rusty remarked. He was probably scanning the locator box from the military aide's overnight duty room in the White House shelter.

"I'm on my way in," I said, as I hung up and dashed into the bathroom to shower, and then I'd change and pack a bag.

Virginia Kelley had breast cancer, but no one in the first family knew that her disease had progressed. Amidst the joy of her son's inauguration and move into the White House, Virginia was dealing with the personal sorrow that her days were numbered. But she gave no hint of her suffering to anyone, including her son.

A few days before the Clintons' first Thanksgiving at the White House, Virginia asked me to see her in the Queen's guestroom where she was staying on the second floor of the residence. She had noticed some bleeding, but refused to be sent to a hospital when I recommended it. She was willing to let me examine her and to have blood drawn and sent for analysis. The blood test returned as abnormal.

Her cancer and prior chemotherapy had destroyed her bone marrow, and she didn't have enough red blood cells and platelets. As a result, she began bleeding spontaneously.

I called her oncologist in Arkansas, who told me of her grim prognosis. He advised me to treat her "conservatively and symptomatically." This meant in doctorese to "provide comfort." Virginia was adamant that nothing further be done to work up or treat her cancer or the complications from it.

"I don't want to worry Bill about this," she shared with me. Virginia squeezed my hand as we sat together on the canopy bed in the Queen's Bedroom after I told her the blood test results. She understood fully the deadly prognosis, since she had been trained and worked as a nurse anesthetist.

Virginia chuckled when I told her I'd like to give her a blood transfusion. "Oh, Dr. Connie, that's all I need, a little blood and platelets. Just fill me up!

"But I don't want the family to know I'm getting any blood," she added, her tone suddenly very serious. "I don't want any fuss over this."

She and her husband, Dick Kelley, were scheduled the next day to join the president and first family for their Thanksgiving holiday at Camp David. I was the duty physician for that trip and was looking forward to spending Thanksgiving with the Clintons. We were to leave the next day, but my mood about that holiday trip had now changed from joyful to somber knowing that Virginia was dying.

I nodded my head, torn between her wishes and my duty to the president. "Yes, ma'am," I responded. "Let's plan on filling your tank at Camp David tomorrow. You'll be in a private cabin, and it will be easier to administer the blood."

The three buzzers rang from the elevator, alerting us that President Clinton was on his way down to the ground floor from the private family quarters. I arrived at the White House forty-five minutes after the military aide's grim phone call, and had just enough time to scan my messages before the president's arrival. I stood at my secretary's desk in the front room of the doctor's office on the ground floor. I kept the door of my office open so I could eye the president as he walked past on his way to the Oval Office. I wanted to let him know by my presence there that I was available to talk about his beloved mother's death that morning. He knew that I, too, was in sorrow over his loss.

As I stood waiting for Bill Clinton, I thought of my last house call with Virginia at Camp David the previous Thanksgiving.

A crisp autumn morning had greeted us at Camp David in the Catoctin Mountains the day before Thanksgiving in 1993. The duty nurse, Deb Beatty, had drawn Virginia's blood at the White House the day before we left and sent out an extra tube for type and cross match for blood and platelets. She had arranged through a courier from Bethesda Naval Hospital to deliver the blood products to us at the camp.

Deb and I were up early that morning, before the president was awake, so that we could visit Virginia in her cabin across the road from presidential cabin Aspen, where the Clintons were staying.

Virginia greeted us at the door of her cabin with a wide smile and led us to the bedroom. Her complexion was pale from anemia, but despite her condition she wore makeup, including false eyelashes, and her signature bouffant hairdo that flashed a wave of silver atop her chemically blackened mane. Deb, a seasoned Air Force critical care nurse, had no difficulty inserting an IV into Virginia's vein and began slowly to administer the red blood cells followed by the platelets. I carried an emergency anaphylaxis kit in my bag in case Virginia developed any reaction to the blood. I had also alerted the hospital corpsmen at the camp clinic, located in a cabin named Eucalyptus, to be on standby with their ambulance in case we needed assistance.

As the blood dripped into Virginia's hungry veins, she sat on the edge of the bed and told us stories of her youth. Deb and I stood in front of her, entranced not only by the vivid stories but more so by our colorful storyteller. At times, Virginia's tales made us laugh so hard that Deb and I were reduced to tears. Other more tender stories made us almost cry and she would reach out and hug us. We would hug her back. She felt like our "mom," too.

At one point the television set in her bedroom began to show footage of the president during a recent speech. Virginia stopped talking and looked up at her son on the screen. "Whenever I see him on TV," Virginia said slowly as she scrutinized her son's face, "I worry about him because he looks so very tired."

"Did you ever have a feeling when he was a little boy that he would wind up being president someday?" I asked, trying to lighten the mood in the room.

Virginia's brilliant eyes lit up. Beaming with pride, she said, "I knew when he was very young that he would grow up to be someone very special."

Deb and I, both mothers of young children, smiled. Virginia turned her gaze away from the television and looked directly at our eager faces. "When Billy was about seven or eight years old, I sent him to the store with a friend of his, a younger boy about five, to pick up some groceries for me." Her mood had shifted from worried self-concern to wistful pride. "When Billy returned from the store, I was surprised to see that he wasn't carrying any bags. Instead, the little boy with him was carrying the bags of groceries."

Virginia held up her hands and continued. "I looked at my son and asked him why the little boy was carrying the groceries and he, who was older, wasn't. He looked at me and said, 'Mother, why use these (holding up his hands) when you can use this (pointing to his head)?'" The three of us laughed at how her son had figured out early on how to use his brain to convince others to use their brawn.

Deb and I spent most of the day in Virginia's cabin administering blood. Fortunately, the president decided to stay at the camp that day and not venture into town to play golf, so I did not have to leave Virginia's side. While we visited with her, we talked about our lives, our children, and our dreams. At one point Virginia looked at me and said earnestly, "I know you take very good care of my son. You must promise me you will continue to take care of Billy and not leave him."

I was taken aback by her request. I told her, "Well, Virginia, my tour of duty depends on how long the president wants to keep me around."

"I guarantee you, he wants to keep you around," the first mother assured me. "But promise me you will stay and take care of him."

I couldn't argue with a dying mother's request about her eldest child. "Yes, ma'am," I answered, wondering if she had a premonition about dying soon.

It was after Virginia had died, without us having more time together, that I realized that her request to take care of her son was made knowing it would be her last chance before she died. In preparing for her exit from her son's life, she was building up a circle of people at the White House who would be supportive of him in the years ahead. I reflected on the promise I made that afternoon of blood giving, hugs, and tears with Virginia. There were several times in the years after Virginia's death that I had wanted to leave my job at the White House, thinking my mission was accomplished and that I needed to move on to another assignment in the Navy. But I couldn't leave. While the president and first family had told me many times how they appreciated and needed me at the White House, what really kept me from leaving was a promise to a mother. My own mother once told me that a promise made to a mother is sacrosanct, especially if it involves taking care of her child. This is especially so if her child happens to be the president of the United States, and one who would soon be in a battle to save his presidency. Looking back, I realize now that God took Virginia just in time to spare her more sorrow.

2.

It all started with tingling in my hands. Then came the clumsiness; I'd drop coins after I had picked them up gingerly from my purse. Amidst this growing revolt within my own body, I was chasing another rapidly moving body that was intent on its own form of revolution: Bill Clinton. I was accompanying the president on his peripatetic travels all over America and around the globe. And everywhere I went, I would lug my medical bag with its thick strap digging deep into my right upper shoulder and neck. I initially ignored the electrical sensations in my hands, the awkward unattached feeling, and the poor coordination of my fingers. But what finally got my attention was the numbness. At the end of a long day, I would tilt my head back from the warm spray of the shower blasting away the grime of jet fumes and limo exhaust from my neck, chest, and arms. It was then that my body went numb from the neck down. I would look at my hand that held the soap bar. I couldn't feel the bar in my hand, couldn't squeeze it with my fist. I had lost my grip in more ways than one.

They say doctors make the worst patients. This is probably because we try to diagnose ourselves, or we listen too little or too much to our own bodies. Maybe we are in denial over our own mortality or fear becoming hypochondriacs. In my case, I was just too busy doing my job to pay attention to my own aches and pains. Mind over matter? In my case it was more like presidential business over body.

I had dismissed these initial symptoms when they first began in 1994 after Virginia Kelley died. Apparently my body was sending me an urgent message before it was too late. It was during her funeral service in Hot Springs that the director of the military office, John Gaughan, offered me the job of director of the White House Medical Unit. From the time I accepted this position, my life went into overdrive. This meant not only more travel time, but when I was in

D.C. I was usually held hostage in my White House office with medical and administrative duties. I rarely saw my own family except in passing. I left succinct notes and extensive to-do lists for my husband, who became a stay-at-home dad, tending to our two young sons. My quality time with my children consisted of kissing them good-bye in the morning on the way out of our house, a charming brownstone colonial, or stealing a hug in the dead of night as they lay asleep.

I didn't have time to monitor my own health. I was too busy watching Bill Clinton's, upholding the promise I had made to his dying mother to take care of him. As I watched the president become further engulfed in the work of his office in the aftermath of his mother's death, I realized he didn't have any time to grieve her loss. If I and the members of the medical unit missed Virginia's presence after only knowing her a few months, I could only imagine what the president felt in his private moments at the loss of the woman who had been his biggest cheerleader.

The fleeting numbness in my body got my attention the first time it happened. *I need to get this checked out at Bethesda Naval Hospital,* I immediately promised myself, only to postpone my hospital appointments because of travel and work. I dove into my new job as director with unbridled passion and purpose. Not only was I accompanying the president on every foreign trip, I was the primary physician on most of his domestic travels. In addition I worked long hours to mold the ailing medical unit into a robust, state-of-the-art organization that was responsive to the demands of the modern-day presidency. Like my first patient, who was charging forth to bring responsible change to the nation and the world, I was determined to bring much needed change to my organization.

My nonstop travel and numerous improvements in the medical unit during the first two years as director gave me the aura of a superwoman. I was promoted to the rank of captain ahead of my peers. I initiated changes such as twenty-four-hour White House coverage of the president, which the Secret Service had attempted, but failed, for decades to institute. The military aides gave me the title of "warrior queen," for fighting for my troops and the medical unit initiatives. My proximity to, and friendship with, the president and first family, as well as my successes in the medical unit, made me not only the object of admiration but the target of animosity as well.

"Doc, this sure is a good annual fitness report," Captain Mark Rogers drawled in a folksy Tennessee accent as he handed me the report, which had been signed by Bill Clinton. "You know, you are only one of a handful of military officers at the White House who get their fitrep signed by POTUS." Rogers, who was second in command of the White House Military Office, was referring to the annual evaluation all officers receive by their senior officers. A good evaluation keeps you in the military. A superb evaluation gets you promoted. And a stellar evaluation signed by the president gets you promoted one day to general or admiral. Rogers knew this fact and apparently resented it.

"Well, Captain," I responded, trying to avoid sounding defensive, "my predecessors all had their fitness reports signed by the president. As the president's doctor, managing his overall care, it comes with the territory. Who's more qualified?"

Rogers waved off my justifications with a short, stubby finger. "Doc, I know the history." Then he eyed me with a smirk and said, "I also know there are some things you don't share with me or the military office about the president. I guess you'd call them . . . personal."

I felt my face beginning to flush. I sensed what Mark Rogers was attempting. He was sniffing out dirt on the president. We had all heard the same rumors about the president and other women prior to his arrival at the White House. Any tidbit of personal information I could leak about private conversations that I may have had with the president, or overheard him have with others, would put Rogers in a position of power on the eighteen acres. At the White House, proximity to the president was power, but any knowledge of the president's failings gave one power over him.

"Sir," I interrupted his line of questioning, "if the president has a medical issue that impacts his ability to perform the responsibilities of his office, I guarantee that you will be informed. That is outlined in the Succession Plan protocol . . ."

"Well, Doc, let's not go into protocol here." Rogers started to chuckle in a down-home, informal tone. "What I'm saying is this: if you're swinging from chandeliers with the president, that's something I've got to know."

I couldn't believe my ears. I had never heard the expression "swinging from chandeliers" used, but knew what it insinuated about my relationship with the commander in chief, who happened to be my patient. I was incredulous that anyone, let alone a senior military officer, was asking me such a question. I heard later that these kinds of remarks were not unusual for Rogers, and why he eventually was removed from his position.

"Captain," my voice started to rise as I tried to maintain my calm while my neck muscles tightened and my fingers began to tingle, "if I were doing what you are accusing me of, I'd tell you about it because then I'd be *your* boss."

Rogers emitted a hoot, slapped his knee, and then ended our meeting with, "That's great, Doc. Glad you've got a good sense of humor about this. Just wanted to make sure nothing is going on that shouldn't be."

I held my tongue, stood up, and marched out of his office, both my hands completely numb. If I had wanted to strangle the man, I would have been incapable of doing so, and that's when I knew it was time to address my own medical issue.

"How *old* are you?" the radiologist at Bethesda Naval Hospital asked as he squinted at my neck films on display on the view box in the main reading room.

"I just turned forty this January," I said as I stood behind the radiologist. Although I was not an expert at reading X-ray films, I knew instantly that my cervical spine looked abnormal.

"Just turned forty? Well, you've got the cervical spine of an eighty-year-old." Perhaps I had appeared to be superwoman to many people on the eighteen acres, but now this woman had superold bones in her neck. My abnormal films led me to see Captain Morris "Bud" Pulliam, chief of neurosurgery at Bethesda. Bud had operated on the necks and spines of congressional members as well as several celebrities. And now he was recommending I be added to his list of famous patients.

"Tell me again why I need to have this surgery? You know, I have a lot of upcoming travel with the president, including a summit in Nova Scotia. I really don't have time for this." I was trying to bargain my way out of the surgery.

"Connie, the tingling in your hands and numbness in your body are from your spinal cord being compressed by the degenerated disks in your neck." Bud explained this patiently as he reviewed my plain films, MRI scans, and the painful myelogram studies that he ordered after seeing my first set of films.

I shook my head. The only other surgeries in my life had been two Cesarean sections, which were typical for many women physicians. I didn't like being cut on. I didn't want to be hospitalized. I didn't like being a patient. I was a good doctor who, like most, was a bad patient.

"Let me put it this way," Bud said, wanting to drive home his point. "You heard about Christopher Reeve? He just had a riding accident a few weeks ago and broke his neck. Your spinal cord is constricted in the same location as his injury. If you fall, slip on ice, or get a whiplash in your car, you may wind up like him."

Bud had delivered the verbal slap in the face. I thought of the recent stories of Christopher Reeve's tragic accident and how he was on a ventilator and couldn't move his arms or legs. If he survived the ventilator, he would be confined to a wheelchair for life. I could not envision

My neck surgery couldn't keep me from visiting the White House during my convalescence in 1995. One month after surgery, wearing a neck brace, I'm checking on my patient. (WHITE HOUSE PHOTO)

life in a wheelchair. I loved to run and move about too much. I was the lady in perpetual motion. *Wind up like Christopher Reeve?*

My neck surgery took over eight hours to perform. Most of the time was spent harvesting bone chips from my left hip to fill in the holes in my neck after cleaning out bony debris to free up my compressed spinal cord, and where Dr. Pulliam placed a titanium plate. My surgery was a success but I was a wreck. I woke up with a hard collar strapped to my sore neck. My left hip throbbed from where the bone had been chipped away. I had a horrific headache due to the spinal fluid leakage from my surgery. The remnants of anesthesia and pain medication made me nauseated and groggy. But what was most painful for me was that I felt helpless, not in control, certainly not in charge.

I was sent home five days later. My surgeons wanted me to be in the neck collar for eight weeks and to be on convalescent leave for most of that time. My surgery prevented me from accompanying the president to the summit in Nova Scotia. My perfect record of being on every presidential foreign trip with Bill Clinton was broken. I had assigned other White House physicians to travel with the president. I had also temporarily turned over the duties of my job to the Air Force physician in the medical unit. He attended meetings for me, reluctantly ran the unit, and reassured me he had no ambition of ever taking my job. I had become professionally paralyzed by my

White House letter to me from President Clinton after my surgery in which he pens "We miss you."

THE WHITE HOUSE
WASHINGTON

July 17, 1995

Captain Eleanor C. Mariano, MC, USN
7663 Summerhill Court
Lorton, Virginia 22079

Dear Connie:

Hillary and I were glad to hear that you are recuperating well from your surgery. We want you to know that we're keeping you in our thoughts, and we look forward to having you back at the White House soon.

Sincerely,

Bill

We miss you

neck surgery. I couldn't go anywhere, do anything. I thought it was almost as bad as being in a wheelchair.

My home life was also emotionally paralyzed from my surgery. I stayed home with my husband, Richard, who worked on writing legal briefs in his basement office during that time. We sent our two sons back to California to be with their grandparents so the house could be quiet for me. The house was more than quiet; it was a morgue with only the two of us there. I missed the sounds of my sons' laughter, the sweet scent of their presence, and especially their warm hugs. Instead, I stayed home with Richard, who had difficulty comforting me. We had grown apart emotionally during my absentee life, and it was painfully evident during my convalescence. Richard had the impossible task of taking care of the president's doctor. Without any health care experience or prior exposure to postoperative or ill patients, the challenge of nursing me proved difficult for him. There were times I thought he was in more pain taking care of me than I from my surgical wounds. My husband had left a prestigious law practice to be a stay-at-home dad, and now a nurse to an irascible doctor-wife.

The whole situation made me inconsolable. I sat on the family room couch watching daytime soap operas until my head would hurt. I would then fall asleep under the influence of pain medication and dream of being on the road again. The tingling in my fingers and numbness in my body were now gone. This was only to be replaced by a growing numbness in my heart over my dying marriage.

3.

When people learn that I had been White House physician during the Clinton presidency, the most common question they ask is: What is Hillary Clinton *really* like? Having spent eight years with Hillary at the White House, aboard Air Force One, and on the road both in the United States and overseas, I have a strong sense of her. As I have often told my patients, I'll be with them both in "sickness and in health."

If Bill Clinton is known for feeling your pain, Hillary Clinton is known for privately bearing her own pain, which must have been a huge burden during those stressful years. Unlike most other patients who are eager to share a litany of symptoms with their physician, Hillary rarely had a sick day nor did she complain of feeling ill unless her illness risked compromising her scheduled activities. As they say in sports, she knows how to play hurt. Even when she suffered a blood clot in her leg during the midterm elections of 1998, I had to force her to take it seriously. It was early Saturday morning, but not too early because she would have waited in pain to call at a decent hour. I was awakened by a phone call from the White House operator, who patched me through to the first lady.

"Connie, I'm so sorry to bother you, but I think I might've pulled a muscle in my leg," she began.

"Where's it swollen?" I asked, realizing that my day off was probably shot.

"In the calf," she replied.

"When did this happen?" I asked, my concern growing.

"It started bothering me yesterday while doing a fund-raiser in New York."

"I'll need to examine you," I said, as I got out of bed and started to dress.

"I'd hate for you to have to come in on a Saturday," she said softly.

"Mrs. Clinton, I'm worried about your leg. You've been out on the campaign trail for months now, sitting in cars for hours at a time. You're at risk for a blood clot." I said this in my most concerned voice, trying not to alarm her but making it sound serious enough to warrant attention.

"Well, if you think so," she said, and then added, "but . . ." She caught herself. "I'll see you upstairs." I'm sure she was about to protest about having any downtime before even getting a diagnosis.

I was at the White House within an hour, examining Hillary's swollen calf. Based on her history and this exam, I felt she needed an ultrasound. As I reached for the phone to contact Bethesda and alert them to her visit, she squinted at me. "Oh, it's not that serious, is it?" I gave her my best doctor's look; she smiled and didn't give me an argument.

Mrs. Clinton invited me to sit with her in the back seat of the unmarked limo, as we drove to Bethesda with a small contingent of Secret Service vehicles and one police car as an escort. As we rode in her limo, she went through a stack of papers on her lap including her upcoming travel schedule, speeches, and correspondence. She was always working, reading, or writing notes on our trips, be they short or long. This was only weeks after Ken Starr had sent his report to Congress recommending impeachment proceedings. As I watched, I sensed that she was internalizing some deep hurt, but she refused to be a victim and was working even harder to turn it around. You had to admire her. I certainly did.

At Bethesda, the ultrasound revealed a clot in the blood vessel behind her knee. Fortunately, the deputy commander of the naval hospital, Captain Frank Maguire, was at the hospital that day assisting with her examination. "Mac" Maguire had been with me during my internal medicine internship and residency at the naval hospital in San Diego. A brilliant clinician who was board-certified in pulmonary medicine and critical care, Dr. Maguire's medical judgment was respected by fellow physicians. Because of the blood clot in her swollen leg, we recommended she be hospitalized to treat it. She balked at the mention of the word "hospitalize." She wanted to get back on the road. So we came up with a different solution and agreed to treat her as an outpatient with a newly released blood thinning drug.

Hillary was back on the campaign trail within days. And despite the Lewinsky scandal and the threat of impeachment, Bill Clinton was the first president whose party won back five seats in the House of Representatives in a sixth-year midterm election. Very few people knew of Hillary's blood clot at the time; she wrote about it after she left the White House. She did have pain in her calf, but her staff thought she had pulled a muscle exercising. If my slogan was "Don't let them see you sweat," Hillary's must've been, "Don't let them see the pain." I assigned a female nurse in civilian attire to accompany Hillary on the campaign trail. I also notified the Secret Service that she was on the medication. In the event she was injured, excessive bleeding would be a dangerous complication.

As I look back at this episode, what impressed me most about Hillary Clinton's reaction was that despite the physical pain she experienced in her leg and the threat of a more serious complication, she never complained, never played the victim or the martyr. She got back on the horse and rode it to victory. As we would say in the military, she "carried out the mission." In fact, her behavior reminded me of fellow military officers, who despite illness or injury, accepted that the mission came first and focused their efforts on getting the job done. This could be why she is never deterred by political or personal setbacks, to put it mildly, and instead is ever focused on the big picture, or service to our country, as we say in the military.

THIRTEEN

Rough Seas Ahead

1.

P OTUS *bait*. That was the term we used to describe the tall, slender, long-haired beauties who would predictably try to capture the attention of President Bill Clinton.

"Is *she* a security threat?" I asked a male agent as I pointed to a comely candidate in the crowd at a Dallas fund-raiser. The bait had big hair and a matching bosom. I immediately spotted her from where I stood at the side of the stage next to the Secret Service shift leader. The woman, who I estimated to be in her mid-forties, looked like she had been surgically preserved and enhanced. She caught my eye when I saw her jump up and down, clapping her hands excitedly while standing at the rope line. This was one of the White House's many forays that year into the Southwestern states to fund-raise for the Democratic National Committee. No visit to the heart of Texas would be complete without a dinner, speech, and a grip-and-grin in glittery, affluent Dallas.

Bill Clinton had finished his speech and was walking off the stage toward the rope line. As he approached, the crowd rushed to the cord where agents and staff stood post to keep the donors from jumping across the velvet rope. Clinton's staff went into their automatic rope-line mode by anticipating autographs that the guests would want signed. Scraps of paper, books, and photographs were handed to Clinton by several of the donors as he greeted them. Without breaking eye or hand contact, Clinton would receive the item and pass it smoothly to an assistant who stood glued to his side. After he had finished working the rope line, the president would be pulled over to the hold and handed items to sign. The aide would then dash back to the crowd and with uncanny accuracy return the autographed item to the correct person. And this was done quickly so he would not miss the president's motorcade preparing to leave.

"Security threat?" The trained killer in the generic dark blue suit smirked at my half-facetious query. "Just watch."

I was one of only a small number of doctors in America who actually got to observe a patient doing his job. I watched that evening as the president spoke eloquently to a crowd of wealthy Texans, who gazed at him adoringly with mesmerized faces. At the end of the speech, the band struck an upbeat tune, and Clinton sprinted down the stage and toward the rope line. He performed his usual magic with the crowd: shaking hands, sharing high-fives, pointing to other guests in the crowd who were too far from his touch but close enough to be under the spell of his charisma. Both men and women were generally entranced by Bill Clinton. A handful of well-groomed middle-aged women in designer suits screamed like teenagers at a rock concert when Clinton started walking along the rope line toward them. I felt as though I were watching a rock star work a crowd of groupies.

Finally Clinton made his way to the POTUS bait I had singled out to the shift leader. The Dallas darling reminded me of a former beauty queen waiting for her bouquet of roses. In her four-inch heels, she was almost as tall as the president but towered over her pudgy, bald husband. He stood beaming beside her, but she had completely

abandoned him for the tall, youthful man from Hope now stepping up to her.

As Clinton reached out to shake the beauty's hand, the woman leaned into his grip, her bountiful breasts brushing against his arm. The agent standing beside me nudged my arm with his elbow and whispered, "And now, Doc, stand by as she moves in for the kill."

The "security threat" then drew her body closer to Clinton, rubbing her breasts into his side as she leaned forward to whisper something into his ear. He laughed loudly and shook his head, making fleeting eye contact with the woman's plunging neckline. And then, in an instant, back to business, he moved on to the next former beauty queen in line.

I blinked in astonishment at the woman's behavior. Her brazen public display of affection in front of her husband, the crowd of donors, and in full sight of the Secret Service agents was overtly flirtatious and bordering on openly seductive.

"See what I told ya?" The agent smirked again. "POTUS bait. They are drawn like moths to a fire."

Bill Clinton's amorous reputation preceded his arrival at the White House. When he was a candidate for the presidency, there had been

Bill Clinton and I used to joke often. Here he catches me in my bad habit of eating potato chips. Taken in 1995 in the medical compartment onboard Air Force One while the nurses look on.
(WHITE HOUSE PHOTO)

numerous rumors about former girlfriends, including one who was interviewed in *Playboy* magazine. I caught one of the physician assistants with a copy of the magazine interview a week before Clinton was inaugurated for his first term.

"What are you doing with this in the clinic?" I said, disgusted at finding the glossy magazine on the PA's desk. "Didn't you learn enough gross anatomy in PA school?"

"Dr. Mariano, I'm just doing research on our new patient," he answered with a sly smile on his lips.

I shook my head as he tried to defend himself. "Well, keep that stuff out of the clinic." And as I walked out of his office to see a patient in the waiting room, I turned and asked, being curious myself, "So, did you learn anything useful?"

His answer was quick. "That women can't resist him."

"So we've been told," I said impatiently.

He now gave me a wink. "I bet *you* won't be able to resist him either, Doc."

I didn't take the bait, but to show the PA that I was unaffected by him teasing me about Clinton's purported charms, I repeated my question. "Again, learn anything useful?"

Clinton was always thoughtful about mentioning his staff. He mentioned me during his commencement speech at my alma mater, University of California, San Diego, in June 1997. I am greeting him in the hold after his speech. (WHITE HOUSE PHOTO)

"Yeah, I think so," the PA said, nodding his head. "He seems to be a very lucky man."

"Well, in this town, luck can only take you so far," I blurted out, a prescient statement that would haunt me and my patient in the years to come.

2.

At first I thought I was dreaming and the sound was from birds tapping on a window, like something out of a Hitchcock film. I was lying on my hotel room bed, having just collapsed into the sheets fully clothed. But the frantic tapping was actually someone knocking at my door at two o'clock in the morning. This meant that I was still awake and this was not a dream. It was, however, symbolic. For I was about to experience a waking nightmare.

An hour earlier the Support Van had just dropped me, the advance site Army nurse Greta Krapohl, and a ragtag team of White House staff and press at a small hotel a few miles from where the president was spending the night. It was nearly one o'clock in the morning on March 14, 1997. We had all survived another eighteen-hour day following Bill Clinton from the moment he lifted off on Marine One from the South Lawn to when he touched down in Miami aboard Air Force One. Our day ended with a helicopter landing at an abandoned field in Jupiter, Florida.

How appropriate, I thought, this might as well be the planet Jupiter, since nothing appeared beyond the reach of Bill Clinton at this point. He had easily won reelection only two months earlier, and despite attempts by his political enemies to distract the American public with allegations of wrongdoing, Clinton still received the highest poll ratings for his performance in office. And the crowds continued to show their admiration, both in the United States and overseas. Clinton was riding high when he landed in Jupiter. His entire staff and those of us who were part of his traveling entourage basked in the glow of his success. Having been Clinton's doctor for over four years at this point, it was an honor to be part of his team. When he had won reelection, the president and Mrs. Clinton had asked me to stay on as their physician. I was looking forward to an exciting but medically uneventful four more years.

The motorcade pulled up to the estate of Greg Norman, the professional golfer, who invited Clinton to spend the night. On the front steps, I was relieved to see a smiling Bill Lang, the Army White House physician, standing beside the military aide. After a full day of duty, I anticipated that I would be exhausted, unlike my energetic patient, who only got stronger as the day wore on. I assigned Dr. Lang to meet me at Norman's estate. Lang would assume the duty upon my arrival and then share a room with the military aide at the compound. Private bedrooms were scarce at the Norman compound, and since the military office frowned on coed duty rooms, it made sense to bring in Dr. Lang to pick up the duty and spend the night at the estate, close to the president.

After handing off the medical bag and the first patient to Dr. Lang, I climbed in the van with Nurse Greta and headed to the hotel. When I got to my room, I was in bed within minutes, but it seemed like only seconds before I heard the ominous tapping sound. Blurry-eyed, I stumbled to the door and peered through the peephole. It was Greta, to whom I had just bid a "good night/good morning" less than thirty minutes ago.

"Greta, what's up?" I asked as I opened the door.

"Doc, POTUS fell . . ." she whispered, looking cautiously up and down the hallway. I later learned that the White House press corps had rooms on our floor, and Greta didn't want to be overheard.

I thought I hadn't heard her correctly. "What, Greta? What's this about POTUS?"

"POTUS *fell* . . . " She emphasized the verb and then quickly added, "and Dr. Lang and the agents are on their way to the hospital with him now—"

"What!" I interrupted. "We gotta meet them there. Do you have a car?" I quickly turned and went back into the room and grabbed my glasses and purse, which contained my "flip pass," the official White House credential. I snatched the jacket that I had just hung in the closet, and stuck my hard pin into the collar with such force that it pricked my finger. A drop of blood beaded up. I rubbed my bleeding finger against the side of my dark jacket. My cell phone then rang. It was Dr. Lang.

"Connie, we are on our way to St. Mary's Hospital in West Palm Beach," he reported calmly. "The president was walking down some steps at Norman's house when he felt his quadriceps muscle snap. I think he tore it pretty badly."

"Is he in a lot of pain?" I asked, trying to feel Bill Clinton's pain. My patient was hurting and I wasn't there to take care of him. Dr. Lang was our junior physician, and while we trained him for worst-case scenarios, I couldn't help but feel guilty that I wasn't there with my patient.

"Yes, he was hurting pretty badly," Lang admitted. "But once we got his leg immobilized, he felt a lot better. We had no choice but to load him into the ambulance, and head out. We left the compound so quickly that the press didn't even get wind of it."

"How far are you from the hospital?" I asked, looking at my watch.

"About forty minutes," Lang estimated.

"See you in the emergency room."

I sat in silence for a moment reflecting on the situation. It was hard to estimate the damage without a physical exam. Fortunately, this type of injury wasn't life-threatening. But I was anxious to get to the hospital.

"Greta, can't you drive faster?" I asked impatiently as she trailed behind the car carrying the agents. We were making our way along the interstate to West Palm Beach, following the agents' car with the flashing red police light on its hood.

"Ma'am, I can't go any faster than the agents' car," she replied. Greta was quiet and tense, and my anxiety wasn't helping. This was one of her first advance trips, and it had already been marred by a medical event. Neither of us had gotten any sleep and would be up for many more hours.

"I'm sorry. Just want to get there before the president." She sped up and came closer to the lead car, which got the message and accelerated.

If the president was really that badly injured, that would mean surgery. I needed to keep my focus and be calm. I tried to reflect and quiet my mind as we sped along the interstate. The red flashing police lights from the agents' car had an eerie hypnotic effect on me.

POTUS fell. Those were the words uttered by Greta at the start of this nightmare. In retrospect, it sounds like a line from Shakespeare's *Julius Caesar.* At the time, this bad dream seemed localized, specific to a physical injury and my first patient's recovery. But the real wound was much deeper and would have catastrophic consequences.

"Dr. Mariano, we're about five minutes from St. Mary's Hospital." Greta's voice pulled me back from my daydreams to the passenger seat of a car going 75 miles per hour. I blinked and wondered if I had dozed off during the thirty-minute drive along the rain-slicked highway.

The local police, who had barricaded the emergency room driveway, allowed us to enter after the agents in the lead car pointed to us and we flashed them our flip pass credentials. I jumped out of the car and joined the agents hurrying to the emergency room. Greta had performed the advance tour of this hospital only three days prior to our visit, and she was familiar with the hospital staff and layout. The trauma team had just finished stabilizing a patient who sustained a gunshot wound. Part of me was grateful that *my* patient didn't have such severe trauma. A torn tendon was painful and debilitating, but it was not a bullet wound to the chest or head, which had been injuries sustained by previous presidents.

"I don't think we'll need the trauma team," I told the nursing supervisor, who appeared relieved by my decision. The team would be used instead for patients who had life-threatening injuries during the

Enroute with the president on Marine One to Bethesda for his annual physical in October 1997. (WHITE HOUSE PHOTO)

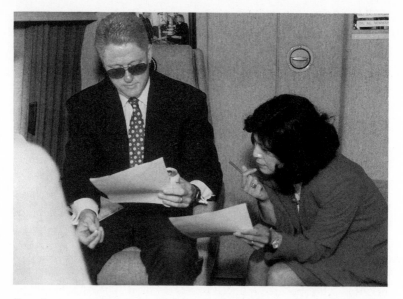

Preparing a press statement summarizing the president's annual exam findings from Bethesda Naval Hospital while flying Marine One back to the White House in May 1996. (WHITE HOUSE PHOTO)

president's impromptu visit. "All we'll need this morning is an MRI scanner and an orthopod"—an orthopedic surgeon.

The nurse supervisor was friendly and upbeat, despite the growing number of men in black suits filling her ER in the wee hours of the morning. "We'll have both ready for your patient."

"Doc, Eagle is five minutes out." The agent's voice jarred me. Eagle, Clinton's Secret Service code name, was the wounded eagle tonight.

The ambulance arrived without flashing lights. It was a generic box-shaped vehicle that pulled up to the driveway without the fanfare befitting a world leader, other than the black Suburban SUVs that sandwiched it. I went to the rear door and Dr. Lang hopped out, smiling. His chipper nature sometimes unnerved me, especially tonight when I was sleep-deprived and knew that I had another very long day ahead of me.

"Here's your patient." He pointed to the ambulance's rear door.

"Bill," I cautioned him, "you're starting to develop your own black cloud." He shook his head in despondent acknowledgment. I put my hand on his shoulder. "Let me talk with the president for a few minutes and then let's get him into the ER."

I opened the rear door of the ambulance and stepped inside the space, crouching down as I entered. The president was seated on a gurney facing me.

He didn't look like the Bill Clinton I had come to know. The twinkle in his eye was replaced by a look of dread, almost bordering on fear. The mouth was in a grimace. He didn't look like a powerful world leader. Instead, he looked helpless, almost childlike and frightened.

"Connie, I'm so sorry this happened," he began. Typical Bill Clinton: apologizing for his own unavoidable injury and its impact on all of us.

"Mr. President." I touched his arm. "Are you in any pain?"

"Just a little," he said with a downplaying gesture of his hand. I took a blanket from the bench beside me and covered his chest and legs, trying to keep him warm. "We are going to wheel you into the emergency room. I've asked the orthopedic surgeon on call to see you. Most likely we'll do an MRI scan of your leg. Chances are you'll need to have surgery."

Clinton let out a moan. "Damn! I'm supposed to visit a school this morning. The kids will be disappointed."

"I'm sure they'll understand," I reassured him. The door opened and Dr. Lang and a handful of agents reached toward his gurney and pulled him into the chilly, dark air.

I followed him into the hospital and did not leave his side for the next three days. We flew back to Andrews Air Force Base that morning, and that afternoon Bill Clinton underwent repair of a torn quadriceps tendon, followed by a few days postop at Bethesda Naval Hospital.

During his surgery, we decided he would receive spinal anesthesia instead of a general anesthesia, which would have required institution of the Twenty-fifth Amendment. He wanted to be awake and aware during the surgery. We played country-western music in the OR suite, and I sat chatting beside him during the procedure. He joked with the surgeons and anesthesiologists during his surgery, trying to lighten the mood in the operating room.

Clinton appeared innocent, almost angelic, throughout the whole ordeal of his surgery and hospitalization. As an injured patient, the president emanated an almost childlike vulnerability that I did not expect. But what surprised me more was my reaction to my patient's injury. I became defensive and very protective of him: the mother hen watching out for her young. I went head to head with his staff, who tried to overbook his schedule in the weeks after his surgery. When his advisors tried to engage him in activities that would fatigue him and risk reinjury to his leg, I invoked the name of the first lady. All White House doctors know that when the staff refuses to listen to you, go directly to the first lady for her support. "Well, I guess I'll just have to let Mrs. Clinton know about this," I would say to the White House staff. Issue resolved.

I stepped softly into the president's room at Bethesda in the early morning of March 15, almost twenty-four hours from the time Greta knocked on my door and whispered that POTUS had fallen. Bill Clinton lay asleep, snoring peacefully while the heart monitor beeped at a steady rate of 55 beats per minute, his usual resting pulse. I sighed and was relieved that the surgery was over. But he had weeks and months of physical rehabilitation ahead. Before I left his bedside to catch a few winks in the duty room across the hallway, I noticed that his blanket had fallen off his shoulders. As I gently lifted the cover, I thought of my two small sons. It seemed like a long time since I had been at their bedside, watching them sleep soundly. I hoped that one day they would understand my absence and that I had a duty to fulfill and another mother's promise to keep.

3.

There is a perennial sick joke in medicine: the surgery was a success, but the patient died. In Bill Clinton's case, he successfully survived his surgery but endured a political near-death experience in the ensuing months. As the president hobbled about on crutches and underwent painful twice-daily physical therapy to regain the use of his right leg, his enemies took advantage of his weakened condition to mount a vicious campaign to destroy his reputation.

I had begun to notice a startling change in the tone of the press coverage about the president. No longer did he enjoy the media love-fest that greeted him upon entering the Oval Office in 1993. Instead, I was hearing more in the press about other women, a potential scandal involving Whitewater, and rumors of an independent counsel being appointed to investigate the president and the first lady. Even before his injury, during the reelection campaign, rumors had surfaced about the issue of his honesty. I dismissed them as the typical character assassination and campaign mudslinging that I had witnessed in the past at the White House.

Even surgery didn't slow down Bill Clinton. Four days after his tendon repair, he was on Air Force

Roasting President Clinton during his birthday celebration in August 1997 on the South Lawn. Clinton covers his face in response to my commentary, while Dr. Richard Tubb (on the right) observes. (WHITE HOUSE PHOTO)

One on his way to Helsinki to meet with Russian president Boris Yeltsin.

"Mr. President, I again strongly urge you to postpone this trip. You've just had surgery. You're not supposed to bear any weight on your leg," I pleaded with him on the second floor of the residence as he sat with his knee elevated on a stool. This was a day before our scheduled departure.

"Sorry, but I need to meet with Yeltsin, Doc. Make it happen," the president ordered.

I didn't have my usual health advocate to turn to for support. Hillary and Chelsea were not at the White House. They had just left for a two-week trip to Africa that had been planned months in advance. They had delayed their departure two days during the president's hospitalization at Bethesda. But once he was cleared to go

During his reelection campaign in 1996, President Clinton reads the statement I've prepared regarding his health while Chief of Staff Leon Panetta (on right) and Press Secretary Mike McCurry observe. (WHITE HOUSE PHOTO)

A house call to see the president at his desk in the Oval Office in 1997 when he came down with stomach flu. I recommended he cancel his photo-op that day and stay home and rest. (WHITE HOUSE PHOTO)

home, the first lady unwittingly abandoned me, leaving me alone to be the gatekeeper and physical warden of the first patient.

"Call me if anybody on the staff gives you any problems," Mrs. Clinton advised as she was headed out the door for the motorcade to Andrews.

"Does that include the president?" I asked, realizing that my most difficult task would be to keep him medically compliant with his physical limitation.

The trip to Helsinki was painful for the president. He sat in a wheelchair during the summit meetings with Yeltsin. Clinton wasn't happy being unable to stand tall to meet his Russian counterpart. Although sitting in a wheelchair may have evoked memories of Franklin D. Roosevelt, it wasn't the presidential image Clinton wished to project at this time. It was, however, symbolic of his general vulnerability.

Chatting with the first lady and president in the Oval Office before a special photo-op with the medical unit to thank them for helping the president recover from his knee injury in 1997. (WHITE HOUSE PHOTO)

But when Clinton experienced pain, I also shared that with him in many ways. One of the distinct "privileges" of being close to the president was to experience his many moods, including his irritation. I allowed him to vent when that would happen. On such occasions it was usually in response to my limiting his schedule or his activities, citing that he hadn't been cleared by the surgeons yet for golf or to walk a certain distance. There were times I found myself raising my voice when the first patient insisted on pushing the envelope. *Connie,* I would tell myself, *do you realize you are yelling at the president of the United States?* Visions of court-martial danced in my head.

But the president recovered rapidly from his injury and healed faster than anticipated. His twice-a-day physical therapy was the main factor, but the medical unit also watched him closely twenty-four hours a day to make sure he didn't trip or reinjure his leg. This was usually me, constantly nearby watching every step, every move, and ensuring that he followed doctor's orders.

The president grew stronger each day and lost twenty-five pounds during his recovery, which delighted him. Despite the arguments over his schedule and limiting his activities, we remained friendly. In fact our disagreements allowed us to grow closer. He knew I was doing my job to keep him healthy and that all along I was on his side. That would mean a lot to him, especially in the treacherous months ahead, but that commitment was to be thoroughly tested.

FOURTEEN

Eye of the Storm

1.

It was a stunning piece from the Robert Talbott collection: an exquisite silk, rich-red tie embellished with bright yellow Maltese crosses. It was to be my Christmas 1997 gift to Bill Clinton—I had exchanged gifts every year with the president and first family. Each Christmas I had spent with the Clintons at the White House or Camp David had been a joyful family gathering with the hopeful sense that peace on Earth would prevail in the coming year. But this holiday season was far from peaceful. Vicious rumors were rampant, and whispers percolated through the press about a White House intern.

When I first heard the term "intern" being bandied about, the only context I could place it in was a medical one. Interns were the lowest entity on the hospital totem pole, someone who had just graduated from medical school and who had a degree but no real doctoring experience. Every seasoned hospital physician knows that interns have just enough knowledge and contact with patients to be danger-

Christmas was usually a happy time at the White House. I escort the president back to the residence in December 1996. (WHITE HOUSE PHOTO)

ous. I wondered what relationship this intern had to my first patient. And if she were like a medical intern, would she have enough knowledge and proximity to be a danger to him?

The atmosphere at the White House felt like a battle zone with each late-breaking news report that blasted across the airwaves. The enemy seemed to be everywhere: members of Congress, investigative reporters, and television talking heads. The tension continued to grow with the threat of an independent counsel being appointed to investigate any wrongdoings by the president and first lady.

Even I was not immune from attack. At medical conferences where I was invited to speak about the history of presidential care, someone in the audience would invariably raise their hand and ask me if I ever treated Bill Clinton for a sexually transmitted disease. I would look at them directly and answer in a matter-of-fact tone, "No. Next question please." What also became an issue was me being both Clinton's personal physician and a relatively attractive woman. Often times at these conferences, male physicians would nudge each other when I stepped onto the stage to speak. "Of course, Clinton's physician would have to be an attractive Asian woman," I could almost hear them sneer. Being an attractive woman had become a liability in the Clinton White House.

But I wouldn't allow the tension at work to spoil my celebration of Christmas. I found myself seeking normalcy and refuge at my favorite Nordstrom's in the Fashion Centre at Pentagon City the week before Christmas. I discovered the stunning Robert Talbott tie for the president there. I had often purchased ties for President Clinton for his birthday and for Christmas. The president's valets would frequently pick out my ties for him to wear at major events, such as press conferences and the State of the Union address. Clinton would always write a personal thank-you note as well as point out the tie to me on days he was wearing my gift. I used to smile and think, "These are the ties that bind," feeling special when the president of the United States was wearing my tie. But I later learned other people,

President Clinton shares a joke in the medical compartment onboard Air Force One in September 1996. (WHITE HOUSE PHOTO)

Punch line! (WHITE HOUSE PHOTO)

including the intern Monica Lewinsky, had also given the president ties. There are ties that bind and those that ultimately turn into nooses, as I would realize later when one of Lewinsky's ties was used as evidence against the president.

But I felt a pang of guilt the week before Christmas purchasing gifts for the first family when I hadn't bought anything yet for my husband and two sons. I guess the Clintons were really the first family in my life during that time. I would later pay the price for that allegiance with my broken marriage and alienation from my children.

"May I help you?" The sweet voice of a saleswoman caught my attention as I strolled into the women's fashion section in search of gifts for Hillary and Chelsea.

I glanced up at the refined, elegantly clad middle-aged woman, almost too classy to be a salesperson. For a moment I wanted to ask her, "Yes, can you please direct me to the first-lady section?"

Instead, I declined her help and moseyed over to a table that had

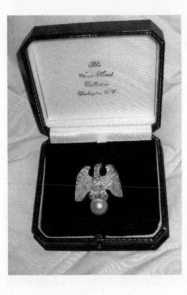

The first family and I exchanged Christmas presents. An Ann Hand pin given to me by the first lady. (FAMILY PHOTO)

woolen scarves and turtleneck sweaters. Practical gifts for the ever-practical Hillary Clinton. "Cover up your neck, you don't want to get cold," I can still hear her advising others. I wondered if Marie Antoinette had the same premonition about protecting her neck. Hillary was at this time under attack about her involvement with Whitewater while working at her previous law firm. Yet she continued to be calm, friendly, and caring toward the people around her. I admired her strength under fire.

Not everyone on the eighteen-acre White House battlefield bore Hillary's Kevlar mantle. At this time the outpatient clinic in the Old Executive Office Building was often filled with the walking wounded: junior staffers who were stressed out. They suffered from

Even after the Clintons left office, we continued to exchange gifts. Bill Clinton's handwritten note in July 2007: Connie Thanks for coming to see me—and for the tie. It's beautiful. Best, Bill

WILLIAM J. CLINTON
7/17/07

Connie —
Thanks for coming to see me — Hillary too —
It's beautiful

Best,
Bill

an array of maladies: insomnia, stomachaches, headaches, frequent colds, and overall anxiety. The medical unit medics, who frequently treated the junior staffers, had created a new disease category: "fear of impending subpoena." Rumors that the independent counsel would want to interrogate the staff drifted down the halls of the West Wing, causing panic. Clinton's valets, who lived and worked in the shadow of the president, feared they, too, would be questioned. Proximity to the president, or life in the kill zone, had taken on a new meaning.

If you were close to the president, especially if you traveled with him, you were at risk of being interrogated about his personal life. As I went about treating and reassuring the fearful White House staffers, I found myself becoming anxious as well. I was his personal physician, yet I knew nothing about the intimate details of his daily life, let alone his involvement with an intern behind closed doors. I knew his health history but respected his zone of privacy in day-to-day activities, and I didn't inquire into private matters unless they had a medical impact on his ability to do his job.

As I drove through the gates of West Executive Boulevard into the compound every morning, cameramen would come scurrying out to my car to film me. What are they going to do with the film coverage, I would wonder. I was just going in to work to do my job, which was taking care of people. It felt like I was in the middle of a brewing storm: a growing maelstrom that was oblivious to anyone who stood in its path. As a doctor, all I could do was take care of the ill and injured who were battered by the storm. I sought to be the healer and offer my patients a sense of calm; perhaps I could be the eye of the storm for them.

But it was not only healing the wounded that was the pressing issue. It was about sheer survival, the survival of my patient's presidency. How could I as a physician help him with that? I was powerless. I thought of my colleagues who at this time were deployed in battalions in the Persian Gulf or onboard hospital ships. I would have jumped at orders to deploy to the Gulf and to serve with the "real Navy" practicing "real medicine," far away from West Wing politics and the Washington rumor mill. But my loyalty to the president and first lady kept me at the White House, to weather the storm that was going to blast us and to do what I could to comfort them.

The beautiful tie I gave the president for Christmas appeared on national television, but did not bring him good luck. The president was to broadcast a statement from the Roosevelt Room. The first lady was to join him. I would watch the press conference from my office, located less than a minute's walk from where the president was speaking. I sat eating my takeout lunch from the Mess with the duty nurse, watching the small television in my office. The cameras switched to President Clinton in the Roosevelt Room. He looked good on camera, wearing my Robert Talbott tie. Mrs. Clinton stood to his side, looking beautiful in a yellow silk suit, hair styled in a flattering way.

As the president spoke, I munched quietly on my salad and then stopped chewing when he said, "I did not have sexual relations with that woman, Miss Lewinsky . . ." How I hoped that was the truth and would put an end to the rumors.

2.

From the start of Clinton's legal woes back in 1994, I was surrounded by attorneys. Not only was I married to one but I took care of at least two at work, Bill and Hillary Clinton. Despite both familial connections with lawyers, I had always tried to stay away from them as much as possible. As a physician, a call from an attorney could only mean bad news. At the White House, a call from one of the president's attorneys meant the worst news of all.

Despite my aversion to attorneys, I admit that I did like the president's attorneys. I even enjoyed working with Bob Bennett, who handled Clinton's defense against Paula Jones. Bob was known to be brash and brusque, reminiscent of a tough Teamsters leader. David Kendall was Bennett's perfect foil. He was Clinton's attorney during

Ken Starr's investigation, and was gracious and genteel, soft-spoken and polished. When the operator would connect me with the president's attorney, I would always welcome a call from Kendall. It wasn't that he had good news, not in the least, but because it was so pleasant to talk with him, and despite the general unpleasantness of this case, it was almost a pleasure to take the call. He was that smooth.

"Connie, I have some bad news for you," David said, preparing me by phone in the midst of the grand-jury investigation about the president's relationship with Lewinsky.

"David, remember, I work at the White House. Nowadays all news is bad news! Just give it to me." I braced myself.

"One of the key pieces of evidence the independent counsel says they have against the president is a dress that Monica says contains the president's DNA," David said to me clearly. I had heard rumors about the infamous navy blue dress that bore the presidential stain. "Ken Starr has submitted an order that you, as the White House physician, draw the president's blood for DNA to see if it matches the DNA sample from the dress."

We were entering the realm of forensic medicine. And now I had just been saddled with the responsibility to extract the president's blood so the FBI could do a DNA match. I was stunned by the indignity of it all. Not only did Ken Starr order Clinton to turn over his DNA in the form of a blood sample, but he picked me, the president's personal physician, to draw the blood. However, I was not just Clinton's physician, but I was also a military officer who had sworn an oath to support and defend the Constitution. Starr took advantage of my duty as a naval officer, regardless of my personal loyalty to my patient, to perform this odious task.

"I guess Starr is really serious about this," I began. "Dave, you must know that I don't normally draw blood on patients. It's usually the White House nurses and medics who are the experts at venipuncture. I'm pretty rusty at this."

"Connie, you have no choice. You're being ordered to do so," David said apologetically.

My training won over my insecurity. "I'll do it, David. Hopefully, it will clear the president of these charges, and we can be done with everything once and for all."

"I hope so, too, Connie. I really do."

The Map Room is located next door to the doctor's office on the ground floor of the White House. This room was used as the Situation Room during World War II, where President Franklin Roosevelt and his generals and admirals would review the maps and monitor the progression of the American and Allied forces. I wondered if Starr knew the history of this room when he specifically ordered that the blood be drawn there instead of my treatment room, doctor's office, or even in the Medical Unit Clinic in the Old Executive Office Building. I thought of FDR as he weighed the movement of troops during the war. Clinton, too, was now embroiled in his own war. The battlefield this evening would be the Map Room, and there would be blood shed, as ordered by Starr.

David Kendall and I arrived in the Map Room about thirty minutes before the president. We were informed that Robert Bittman, Starr's deputy, and an FBI agent were en route to the White House to witness the blood draw.

I set a blue disposable chux pad on the room's antique mahogany table. This wasn't the usual setting for the medical unit to draw blood: crystal chandelier dangling from the ceiling, Georgian-style wood panel, Chippendale cabinets, and plush carpet. Atop the pad, I carefully laid a rubber tourniquet, alcohol pads, a Vacutainer syringe, needles, purple-top tubes, and gauze and Band-Aids. I positioned each item carefully so I would not have to fumble locating them when it was time for the procedure. I was ready to perform my duty and, in essence, carry out Starr's dirty work. I was a soldier in Clinton's war but a mere pawn to the enemy.

Starr's deputy Bob Bittman arrived with a woman FBI agent and had come through the Diplomatic Reception Room. Bittman hardly made eye contact with me. The FBI agent was businesslike but pleasant. A few minutes later Clinton came into the room, having completed an event on the State Floor of the White House. He was in a quiet mood. The president was introduced to Bittman and the agent, and then he sat down in a chair in front of me and rolled up his right sleeve to expose the antecubital vein in his arm.

"Okay, Doc," he said to me, averting his eyes from the sight of my needle. "Let's get down to business."

I wiped the inner part of his forearm with an alcohol pad and felt for a vein. He had a nice-sized vessel there. I inserted the needle, which was connected to the vacuum suction device and from that to a purple-top tube. Dark-red blood squirted into the tube. I let out a quiet sigh of relief as I undid the tourniquet from Clinton's arm while the tube filled with 4 cc of his precious blood. I handed the warm tube to the FBI agent, and then turned and placed a 2×2 gauze over Clinton's puncture wound. He folded his arm to keep the gauze in place, before I put a Band-Aid over it.

Bittman seemed pleased with my handiwork, not saying a word. The agent then had both Kendall and me sign forms indicating that we witnessed the blood draw and that I had performed it. The time marked was 10:10 P.M.

They left quietly, stealing away into the night with the president's blood. I don't recall them even thanking me. But what was there to be thankful for? The purpose of the blood draw was to prove my patient guilty. And if he was, I would have helped them to do that. His blood was figuratively on my hands. I felt pain in the pit of my stomach afterward for having been used in this way, and even if done reluctantly, it was still a form of betrayal.

The DNA in the blood that I drew on Clinton that night proved to be a match to the DNA sample from the stained dress. Clinton didn't contest the evidence. Instead, he confessed.

3.

Bill Clinton was to return to the Map Room on August 17, 1998, for more "bloodletting." Two weeks after he had submitted his blood for DNA testing, Clinton was brought back to the same room to testify in front of the grand jury and independent counsel Ken Starr. Until then I had not received any word about the results of the DNA test, although I had anticipated that I would be the last to know. What role did I play other than to draw the blood handed over to the FBI? What did I expect? I had believed all along in the president's innocence, and that he was being framed, set up by his political enemies.

My office, which was located next door to the Map Room, was to be vacated on the day of his testimony, except for me. I sent my secretary and the duty nurse to help in the clinic across from the West Wing. Despite the chaos wrought by this political storm, the medical unit continued to practice medicine as usual, seeing patients and preparing contingency plans for the president's busy travel schedule. Although it was an awful time for the president personally, an NBC poll showed his job approval rating at an all-time high of 70 percent. And despite the allegations against the president, the economy was doing well: the Dow Jones Average jumped 150 points the day Clinton was to testify before the grand jury.

No one was supposed to be on the ground floor near the Map Room during the president's testimony, except for the Secret Service and the president's senior aides. I sat in my quiet space and tried to imagine what was transpiring on the other side of the wall. I had read the newspapers and heard the reports of the alleged affair with Monica Lewinsky, including an intimation of sordid details. I didn't want to believe that the man I knew as my patient had engaged in such behavior.

Suddenly I heard over the radio the voice of the senior agent whisper, "Eagle leaving Map Room." I glanced at my watch. His testimony had just begun a few minutes prior to the announcement.

What happened? Did he lose his temper? Did Starr antagonize him? Had Clinton become suddenly ill?

"Eagle, headed to the doctor's office." I stood up as I heard the door to my office open. Clinton walked inside. He looked fine, not red-faced or upset. Deadly calm. He walked past me without saying a word, headed toward the bathroom.

Clinton's senior agent opened the door to my office and poked his head inside.

"Is everything okay?" I asked the agent.

"Eagle said he needed to use the bathroom," the agent responded, turning his head in its direction. We heard the toilet flush a minute later, and the agent ducked out of my office, disappearing into the hallway.

Clinton walked toward me blowing his nose with a Kleenex. I sat at my secretary's desk trying to look busy shuffling papers.

"Everything okay, Mr. President?" I was hesitant to ask. It was like asking Mrs. Lincoln how she liked the play.

Clinton blew his nose and tossed the tissue into a wastebasket near the desk. He then stood before the mirror to the side of the door, adjusting his tie. When he was done, Clinton looked one more time into the mirror and with a voice loud enough for me to hear, uttered his familiar refrain, "Well, it's show time." Clinton stepped out of my office and went back into the Map Room to complete his testimony before the grand jury.

The day had gone by quickly, although I was imagining that time couldn't go fast enough for Clinton while he was being grilled by Starr. Rumors spread like wildfire throughout the West Wing that the president was going on television in the evening to speak to the American people in the aftermath of his testimony. I stayed late in my office that day to watch the broadcast that was coming from the Map Room next door. The final battle, I thought. Would Clinton finally win this war? Or would this be his Waterloo?

Clinton's senior aides Paul Begala and Rahm Emanuel rushed in and out of the Map Room, occasionally dropping by my office to use the restroom. I kept the television on, looking up periodically at the screen to see what time the networks anticipated airing the president's address. Even though Clinton's senior staff was in and out of my office all evening, I had no idea. I wanted to stay out of the loop as much as possible. Clinton's senior communications staff was focused on the message the president would deliver. For tonight's broadcast, I would just be part of the American public that was his audience. Begala and Emanuel were in the loop; they were his spin doctors.

The president went live at 10:02 P.M. I held my breath as the cameras focused on his face. I had seen him throughout the day, and when his face appeared on my television screen instead of in my doorway, he looked very tired and deadly serious. The duty nurse sat in my office in a chair next to me, our takeout dinners from the Mess on the coffee table. As the president launched into his prepared remarks, Rahm Emanuel dashed into my office. Slender, handsome, and arrogant, Rahm had worked closely with the president on tonight's speech. He sat in the chair opposite me and I turned to watch his expression while the president spoke, trying to gauge what would happen next.

What happened next was a painful and defiant admission that Clinton did have an inappropriate relationship with "that woman." It was not the news I wanted to hear but deep down inside it was what I feared would be coming. As Clinton spoke, Rahm uttered an expletive and then said, "This is not going well at all." He then jumped up and rushed out of my office.

"This is not going well at all" was an understatement if there ever was one. My first thoughts were with Mrs. Clinton. I hadn't seen her all day. I assumed she was upstairs on the second floor of the residence watching this address on television. Was she alone? Who was there to comfort her? I wondered. And if she didn't know this news already, she knew it now, along with the American public and the world. And as his doctor who covered him twenty-four hours a day, who conducted his physical examinations, took care of him when he was ill, traveled with him around the globe, joked and laughed with him, exchanged birthday and Christmas gifts with him, I only heard his confession on CNN. I did not hear it in the privacy of my office or in the sanctity of the family quarters on the second floor, but on prime-time television. Did he not trust me enough as his personal physician to talk with me privately? Or was he too ashamed to let me know what he had done? I hoped it was the latter.

As I sat watching while Clinton defended himself on television, anger rose within me. He had lied to his wife, his daughter, and his loyal office staff and even his valets, who were dragged before the independent counsel to testify. As director of the White House Medical Unit, my first word of caution to newly reporting staff was: *Never lie to me. You lie, you die.* I felt the same standards of conduct that applied to me and my staff as military personnel should also apply to the commander in chief. Or was I naive in believing so? Sitting in my office listening to the president's address, I thought of my father's cousin, Marciano "Rocky" Mariano, who had served under Kennedy and Johnson. In my childhood I had heard stories from my Uncle Rocky of "all the women" in both prior administrations. He made it sound like extramarital relationships were par for the course for the presidency.

But this thought did nothing to comfort or reassure me as I sat painfully listening to the president that August night. My nurse squirmed nervously in his seat watching me. Our dinners sat untouched and cold on the coffee table in front of us. I had no appetite. I defended him and his character over and over to friends and family. And now what was to happen? How would my relationship with him ever be the same?

In the midst of this mental storm that blew through me as I watched Clinton on television, the thought of Virginia Kelley, the president's mother, came to mind. She did not live to see her son's painful confession today, and I was thankful for that. But I could still hear her plea to "take care of my son." I promised her I would do that and that I wouldn't leave him. And then I was reminded why I was at the White House. And that reminder came from the most unlikely source: Burt Lee, my old boss under President Bush Sr. He had picked me for this job six years ago. Burt had toughened me up for the White House duty in order to face the criticism and derision. I realized in order to survive this disaster, I had to be tough like Burt, loving like Virginia, and like my father and the valets before him, I had to stay and serve the president of the United States in "sickness and in health."

FIFTEEN

It Takes a Village

1.

I've got the worst headache of my life."

These were the first words uttered by a patient to Mac "Black Cloud" McLeod during his first week with the White House Medical Unit in 1998. After a year as an independent duty medic at an isolated air base in Turkey, McLeod was used to being on his own when taking care of patients, hours away from the nearest hospital or doctor. He almost turned down the White House position since he craved the "blood and gore" emergencies in the field over "bread and butter" medicine. But when McLeod interviewed with me, I convinced him that I wanted someone like him, who was cool under pressure. So he took the job, anticipating that the only medical problems he was going to treat in the outpatient clinic or on the road with the medical unit were run-of-the-mill colds, sprains, and occasional headaches. But the "worst headache of my life" is not what McLeod was expecting as he sat down at the clinic check-in desk at lunchtime.

The clinic doorbell binged cheerfully, announcing the arrival of a heavyset, middle-aged African American man wearing a plain dark suit. McLeod leaped to his feet when he heard the chime. "May I help you, sir?" he asked the man who came through the clinic door clutching his forehead.

The man talked slowly and softly, his eyes tightly shut, beads of sweat forming above his brow. "I've got the worst headache of my life."

Medical personnel are conditioned to experience chills down their spine when they hear that phrase. It means the patient may be experiencing a subarachnoid hemorrhage, a sudden bleed in the brain from a ruptured blood vessel. The condition is almost always fatal.

McLeod had that reaction as he took the man's pulse and strapped a blood pressure cuff to his beefy arm. His instincts told him this was an emergency so he better act fast. Time was of the essence as he noticed the man's face beginning to droop. McLeod began to pelt the patient with a litany of questions before he passed out: "Do you have any allergies? Did you hit your head or experience any trauma? Do you have high blood pressure, heart disease, diabetes? Taking any medications?"

The man responded no to each question as McLeod placed an oxygen mask over his face. Weighing over 240 pounds, the patient barely fit the width of the exam table. As Mac checked the man's blood pressure, the patient groaned and then suddenly became silent, slumping to the right side. Mac grabbed the man and pushed him back onto the table and yelled, "We need help in here!"

Physician assistant John Chitwood was at the back of the clinic eating a sandwich and chatting with Navy nurse Vince Starks.

"Did you hear something?" Starks asked Chitwood, abruptly stopping their conversation in midsentence.

"It's probably the new guy," Chitwood responded, grinning. "They all get nervous during their first week. No matter how experienced they are in the field, they're all a little anal the first few months here."

Luckily Vince stood up and walked to the hallway, calling out in the direction of the medic's voice, "Mac, did you call us?"

McLeod had begun CPR on the patient. "Need help in here STAT; we've got ourselves a code!" McLeod yelled between compressions, with only a twinge of anxiety in his voice.

"Is he kidding?" Chitwood asked, standing up slowly and following Starks into the treatment room. A few seconds later they witnessed the patient's first grand mal seizure.

"This is not looking good," McLeod muttered, shaking his head as he observed the seizure. The waves of severe jerking that overwhelmed the large man's entire body passed in what seemed like the longest fifteen seconds of the medic's professional life. When it was over, the patient groaned, saliva drooling down the corner of his lips.

Chitwood and Starks joined in after the seizure had passed. Chitwood stood opposite McLeod taking turns bagging the patient with an oxygen bag mask and compressing his chest. Meanwhile Starks took the patient's limp hefty arm and tried to find a vein to place an IV. McLeod reached for the phone and punched out 911 first and then alerted the Uniformed Division security that a D.C. Metro ambulance would be dispatched with sirens and lights blaring. He also paged Dr. Barry Nash, the White House physician on duty, who was eating lunch in the cafeteria.

Airway. Breathing. Circulation. Disability. McLeod, Starks, and Chitwood had to focus on sustaining breath and pulse in a patient who was rapidly losing brain function. They couldn't do anything about the blood vessel that had exploded in this man's brain, pouring blood into the closed space of his skull. This patient needed to be on an operating room table with a neurosurgical team working on him. It seemed like hours but was actually only minutes when D.C. Metro arrived escorted by the Uniformed Division agents. The tiny outpatient clinic became flooded with men in uniforms carrying radios and medical gear. Dr. Nash, after receiving the page, dashed to the clinic and arrived the same time as the ambulance crew.

McLeod gave a quick report to Dr. Nash and the paramedics, who quickly assumed care of the patient. It took several minutes to "load and go" as they continued CPR, placed an IV in the man's arm and EKG pads on his chest, and lifted him onto the ambulance gurney.

The paramedics wheeled the man out of the clinic, into the ambulance, and rushed him to George Washington University Hospital down the street from the White House. As the sound of the ambulance siren faded in the distance, a hushed stillness descended upon the clinic previously overwhelmed by the buzz of a medical emergency. Dr. Nash sat down in the reception room with McLeod, Starks, and Chitwood to discuss the code. The four men sat quietly, dazed in the wake of the patient's trauma.

"Well, Mac, welcome to the Medical Unit Clinic!" Dr. Nash broke the silence. "I want you to know that wasn't our typical sick-call patient."

McLeod grinned and spoke up, "Well, I've got to admit that I haven't treated too many patients like that one. But I also have to admit to something else."

Nash and the other two men listened closely, their interest piqued.

"I tend to have a black cloud around me. And I've had it in every command. Whenever I've got the duty, bad things like this tend to happen," McLeod confessed in a tone that was part apology, part braggadocio.

"That's good that we know that," Dr. Nash said. "And even better that you know what to do when bad things happen."

The patient was admitted to GWU Medical Center where doctors confirmed that he had sustained a large subarachnoid hemorrhage. He was beyond rescue. Although the patient was under the care of the staff at GWU, the medical unit remained involved in his care and disposition. The patient was an active duty Army warrant officer who was assigned to the White House Communications Agency. As a fellow military officer assigned to the White House, he was considered family, one of our own. After he had left the compound, a flurry of phone calls were generated to notify the chain of command of his medical condition.

Dr. Nash phoned me on my cell phone as I sat in a golf cart in Martha's Vineyard, watching the president complete eighteen holes on his family vacation.

"You've notified everybody, Barry?" I asked, after Nash had given me the story of the code and the patient's status in the intensive care unit at GWU.

"Yes, ma'am," Nash answered. "We contacted the WHCA commander and the director of the mil office. A car has been dispatched to pick up the patient's family and take them to the hospital. It doesn't look good. He's on life support."

"Make sure our medical administrator works closely on this one. If the patient stays on life support for a few more days, we'll have time to retire him from active duty, so his family gets full benefits when he dies."

"Got it," Nash agreed.

"One more thing, Barry," I said. "How did the new medic handle it this morning?"

"McLeod did everything we would expect of him, Connie," Nash responded. "Never broke a sweat, and was calm, cool, collected. It was quite a test his first day in clinic."

I was happy to hear this report. "So you think he'd pass the final exam if that ever happens?"

"Final exam?" Nash asked, confused by my question.

"What he'd do if the patient today was the president? Would he do the exact same thing medically? How would he handle it?"

Nash paused to think. "Well, he'd probably soil his underwear like the rest of us, but I think he would've done it the same way in taking care of POTUS."

I smiled. "Right answer. Everyone has to be prepared for the final exam. You hope to never take it. Until then, every other patient is a dry run. That's why we're here."

"Got it, boss."

2.

The medical unit was charged not only with taking care of the first patient and his family, but the vice president and his family as well. I guess you could call him the second patient, but of course the care and attention afforded him and his family, as it was for everybody on the eighteen-acre White House compound, was first-patient quality. We would just get stretched thin sometimes, especially if the president was overseas or on the road, and there was a medical emergency back home. And when you considered that President Clinton sometimes extended our medical net to include foreign heads of state, the village became a small city at times.

Vice President Al Gore grimaced when he heard the orthopedic surgeon's diagnosis.

"Mr. Vice President," the physician said cautiously and politely to the second most powerful man in America as they sat in the Medical Evaluation and Treatment Unit—METU—suite at Bethesda Naval Hospital. "Your Achilles tendon is torn. We're going to need to reconnect it in the operating room."

Gore was hoping it was a simple sprain, treatable by ice and an Ace wrap. What the doctor told him was not the diagnosis he would have made himself. And, if the vice president's left ankle wasn't hurting so badly, he would have just walked out of the hospital. He had no time for any surgery, his calendar was packed, and he was traveling overseas in the next few weeks. But since Gore couldn't even manage a single step without wincing, he gave the surgeon's opinion a second thought.

It was August 1994 and Gore had capped off another busy day on

Capitol Hill with a pickup basketball game with two members of Congress. Without any warmup, Gore tossed his suit coat into the arms of his personal aide, who stood beside the bleachers with Gore's entourage of agents, assistants, and the medical unit's physician assistant. The whole group had accompanied him into the gymnasium in the House of Representatives. Gore jumped up to snag the ball in midair and then came down onto the court, pivoting sharply with his left foot. He then heard a sudden snap and felt something slap the back of his left leg. What the vice president felt was his Achilles tendon rip from its attachment to his left heel, with the belly of the tendon bunching up under his calf muscle. He tried to step forward but excruciating pain knocked him to the floor.

The on-duty Navy physician assistant, Mike Grant, heard the snap across the court and rushed to the vice president's side, pulling out an ice pack from his medical bag as he sprinted to him. Grant examined Gore and recommended they go directly to Bethesda to get a CAT scan of his ankle and to see the orthopedist. The PA knew from his exam that Gore's tendon was torn and called me on my cell phone as the vice president's motorcade made its way along the George Washington Parkway. My first call was to the METU coordinator at Bethesda. This set into motion a chain reaction of phone calls that activated the presidential suite for the VP's impromptu visit.

Activation of the METU meant that the nurses and corpsmen assigned to the private suite reported to that space immediately, ready to assume their roles in ensuring the visiting patient received the most expeditious and responsive care possible. The METU suite is a private ward located in the heart of Bethesda Naval Hospital's historic tower. The floor is specially outfitted with protective devices and communications gear used in support of the president. The decor is modest but elegant, resembling the West Wing of the White House. It remains locked most of the time until it is activated by me, as the director of the White House Medical Unit, for the evaluation and treatment of the first and second patients and their families.

This secure space has served as the inpatient ward for previous hospitalized presidents. White House archive photos show President Lyndon Johnson recovering from gall bladder surgery in a hospital bed in this suite, and President Ronald Reagan and First Lady Nancy Reagan waving from a window in the suite during his hospitalization there.

The METU ward is also autonomous; the president could be hospitalized in the METU while the rest of the hospital carries out the business of taking care of patients as usual, oblivious to the presence of the commander in chief and his entourage in the private wing.

"Hazelnut coffee with cream and two packs of sweetener, just as you like it, ma'am," said Lieutenant Bill McGee; he greeted me with a steaming cup bearing the gold logo of the hospital. McGee knew from prior presidential visits how I liked my coffee. No detail is too trivial for the METU team, staffed by handpicked nurses and hospital corpsmen. Even the official portraits that greet the guest as they enter the suite are personalized: with Gore's visit, his portrait and that of his wife, Tipper, were immediately hung on the wall in the reception room. If President Clinton or the first lady were to visit, their portraits would be hanging on the wall.

I met up with the vice president's motorcade right as it was pulling into the driveway outside the suite. Tipper and two of the second family's children arrived in a separate motorcade a few minutes later. We were met by a Navy security guard and a Secret Service agent and escorted to the suite.

Blonde, lovely, and vivacious, Tipper was the epitome of the concerned wife as she stood beside her husband, listening intently to the surgeon's recommendation for surgery. She looked thoughtfully at the surgeon, then her husband, and then finally at me, seeking my reaction.

"I agree with going to surgery," I told Gore and his wife, then turned to the orthopedic surgeon. "How soon can you get the operating room ready?"

"It's ready right now" was the reply I had anticipated. The vice president grudgingly nodded his head in acquiescence, and we were off to the operating room.

Al Gore's Achilles tendon repair was the first of two presidential hospitalizations during the Clinton administration. Occurring a little over a year and a half into the first term, Gore's surgery at Bethesda allowed the METU and White House Medical Unit to work closely together. In many ways, the vice president's surgery prepared me for President Clinton's quadriceps surgery three years later. Not only did I learn to institute the procedures that would lead to a smoother hospital visit, but I was later ready to face another patient who insisted on traveling overseas as soon as he left the hospital.

The vice president was wheeled into the operating room a few hours after our short discussion in the METU suite. Tipper and the children observed the surgery from the glass viewing platform over the operating room. Two of Gore's shift agents donned scrubs and gowns, and joined me with the orthopedic surgeon, anesthesiologist, and operating-room team.

The repair of the torn tendon took one and a half hours, and the surgery went without a hitch. During the procedure, I would periodically look up at Mrs. Gore and the children, who hovered overhead watching the surgery. I would give them a thumbs-up that everything was proceeding as planned. Tipper would beam and reciprocate with two thumbs-ups.

Hospitalized for only one day, Gore was eager to be discharged home. Before he left the hospital, I met privately with him and Tipper after the orthopedic surgeon had informed the vice president that he would need to wear a full leg cast to immobilize his leg for three months, to allow the sutured tendon to heal properly.

"Okay, I know I have to be in a cast and use crutches," Gore said grudgingly. "But I'm still traveling overseas next week."

I counseled the vice president about the risks of blood clots post-operatively, as well as the difficulty he would most likely encounter getting around on crutches. "I recommend you postpone your trip till you're out of the cast, sir," I spoke, looking at Gore and then at Tipper, who was nodding in agreement with me.

"Thanks, Doctor, for your opinion," Gore spoke brusquely. "But I'm still going."

And Gore did go, along with a physician assistant from the medical unit who had specialized in orthopedics. In fact, the cast and crutches didn't slow down the vice president at all. He traveled to forty-three states and a handful of foreign countries while on crutches that fall.

But Gore's three-month recovery was not without incident. During one event in which he was hobbling on his crutches into a church in D.C., Gore lost his footing while going up the steps. He fell forward on his knees onto the steps, his metal crutches tossed to the side with a loud clang. But what the Secret Service agents on the counter-assault team witnessed from their black suburban on the street was the vice president going down suddenly to his knees, and the loud report of metal on pavement. Thinking that Gore may have been shot, the agents rushed forward with their guns bared to surround and cover the vice president. Fortunately, no one got hurt and the vice president recovered from his torn Achilles tendon well enough to complete the 1997 Marine Corps Marathon.

3.

The strain of working for the president of the United States affected everybody on this detail, whether you were a young advance-team member with personal problems or an elderly cook working in the kitchen. You didn't have to be on the front line for it to affect you. The threat of physical violence, from a sniper on a rooftop or from someone trying to poison the president's food, was ever a concern. And it took its toll.

Irish eyes were indeed smiling upon Bill and Hillary Clinton when they arrived in Ireland on December 1, 1995, on day three of Clinton's five-day swing through Europe. Ireland held a special place in Clinton's heart; his mother's Cassidy family claimed Ireland as their homeland. While Dubliners waved the American flag to welcome the Clintons at the airport, the medical unit nurse, Michelle Adams, greeted me at the foot of Air Force One's rear airstair with an alarming message.

"Doctor," Michelle whispered to me as I stepped off onto the tarmac. "I got a call from a woman psychiatrist in D.C. just before you landed. It was very disturbing."

I knew then that this trip wasn't going to be uneventful. "What's up, Michelle?"

"It was about a patient of hers who's one of ours," Michelle continued. "She's a young White House staffer who was sent to Dublin to cover this trip. She called her psychiatrist in D.C. today, after breaking up with her boyfriend, and told her that she was very depressed and planned to kill herself at midnight at Dublin Castle."

We walked briskly toward the ceremonial site, passing the White House press corps, which had also deplaned and was working on their camera gear to film the arrival ceremony. Without missing a beat, I smiled and waved to them.

Speaking under my breath, I told Michelle, "Wave and smile at the press. Don't let them see us looking stressed out. They'll sense that something is wrong."

Michelle, knitting her brow, dutifully imitated my press greeting. Some of the guys waved and went back to setting up their cameras and microphones.

"Possible midnight suicide at Dublin Castle," I summed up the situation as we walked toward the spare limousine. "Not good, for her or us. I suppose she knows this is the site of tonight's state dinner for the president and first lady."

Michelle hadn't made the connection. "Oh my God, you're right. That's the trip's big event."

"I know it sounds callous, but a suicide during the president's trip by one of his staffers would overshadow all the goodwill this visit could bring. It's all the press would cover, the suicide." I looked at my watch to calculate the time difference with Washington. "Do you have the doctor's phone number?"

As I dialed the D.C. number of the psychiatrist, I glanced over at the Irish Army Corps, which had assembled on the tarmac, decked out in vibrant military regalia. The Clintons were now gracefully coming down the front steps of the plane. I pondered the awesome power of the press in creating the image of the American presidency. One of the truisms I learned early at the White House was perception is its own reality.

For instance, if the president were to miss a step and fall while coming down the stairs, even if he only had this one mishap, the perception would be he was clumsy. How would a suicide associated with the president's visit to a foreign country be perceived? Would the press make it look like the White House didn't adequately screen their staffers? Perhaps they would investigate if the young woman had a relationship with Bill Clinton. A variety of conspiracy theories would erupt. Of course that was the spin doctor in me; every White House staffer has this side. But the part of me that sprang into action that morning in Dublin was the medical doctor. Someone out there was in urgent need of medical help, and we needed to get to her right away.

I spotted Dr. Jeff "Doogie Howser" Eschbach, the medical unit physician assigned to cover the Dublin events. Looking like a Secret Service agent, Jeff stood post beside the president's limo, one hand on the limo door handle, the other carrying the medical bag, and both eyes fixed on the president. Jeff was part of the advance team and would cover the president during our events in Dublin, while I stayed at the hotel to catch up on sleep, see patients from our traveling party, and perhaps steal a few hours of tourist time in Dublin town. I had a sinking feeling I wouldn't be doing any sightseeing this trip.

The psychiatrist was pleasant and concerned over the phone. Her patient "Mary" had been under her care for depression prior to this appointment. It had been controlled with medication, and she was certified to work this job. But Mary had become fragile when problems developed with her boyfriend. When he called long-distance to break up with her that morning, she had lost all emotional reserve. She frantically called the doctor, deeply depressed, and made threats about killing herself.

"I'm very concerned about this young woman; she may try to take her life," the psychiatrist reiterated. "I'm sorry all this has to fall in your lap."

"Although our primary job is to take care of the president, Mary is part of our family. We'll do our best to help her, once we find where she is."

As I finished the call, I made a list of team members that I had to notify immediately to help find this young woman before she killed herself.

Don Flynn's Irish eyes weren't smiling when I told him about the missing and presumed suicidal White House staffer. After firing off an expletive, the veteran Secret Service agent radioed several agents to come to our site. We huddled on the tarmac with the White House advance-trip lead, Brian McPartlin, and the military aide to discuss our game plan. The agents would search the event sites and be on the lookout for the young woman at the castle that evening. Brian and the military aide would return to the hotel, searching for the woman in her room. Michelle would contact our medical counterpart at the American embassy to get the patient admitted to a local hospital for care, when and if we found her. And I would now accompany the president to Dublin Castle that night in case we wound up with more than one patient this evening.

The spare limo trailed the president's stretch limousine as we rattled across the cobblestone courtyard that led to the grand entrance of Dublin Castle. I jumped out of the spare limousine, Jeff Eschbach behind me, when the cars came to a stop. Jeff then followed the president and first lady into the grand hall, while Brian McPartlin and I were diverted from the entourage on our own private tour of the grounds.

The moon half lit the velvet night as I glanced at the austere Norman Tower to the side of the castle. The grand hall was lit by dim candlelight, which was intended to project an elegant, romantic ambience. Instead, the effect made the castle look eerie from the outside. Images of medieval dungeons, moats, kings, and queens filled my worried mind as I now treaded cautiously into the stone castle, still searching for a damsel in distress.

"We found nothing at the hotel, Doc," Brian reported to me on our way into the castle. "Her room was empty. We did see a suitcase of pill bottles." Brian named the medications one by one. Most of the bottles were full, suggesting that the patient had not been taking her medications.

"Any clues where she may be tonight, other than here at the castle?"

Brian shook his head as we met up with the agent who was the lead for tonight's state dinner.

The president and first lady were toasted and regaled at a memorable dinner in the grand hall. I sat in a back room with the military aide, Michelle, Jeff, and Brian. All of us were tuned closely to the radio traffic, ready to jump up at the mention of any irregular activity noted by the numerous agents posted throughout the castle.

Midnight arrived and faded without any disturbance at the castle. As our motorcade left the grounds, I sighed deeply but without relief, knowing that although no one committed suicide at the castle this night, there was still a troubled young woman missing in Dublin and we had to find her.

I returned to the hotel weary and worried. Three patients were waiting for me in the hallway outside my room. Jeff, sensing my jet lag and fatigue, lured them down to his room where he took care of their medical ailments. I checked with Don Flynn briefly, in front of the president's suite; there was no word from the agents about Mary's whereabouts. It was already two in the morning. Michelle informed me before heading to her room that the only way to get Mary admitted to an inpatient psychiatric facility in Dublin was through a local psychiatrist, and that we had to pay cash up front for the hospital.

The situation seemed hopeless in the wee hours of that morning. As I settled into my hotel room for four hours of sleep, my drop line rang. It was Brian.

"Doc, we found her." Brian's voice was jubilant. "Ran into her in a bar across the street from the hotel. She's in my room with me now."

"I'll be there in two minutes."

Mary was subdued, avoiding my eyes. She admitted she was planning to kill herself but at the last moment decided against it. So she stayed at the bar across the street from the hotel, watching the motorcade come and go, feeling awful about herself and how she wasn't doing her job as part of the advance team on this trip.

"We need to get you back to D.C. right away," I told her. "Your psychiatrist wants to see you as soon as you get there."

Brian spoke up. "There's a flight this morning to Dulles. We can book her a seat right away."

I nodded, looking at the young woman who sat across from me with her head down. "Book two seats. I'm sending a nurse with Mary. I don't want her to fly alone."

"Good plan, consider it done."

Mary made it back to D.C. without incident. She arrived at Dulles the next afternoon, accompanied by one of our White House nurses. But when she landed, Mary asked her family to pick her up at the airport. Rather than take her directly to the psychiatrist, they took her home.

Mary resurfaced two weeks later at her regular appointment with her doctor, who admitted her for a month of inpatient therapy. We were forced to relieve Mary of her White House assignment, but we were happy to learn she later found work in the private sector.

4.

The young Filipino-American cook hesitated at the door of my office. He would have turned around and gone back downstairs to the scullery if I hadn't noticed him peeking around the corner to see me typing on the computer at my desk.

"Miguel," I said tentatively, trying to remember his name, "can I help you?" I stood up and walked toward him, pointing to the inside of my office, inviting him in. "Are you okay?"

I had taken care of most of the housekeeping and kitchen staff over the years. The kitchen was right across the hallway from my office, and it was not uncommon to see a cook, or even the White House chef, come dashing into my treatment room with a towel wrapped around a cut finger.

But Miguel wasn't bleeding from a finger. He was in pain, bleeding from his heart.

"Doc," the twenty-five-year-old man began, "I'm worried about my dad . . ."

His father was Johnny, one of the longtime cooks who had been a career Navy steward, like my father. Johnny had retired from the Navy and was hired as a civilian cook at the White House. His son, Miguel, was hired a few years ago as an assistant cook. The two men shared a home together in Maryland.

The young man shook his head and frowned. "Something is wrong with my dad. When he comes home at the end of the day, he just sits on the couch and stares into space."

The description conjured up a list of tentative diagnoses ranging from depression to brain tumor. "Does he drink, Miguel? Take any drugs or medications? Any stressors at home?"

The young man shook his head. "We get along fine, just the two of us at home. He just doesn't want to talk about it."

"Where is he now?"

"Downstairs in the scullery," Miguel responded. "Please help him, Doctor. Something is wrong."

Miguel was right. Something was wrong with Johnny. After thanking Miguel for coming forward with his concerns about his father, I took the stairwell down to the scullery, located in the bowels of the White House.

Johnny was about sixty-five years old, handsome, with a shock of gray in the middle of a headful of thick hair black as polish. He was cleaning pots and pans over the sink when I came upon him. He looked up at me and then back down at the pot he was scrubbing.

"Johnny," I began cautiously. "You have a moment?"

His response was terse but respectful. "Yes, ma'am." Johnny had rarely seen me as a patient at the White House, let alone down in his territory. My presence apparently made him uncomfortable as I spotted a nervous tic on the right side of his face.

"I'm here because I'm worried about you." I chose my words carefully, trying not to reveal my sources. "Several people around here are concerned about your health."

He waved me off with a sponge. "Nah, Doc," he said, dismissing my concerns. "I'm okay. No problems."

"Well, how about you doing me a favor, please?" I wasn't going to give up without taking a thorough history from the man. "Humor me. Come upstairs to my office. Let me talk with you a little more. And maybe do an exam."

That proposal shocked him. "You, examine me?" he stared back incredulously.

"Yes, I'm pretty good at it." I smiled, trying to reassure him. "I perform the president's exam every year. I'll examine you like I do for him. How about that?"

"You're the doc, Doc." The man, who looked like one of my uncles, easily caved in.

"This is Dr. Mariano." I was calling from my office after having examined Johnny in my treatment room a few hours later. I had phoned the radiology department at Malcolm Grow Hospital at Andrews Air Force Base, close to Johnny's home in Maryland. "I'd like to order a CAT scan of the brain for one of our retired servicemen."

Something wasn't right with Johnny's exam. His mental status was off. Although he was alert, and oriented to person, place, and time, his affect, or facial expression, was blunted. His pupils were reactive to light, but his balance was off. I was worried about a brain tumor.

I was home that evening when my pager went off. It was the radiologist at Malcolm Grow calling me with an emergency reading on Johnny's CAT scan. It wasn't a brain tumor; it was multiple brain tumors.

Telling a patient bad news is never easy. It's harder to do it over the phone, but in Johnny's case I needed to act quickly to get him admitted to the hospital because the tumors were compressing his brain. Once the words "you have cancer" leave your lips, patients instantly divide their lives into "before" and "after" the diagnosis. Their lives are never the same and they will always remember how they were told.

"Johnny," I spoke softly but clearly into the phone. "I don't have very good news for you this evening."

Silence on the other end of the line.

"Johnny, are you there?"

"Yup, Doc, I'm here," Johnny answered slowly, almost slurring.

"Johnny, I know why you've not been acting yourself lately. You have several large tumors in your brain. I'm sorry to tell you this over the phone. But I have to get you admitted right away, before one of them presses on the vital parts of your brain."

"Tumors on the brain?" Johnny repeated my words slowly.

"Yes, Johnny, tumors on the brain," I reiterated. "Can Miguel drive you to the hospital tonight? We need to admit you right away."

"Doc, this is Miguel," his son's voice came on the other line. "I can take him."

"Thanks, Miguel. I'll call the hospital now."

Johnny was admitted to Walter Reed Army Hospital, which had a large neurosurgical ward. When I visited him the next day, the resident taking care of him gave me more unfortunate news. The multiple tumors in Johnny's brain were from the large tumor in his lung. He had been a smoker for many years, and the lesions in his brain were due to metastases from the cancer in his lung from smoking. Johnny remained in the hospital for a month for a biopsy of the tumor in his lung, and subsequent radiation treatments to shrink the tumors in his brain.

It was snowing the January morning when Johnny was buried at Arlington Cemetery, about four months after I examined him in my office. I was rushing that morning from Bethesda Naval Hospital, finishing off the preparations for President Clinton's final physical examination there before leaving office. I arrived at the gravesite right as Johnny's casket was being lowered into the ground. The housekeeping and kitchen staff were there. I stood in the periphery, bowing my head, saying a prayer for Johnny, who never complained nor made demands on my time. Even in the final days of his life, when I visited him at the hospital, he thanked me for helping him.

As the service concluded, each of the cooks, butlers, and house-keepers reached out and embraced me. I was to leave the White House in only two weeks, when President Clinton left office. I reflected on this somber farewell not only to Johnny, but to the kitchen staff who had been part of my family before and after I got to the White House. My early memories of childhood had been filled with the scents and sounds of military kitchens. Once again, I was back with my Filipino kitchen family, in this final farewell. I wept quietly for Johnny and for the people I would miss at the White House. They really were my family in sickness and in health, in good times as well as bad.

My term at the White House was drawing to a close and I was frightened about what lay ahead. I would no longer be the president's physician and the director of the White House Medical Unit. I would be retiring from the military and working at the Mayo Clinic in

President Clinton introduces me to Philippine President Estrada in July 2000 on the North Portico during a meeting with Filipino-Americans assigned to the White House.
(WHITE HOUSE PHOTO)

Arizona. But the new job in the civilian sector didn't frighten me. What terrified me was returning to my prior full-time position of wife and mother. I had been missing in action for nine years to take care of the first family. Would my real family still need me when I finally came home to stay?

SIXTEEN

My First Family

1.

It was a rare weekend that I wasn't traveling with the president or taking care of patients on the eighteen-acre compound or at Camp David. It was 1994, and although I had been at the White House for only two years, I had spent most of that time away from home traveling with the president. After nonstop travel as a Clinton "road scholar," a quiet weekend at home was a rare luxury. At this point, having me at home was more of an aberration in my family's daily lives. I was missing in action from the rhythm of their busy lives during most of my nine years at the White House. And, sadly, I was gone when I was needed most: when my husband or sons were hurting physically or emotionally.

"Connie, what does chicken pox look like?" Richard's call came through the signal operator, and it both worried and annoyed me. I was on the steps boarding Marine One, headed to Andrews Air Force Base where I would fly with President Clinton to Haiti to meet with the newly reinstalled Haitian leader Jean-Bertrand Aristide. Richard rarely called me while I was on the road. I, instead, would phone the drop line at home when I got to the hotel at night to check in with him. But his unexpected call diverted my attention from the mission and pulled me back into the orbit of my family. I had just left our house that morning in the darkness before dawn, my husband and sons all sound asleep as I tiptoed out the kitchen door.

"Chicken pox? Which of the boys has chicken pox?" I asked.

"That's not what I asked you," my husband snapped, sounding more like a sharp-tongued plaintiff's attorney than a law-school professor. "I asked you what it looked like. Jason woke up with a rash on his body. He has a fever, feels crummy. I kept him home from school." Richard was never comfortable dealing with medical illness, and before the White House I would always be available to care for the boys when they were ill. I felt awful: I had abandoned Richard with a sick child while I was traveling to the Caribbean with the president.

Jason, my five-year-old and younger son, was sick and I wasn't there. My maternal guilt shot up instantly. But once again I had to be the doctor first before being the mom. So I went into my auto-physician mode to answer this inquiry: "The classic chicken pox lesions are dew drops on an erythematous base, which means water blisters on a bed of red." As I spoke, I began to ache for my little boy, who was home sick without me. "He needs bed rest, Tylenol for his fever, plenty of fluids, chicken soup," I instructed. "He's contagious until all the water blisters crust over completely." I envisioned Richard standing beside the phone in the kitchen, scribbling down notes on a legal pad atop the counter. I wanted to add to the prescription: the young patient also needs his mother's soft words and warm hugs. But once again, she was absent, unable to fill that prescription.

"Very well, Doc," Richard spoke, his voice softening, trying to lighten the tense mood. "I'll keep you posted on the patient's progress. Have a good trip."

I returned from Haiti just in time to see the final crop of Jason's chicken pox crust over. But as childhood contagion would have it, seven-year-old Andrew came down with his bout of "water blisters on a bed of red" ten days later. And predictably, I was again on the road. This time Richard didn't call me. He mentioned the event only in passing during my evening phone call from the road.

Because I was away so often, Richard and the boys learned to live on without me. This was typical of military life, but usually the burden of carrying on the day-to-day activities of home life fell on the wife, who is often better equipped by disposition and experience. Richard became both mother and father to our children as he worked part-time teaching at George Washington Law School at night and doing part-time projects for a D.C. firm during the day. In between his professional activities, he would chauffeur the boys to and from their Montessori school in Alexandria as well as to their Tae Kwon Do lessons in Springfield. He would cook for them, clean the house, and comfort the boys when I was away. For a brilliant attorney, spending most of his day taking care of elementary school children had begun to erode his self-worth.

"So what do *you* do?" the gray-haired woman dressed in St. John evening attire and with three-carat diamonds asked Richard at a cocktail party in downtown D.C. She had just met me at the event and "oohed and aahed" over my position at the White House. Impressed with what I did for a living, she turned to Richard, who stood quietly beside me.

Richard was uncomfortable at such parties, clutching his glass of Canadian Club and water, wishing he could swig it down quickly and disappear. He also didn't like being asked what he did when he felt like a glorified baby-sitter most of the time. So he came up with a clever response, suited for the D.C. status-conscious crowd.

"Me?" he looked at the bejeweled matron. "I'm the domestic advisor to the physician to the president of the United States."

Although it was humorous, it was a painful title for any man. I would be flying around on a glamorous 747, taking care of the most powerful man in the world. I'd return home, and as Richard and I got reacquainted in the evening, sitting at the kitchen table catching up on each other's lives, I'd ask him, "So how was your day, dear?"

His response of "I took the kids to school, picked up groceries at Safeway, took the car in for repairs, and worked on a brief," paled in comparison to my typical day of managing one of the most complex medical practices imaginable.

Like a typical military family in which one spouse is deployed, the remaining spouse and family learn to carry on in their absence. It was the case for us for all of my years at the White House. After the chicken pox episode, Richard never called my cell phone again to report an incident. He just handled it on his own. I would learn about events in a routine evening phone-call update.

"Well, we had a little excitement today." Richard said with very little emotion in his voice, almost as though he were reporting the evening news on television. I had just arrived at the hotel in Warsaw with the president, and I called the drop line at home in Virginia to see how the family was doing. "Andrew's okay but he had to get stitches."

"Stitches? What happened?" I prepared myself for a traumatic story about both, recalling that Richard didn't comfortably "do blood." This is a man who would pass out at having his blood drawn, or would grow pale at a blood pressure cuff being placed on his arm.

"The boys were sledding down the hill after the big snowfall we had yesterday," he began.

"It snowed?" I almost whined, feeling left out of the fun. Like most kids, my sons loved it when it snowed because they not only got out of school, but they could spend the day frolicking in the snow with their friends.

"Andrew was sledding down a hill and ran into a tree."

My doctor mode kicked in as I interrupted him, "Any head or neck injury? Anything broken?"

Richard hesitated, annoyed by my interruption, but continued,

"No, fortunately not. His leg hit the tree. He got up and walked home. When he got home, he was crying."

Maternal guilt stabbed me in the chest. My son hurt, crying. Where was I? Oh, yeah, in Poland with the president, calling from my suite in a five-star hotel. Once again, good naval officer, bad mother.

"Well, he didn't break any bones, but got a huge cut on his leg. I brought him over to Becky next door, who's a nurse."

I felt simultaneous relief and envy. Fortunately, our neighbor the nurse was able to clean Andrew's laceration and recommend the correct action.

"Becky said he needed stitches, so I took him to the clinic at Fort Belvoir," Richard continued. "They put in fifteen stitches."

"Fifteen? Was he okay during the suturing?" I felt sorry for my little boy.

"He was very brave," Richard said proudly.

"Well, when I get home, I'll take the stitches out," I offered. Then I realized I was back in my doctor mode. Having failed at being a mother, I could only offer what I knew how to do best and that was to doctor. I was the first doctor, as some would say, but I was really the doctor first, above all. It was my blessing and my curse.

Even when I would try to get away to spend quality time with my family, work would often follow me. For spring break in 1998, Richard and I took the boys to Puerto Rico to visit our friends Commander Rich and Kitty Miller. Rich had been the dentist aboard the USS *Prairie* when I was the medical officer. He, Kitty, and son Ryan were stationed at the naval base in Puerto Rico and invited us to visit for sightseeing and snorkeling. We had planned this vacation months in advance and were all excited about spending time together in the sunny Caribbean.

On our first day in San Juan, we went to the ancient El Morro fortress overlooking the sea. We followed the tour guide through the ancient ruins, snapping photos as we went along. Then my overseas cell phone rang.

It was Barry Toiv from the White House Press Office, calling on behalf of Mike McCurry, the president's press secretary.

"Doc, I hate to bother you on your vacation," Barry apologized.

"Vacation? Who's ever on vacation at the White House?" I waved my family off to continue on their tour of the fortress.

"Yeah, tell me," Barry added. "Well, we've had a flood of inquiries about Buddy the dog."

Buddy the dog, the president's beloved four-month-old chocolate Labrador retriever, had been neutered by the White House veterinarian. The procedure took place at the veterinary clinic at Fort Myers the day before I left with my family for Puerto Rico. A statement had been issued by the press office in response to inquiries from animal activist Doris Day and from animal organizations, asking the president if he was going to neuter his dog. I didn't anticipate that Buddy's castration was going to make headlines. I was sorely mistaken.

"Just tell them Buddy did fine during the procedure and is resting comfortably at the White House and he's in good spirits," I teased, repeating a hackneyed catchphrase used in press statements for hospitalized celebrities.

"Well, Doc," Barry continued, "the press wants more." So, for the next hour, Barry and I went over a draft of another statement that hopefully would satisfy the press.

An hour of my vacation time spent talking about the first dog's neutering. Only in America, where politicians are treated like movie stars, would I get "pressed" into service over such minutiae. I caught up with my family right as they were concluding the tour.

"What was that about?" Richard asked, looking concerned.

"Buddy's balls," I quipped. "I need a piña colada."

2.

The yellow autumn leaves had already fallen off the trees in a neighborhood now decked out in Halloween decor in the small town of Fond du Lac, located on Lake Winnebago in Wisconsin. It was October 1999 and my cab drove along quiet streets and pulled up to the house of Dick and Leslie Ridenour. A former two-star rear admiral who had been the commanding officer of Bethesda Naval Hospital during my early years at the White House, Dick was fully aware of the stresses of my position. It was on his watch at Bethesda that Vice President Gore and President Clinton underwent their orthopedic surgeries, and Hillary Clinton had her blood clot treated.

Dick had retired from the Navy after his tour at Bethesda and accepted the position of president of Marian College, a Catholic liberal arts college. I had remained close to Dick and his wife, Leslie, over the years; I had been the keynote speaker at Dick's inauguration as college president, and I also served on the board of trustees of his college. I visited Fond du Lac annually for board meetings and stayed with the Ridenours during my short visits.

This trip was for the board meeting and to give a speech to a local physicians group, and it came at the right time for me. I needed to be with old friends now who were grounded and comforting. Dick had also been trained as a psychiatrist, but I really didn't need a shrink; I needed a mentor. The Ridenours were also my role model for a happily married couple in which one spouse had been a career military physician and had gone on to succeed in the private sector after retiring from the Navy. I yearned to follow in the life path of the Ridenours.

During this time in my life, everything on the surface appeared to be smooth sailing, as we say in the Navy. Up to this point, my tour at the White House had been very successful. I had now served an unprecedented seven years there, most of it as the director of the medical unit. Under my leadership, we had instituted a series of groundbreaking achievements that set the benchmark in the care of world leaders. Clinton had also bestowed upon me the political appointment of physician to the president, the equivalent of a senior flag rank in the military.

All these factors were used to justify my nomination by him to rear admiral. If confirmed, I would not be the first presidential physician to become a flag officer. In fact, most of my military predecessors at the White House were promoted to admiral or general as a result of their tour of duty. But I would be the first Filipino-American in U.S. naval history to be a rear admiral. For the daughter of a Filipino steward in the U.S. Navy, this was a significant milestone for me, my family, and my native countrymen.

But I didn't want to dwell on the promotion, partly because I was superstitious and I didn't want to jinx it by focusing on it. Yet I couldn't help but wonder if I did become an admiral, what would that mean for me? Would I stay at the White House and take care of the new president after the Clintons left in 2001? Or move on to another duty station? What about my family? Richard had already lost the chance to return to his law firm in San Diego after my two-year assignment at the White House was extended to four, then to seven, and now to nine years. Although my family liked living in Virginia, all along we felt home for us was in San Diego. Or was it time to retire? If so, what would I do in the private sector?

I was hoping to bounce these questions off Dick Ridenour, who had retired from a career in the Navy and moved on to become an effective college president. And I also wanted to talk privately with Leslie. Blonde, bubbly, with a perpetually positive attitude, Leslie epitomized for me the consummate military spouse: a good household manager and cheerleader for her husband. Did she have any regrets from their military life together? What did she give up to support her husband in his meteoric career? How did she like their new life now? I wondered how my spouse would have answered those questions. Yet part of me dreaded to hear what his answers would be.

"Welcome back," Dick said, greeting me with a warm hug that dissolved the chill of the Wisconsin winter. Tall and lanky, Dick reminded me of Hawkeye Pierce in the television series *M*A*S*H*, and had the same attitude. Nothing fazed Dick Ridenour. Perhaps it was his training as a psychiatrist in which he had seen it all. But I would like to think that deep down he was meant to be a performer: he had stage presence and never hid from the spotlight. I, on the other hand, was tired of the spotlight. I just wanted to settle down, whatever that meant, and I really didn't know which was scarier.

As we finished a light lunch in their family room, Dick looked at his watch as he outlined my itinerary, "Let's see: board meeting at three o'clock, cocktails at five, dinner at six, your speech to the doctors' group at eight." He then made an executive decision. "It's time for a nap." I smiled at his recommendation. I had gotten up at four o'clock in the morning to catch the early flight from D.C. to Milwaukee. Then I stayed awake during the one-hour drive from Milwaukee, with my ear glued to my cell phone catching up on the activities back at the White House. Dick knew I needed to talk with him, but he also knew that I needed to sleep first.

As I lay my head upon the pillow on the bed in the Ridenours' second-floor guestroom, my pager vibrated with an incoming text message:

"CONGRATS RDML MARIANO. LTC WISSLER SENDS FROM PNTGN"

I stared at the screen. RDML was the abbreviation for rear admiral (lower half), which meant one-star rear admiral (versus RADM, rear admiral upper half, which stands for a two- star). The rank was being applied to my last name. Lieutenant Colonel John Wissler had been the Marine Corps military aide to President George H. W. Bush when I first arrived at the White House. Honest and true-blue, Wissler was the ultimate Marine. Since leaving the White House, he would visit my office to say hello whenever he dropped by to visit the incumbent mil aides. Wissler had gone on to the Pentagon and a series of high-level positions. From his text message, it sounded like he was working in a department that dealt with flag officer promotions.

I called the signal operator to get hold of Colonel Wissler at the Pentagon.

"Ma'am?" Wissler's voice was all business. "Did you receive my page?"

I could visualize Wissler's toothy grin as he spoke. "Yes, I did, Colonel. Is this some sort of a joke? I wasn't aware that the nomination made its way to the Pentagon yet."

Wissler responded, "It has and it did."

"What does that mean?" I was starting to get excited.

"It means that your nomination is moving forward and pretty much assured. It goes next to the Senate Armed Services Committee for confirmation, and then to the president's desk for approval."

"How long will that take?" I could feel my heart pounding now. Was this the answer I was awaiting to guide me in my next career move? Or would it sink my family's chances of ever having a normal life again if I were to remain in the military?

"A matter of months" was Wissler's terse reply.

"Well, *if* it does come through, you're invited to the promotion ceremony," I promised cautiously.

Wissler laughed, "It's not *if*, it's *when*. And when it does happen, I'll be there, ma'am."

I jumped up from the bed. I had to tell *somebody*. I wandered down the upstairs hallway of the silent house. Dick and Leslie's bedroom was down the hall. I knew they, too, had planned to take a nap. I stood outside their partially open door and in an almost meek, childlike voice spoke to anyone within earshot, "Hello, Dick? Leslie? I think I'm going to be an admiral."

The Ridenours rushed out of their bedroom and gave me big hugs. They pulled me inside their room and we sat on their divan. Dick shared the story of how he got his first star and became an admiral, his eyes twinkling as he relived the moment in its retelling. I thought it was fitting that I receive the call in the home of my only admiral friend. But there were others close to me with whom I wanted to share the news. But first, I dialed a number in San Diego where I knew a retired Navy couple who, on hearing this news, would be speechless.

"Hallo," my mother's tired voice answered the phone, sounding like she had once again been up all night securing the kitchen. After forty years in the United States, my parents both retained their thick Filipino accents. The main language at home was their Pampanga dialect. I could understand their native tongue but no longer knew how to speak it without an American accent.

"Mom, it's me," I spoke, trying to contain my excitement. "Is Dad there?"

"Oh, he's in the backyard, working on the plants." Dad loved his garden and loved getting his hands dirty tilling the soil, fertilizing his plants, and harvesting his vegetables.

"Can you ask him to come to the phone?" I asked. "I have some news I wanted to share."

I could almost see my mom's eyebrows rise on the other end of the phone.

"No, Mom," I began, preventing her from asking the question. "I'm not pregnant." I started to laugh.

"Oh, okay." She put down the phone and ran over to the window facing the backyard. I could hear her yelling for my father, "Hon-neee . . ."

My father had proudly served twenty-nine years in the U.S. Navy. He enlisted in the 1940s, following in the footsteps of his paternal uncles, who had joined twenty years earlier. They all became stewards, serving in the homes of admirals. In my afternoon phone call to him, my father, with dirt on his hands from the soil he was tilling, tightly clutched the telephone receiver to learn that all along, he had been raising his own homegrown admiral. I could just see the tears of joy spilling down the cheeks of my mother and father. My family had experienced their own American immigrant success story.

The excitement that cut short my afternoon nap spilled over to a lively board meeting at the college followed by celebratory cocktail

hour and dinner at a local restaurant. I gave my forty-minute presentation to the local doctors' association about the history of presidential care. Over the years, I had given numerous presentations to
university medical centers as well as physician groups around the
world, all of whom were interested in "the ultimate house call." As I
spoke, I realized that if I were to be promoted, I, too, would become a
part of presidential medical history.

As the audience applauded my presentation, Dick Ridenour, who
had introduced me to the group, came up to shake my hand. He also
had a special gift for me: a silver star. It was the collar device for a
one-star rear admiral.

"You're going to need this soon," Dick remarked, teary-eyed, as
he handed me the star.

"I'm honored and touched to receive this, especially from you," I
thanked him. And as I held the star in my hand and received congratulations from the crowd around me, I felt a sinking feeling in the
pit of my stomach. In all the hoopla of the news of my nomination
for admiral, had I forgotten to call my husband, Richard, to tell him
the news? He was as responsible as anybody for this promotion, in
allowing me to stay the course, but would be the one to least welcome it and what it might portend for our family.

3.

On a quiet autumn weekend in 1999, as my sons played ball in the
front yard amidst the fallen crimson leaves, I decided to catch up on
some long overdue housecleaning. Grabbing a broom, dustpan, and
a large plastic trash bin, I ventured down into the basement. I was
eager to sort out the remnants of our military family life in the debris that had accumulated over the past seven years in the basement
of our two-story brownstone in Alexandria.

I was in a contemplative mood, and my cleaning ritual reflected my need to triage not only the stuff in my house, but also the stuff that I was mulling over in my mind. I had been at the White House for seven years, and my tour would be over in less than two when President Clinton left office in January 2001. The stacks of odd boxes that greeted me as I descended into the bowels of the house symbolized the accumulated clutter of these past few years. What I needed to do was to take each box, open it, sort out the contents, and decide what I needed to keep and what I had to let go. Maybe then my future would come into clearer focus.

This was a happy time in my naval career. I had been nominated and confirmed for rear admiral and was waiting for the formal promotion to take effect in July 2000. Even my detailer had called me the week before to congratulate me.

"So where do you want to go next?" asked the Navy captain who was responsible for picking my next military assignment.

"You're asking me?" I asked. "This is the first time I've been asked that," I said, pleasantly surprised.

"Well," my detailer quipped, "you've never been both a White House physician and a rear admiral selectee before."

"Please keep this quiet, but I don't know if I'm going to stay in the Navy," I confessed to a man who was used to hearing and keeping secrets. "I will be nine years into a two-year assignment when Clinton leaves office. That's a long stretch of time in the kill zone. I will also have over twenty-four years of active duty, when all I need is a good twenty to retire."

"But the Navy would really like you to stay on. And I have a choice assignment you might be interested in," the captain teased. "Force surgeon of the Pacific Fleet."

I knew the billet well. It was considered a dream assignment among flag officers. Headquartered in Makalapa, Hawaii, it was not far from where I grew up in military housing as a young Navy brat. As force surgeon I would be in charge of all the medical departments onboard the ships of the Pacific Fleet. It was a dream job for me because I had always loved the operational side of the Navy. I started to salivate over the thought of it; that is until reality set in: the effect on my family. I had promised Richard and the boys that we'd go back to San Diego after my first two-year stint at the White House. But I had broken that promise and subsequent ones in my extended stay. I had honored my promise to Clinton's mother, and now it was time to do the same for my own family.

"Let me think about that," I told the eager detailer. I didn't tell him that president-elect George W. Bush had asked if I would be part of the medical team at the White House when his term began. Nor did I share the details of a civilian job I was seriously considering. Over the past few months, I had been exploring privately with the senior leadership at George Washington University Medical Center in D.C. the idea of a Center for Executive Medicine. The plan was to create a world-class facility for executive health care, fashioned after my practice in the White House. My former administrator from the White House, Bill McGee, and I had pitched this proposal to the vice president of the university, and the possibility of its creation looked promising.

"Your problem, ma'am," the detailer said soberly as he ended the call, "is that you may have too many options."

"You may be right, Captain," I admitted. "Sometimes the best option is no option at all."

As I prepared to launch my attack on the boxes in my basement, I glanced over to Richard's office on the other side of the basement. It was a far cry from the law office he enjoyed in San Diego, located atop an emerald-shaped glass building that boasted breathtaking views of the harbor and city. The basement was always damp and cold, with dim lighting. It had a fireplace we never used. In his corner there stood a simple workstation with a desktop computer, printer, and fax machine. And somewhere buried under the heap of papers on his desk was a telephone. Today Richard was not sitting at his desk and typing away as usual. He took advantage of my rare home visit to go to the law library to do some research. I was home; he left.

When compared to the historic luxury and prestige of my office at the White House, Richard's corner in the basement looked like a kind of purgatory. In many ways this confinement and his "domestic advisor" position was just that: painful and unrewarding as he endured my time on the White House stage. My White House years had been an unhappy time for my husband. For every achievement and recognition I had received, he would smile quietly beside me, supportive, yet suffering. I could sense this at some level, but I was in denial. And I would only recognize his pain years later, when it was too late.

As I thought of Richard, I found something that needed my housecleaning attention. By serendipity, as I dug into the boxes, I unearthed one that held an old memento: a wooden plaque that had been given to me during my shipboard days by my medical crew. The plaque had inscribed upon it: "LEAD, FOLLOW, OR GET OUT OF THE WAY." It used to hang in my office on the *Prairie*. When I received it from my corpsmen, Richard sniffed in disdain when he read the message. "Get out of the way?" he reacted defensively. "Does that apply to me?" He resented the implication. I identified with the take-charge attitude of the message, since I had always been the leader in school, career, and even in our relationship. But what about Richard; wasn't he my partner? Or was he a follower? Or, as I feared he had felt for many years, "in the way?" I threw the plaque into the trash.

So many choices, so many possible paths to take, I pondered as I opened boxes, threw out old papers, broken toys, and outdated clothing. I loved my job at the White House but was tired and knew I needed to leave. But what would I do? I could stay in the Navy as an admiral, become force surgeon, and move on to other flag officer assignments. But that would mean the death of Richard's career; he'd have to sit for the bar in whatever state to which we moved. And what about our children, I asked myself? Where was home for them? I was a Navy brat all my life and loved to move; home was where the Navy sent my family. But my sons were different. They missed their grandparents and our extended family in San Diego. They had always considered our house in Virginia a temporary residence. They needed a home. But most of all they needed a mom. I learned that in the next box I uncovered.

The words "Kids' stuff" were scrawled in Richard's cursive handwriting on the front of the box. Inside was a stack of ringed notebooks from the boys' first four years at their Montessori school. I thumbed through each book, admiring the rudimentary penmanship of my little boys on each of the pages. We can't keep all this stuff, I thought. I gently placed each notebook into the trash can. The boys won't be looking for these again. I was about to blindly toss in another notebook when the title caught my eye: "Jason's Journal." According to the date on the inside of the cover, Jason was eight years old when he wrote this diary. I smiled when I read his entry about a trip to San Diego we had made for Christmas and about the gifts he had received. But my smile faded when I read the last entry in his journal:

"Mommy is gone on another trip this week. The house is dark and sad. When she is away, it is as though she is dead."

My hands shaking, I closed the notebook. I felt as though I had been stabbed in the chest. I had been dead to my family for too long, to my two little boys, and to my husband. My decision was made then: it was time to leave the military at the end of my tour with Clinton. I wasn't dead yet. I needed to come back to life for my family and, in the end, renew my own life as well.

SEVENTEEN

A Star Is Worn

1.

George P. A. Healy's portrait of Abraham Lincoln hangs above the ivory marble mantel in the State Dining Room of the White House. The sixteenth president of the United States is seated, leaning forward, his prominent chin resting in the palm of his hand. The expression on his face is contemplative, almost peaceful.

The State Dining Room has always been my favorite room in the White House. It is a place of food, drink, and celebration; where kings and queens are lavishly feted, holiday guests generously treated, and where I performed my first Heimlich maneuver. It is also where generations of Navy Filipino stewards have served the president and his guests. So, when it came time to plan my promotion ceremony to admiral, I honored my kitchen roots, that stemmed from my father and great-uncles before me, who had served their entire careers in dining rooms and mess halls. I, the daughter of a Navy steward, would be promoted in the nation's State Dining Room.

As I stood on the stage, which had been set up that morning in front of the fireplace, I glanced up at Lincoln's portrait. I felt as though his eyes were looking down at me. I smiled at the Great Emancipator and imagined that Honest Abe would have approved of the ceremony that was about to take place.

It was July 26, 2000, and I was to be promoted to rear admiral. With this honor came two firsts: first Asian-American and first graduate of the Uniformed Services University School of Medicine to become a flag officer. I was made aware of these facts when the Senate confirmed my nomination. But I didn't want these firsts to go to my head. The promotion didn't come easily and it was with the support of many people at the White House, the military office, the Navy Bureau of Medicine and Surgery, and President Clinton himself, who gave it his final approval. The honor touched and humbled me. I had so many people to thank and acknowledge. This promotion was more about honoring them than it was about me.

President and Mrs. Clinton joined me onstage, both embracing me and then taking their place at the rear of the stage. They had returned late the night before from a trip, and still had bags under their eyes. I wished they could have slept in that morning, but they didn't want to miss my ceremony and meeting my family.

My parents and brother and sister had flown in the day before from San Diego. My father, Angel, stood nervously in front of the stage, wearing a new polyester suit. He was used to attending events with VIPs, but usually he worked behind the scenes in the kitchen, serving or managing the staff. He was uncomfortable being in front of the stage, with attention focused on him. I sensed his nervousness as I looked at him and my mother. He would rather be serving coffee at the ceremony instead of participating in it; I understood that sentiment and felt the same. I was my father's daughter; I'd rather be the doctor in the shadow than the star on stage. But this was my time and I accepted it, almost numb with the sensation that everything happening was surreal.

My mother, Lourdes, stood beside my father, also in a new two-piece suit. Her back was causing her pain that morning, and she couldn't stand very long, but refused to sit in a chair. My dear, stubborn mother would rather stand suffering silently than sit while everyone else stood. I saw myself in her steely-eyed resolve. My brother, Angel Jr., and sister, Lorie, stood quietly beside my parents, smiling at me. They knew I was anxious about my parents' physical stamina and social discomfort—about feeling out of place in a room full of "important white people," as my father remarked in awe when we talked about the guest list.

Richard, Andrew, and Jason were positioned near my parents to the side of the stage. Around them were fifty close friends and Navy colleagues I had known during my career. I was moved to see in the crowd two former corpsmen from my days on the USS *Prairie,* as well as a former White House nurse who was now stationed in Okinawa and had flown halfway around the world to be here. Several former bosses were in the audience, including Captain John Mitas, who had nominated me in 1991 for the position of White House physician. My promotion to admiral today validated that decision, made at a time when I was planning to leave the Navy.

My old friend Captain Frank Maguire, who had served his internship and residency with me in San Diego, was now the executive officer of Bethesda Naval Hospital. I respected Mac both as a physician and as a military officer. He was my choice to issue the oath of office and stood calmly onstage with me in his summer white uniform.

I was excited and nervous, but not only for me. I felt anxious for the players in this performance. Andrew and Jason, now ages thirteen and eleven, would participate in the ceremony. Quiet and shy, they looked handsome in new suits that their father had purchased for them. Their role was simple: walk to the front of the stage when Captain Maguire signaled them, and remove my captain shoulder boards. They had rehearsed their part the night before at home and were handling the morning's excitement with adult aplomb. They had visited the White House and met the president on numerous occasions. Yet what also thrilled them about this visit was the chance to

see the first pets, Buddy and Socks, who were waiting for them in
my office.

Colonel Richard "Dick" Tubb, who had been my medical unit
deputy for five years, presided over the ceremony. He was loyal and
dedicated, and I could not have asked for a finer number two to help
me run the medical unit and take care of the first and second families. Tubb was slated to run the medical unit when I retired from the
Navy. One of my greatest achievements, I later told him, was picking him to succeed me. A doctor with a heart of gold, Tubb had
unquestionable integrity and would become one of the finest White
House physicians in history. "That's because you picked and trained
me, boss," Tubb said humbly, turning the honor back at me. Tubb
continued to affectionately call me "boss" even after I left the White
House, when he became the next physician to the president under
George W. Bush.

The ceremony went smoothly according to the script: opening
remarks by Dr. Tubb, the reading of my official orders making me
a rear admiral, and removal of my shoulder boards by my sons. And
then the gold shoulder boards adorned with the star of a rear admiral were brought forth to the stage, on a dark velvet pad carried by
my administrator, Barbara Idone, and my executive assistant, Phyl
Green.

Richard and my father stepped up to the stage. Each took a shoulder board and attached them to the shoulders of my white summer
uniform. Richard grinned proudly while my father was silent, tears
forming in his eyes. And as my father, the former Navy steward,
latched on a gold board to his daughter's uniform, something he had
done hundreds of times as he prepared the daily uniforms for other
admirals, his brown, wrinkled hands shook with emotion.

After the admiral boards had been placed, I turned and faced Captain Maguire. I then repeated slowly after him the Commissioning
Oath in which I renewed my vows to support and defend the Constitution. It was like renewing my marriage vows. And as I stood onstage in a uniform of white with gold, shiny braid gleaming in the

light, I realized I *was* married to the military. I repeated the solemn
words slowly, aching inside and knowing that my marriage to the
Navy would soon end, when Bill Clinton left office. For longer than
my marriage to Richard, the military had been my friend, my partner, and my lover, my source of passion, joy, and purpose. This would
be the last time I would repeat the words that bound me to my uniform and my service to my country. I held back tears, which many in
the audience mistook for joy; they were tears of bittersweet sorrow.

". . . So help me God," I repeated after Maguire, completing the
oath. The room erupted in applause as Maguire shook my hand and
saluted, to which I responded by embracing him.

I then gave my remarks and acknowledged my parents, Richard,
and our sons, as well as the handful of people in the room who had
played a part over the years in "helping me get on the stage today."

As I read off the names of the people in the audience, who in turn
stood graciously for applause, I thought of what really got me to

*Having been promoted to Rear Admiral in the State Dining Room, I give my remarks
while the president and first lady look on. July 2000.* (WHITE HOUSE PHOTO)

The president and first lady toast me upon my promotion in July 2000. (WHITE
HOUSE PHOTO)

where I was that day in the State Dining Room of the White House.
The motivation was a simple, all-too-common mantra: *You're never
good enough.* All my life, I felt that I was never the "right" height,
size, color, talent, or intelligence. I never fit in. I was the outcast.
And no matter how hard I tried to become good enough, it was
never *enough* to be enough.

As I stood onstage in the State Dining Room, under the peaceful
gaze of Abraham Lincoln, the admiring smiles of Bill and Hillary
Clinton, and the warm applause of family and friends, for one brief,
shining moment in American history, I was finally good enough to
become a Navy rear admiral.

2.

After my promotion to admiral, life at the White House seemed to
shift into fast forward. In Clinton's last year in office, we traveled

constantly. "You must be using up your frequent flyer miles on Air Force One," Richard would wryly comment to me when I told him I'd be away on another trip.

"Just a matter of months, and I can put my suitcases in mothballs," I reassured him.

The presidential election of 2000 came upon us, and half the medical unit traveled with Vice President Gore on the campaign trail while I accompanied President Clinton on his farewell journey on the international stage. We went to our last of everything presidential. Last G-8, last APEC Summit, last visit to Asia, Europe, and Africa. It was Clinton's farewell to his friends overseas, and it was my farewell to a life on the road.

On election day 2000, I sat in my hotel room in New York City to relish my last presidential campaign. I watched the television screen closely, waiting to see who would become our next president. Down the hall, the Clintons were celebrating Hillary's Senate victory. I was delighted for the first lady; she had worked very hard to win her seat. Hillary was a woman of many firsts as well, whom I admired not only for her achievements, but also because she continued to be caring and down-to-earth. When I accompanied the Clintons to the hotel grand ballroom on election night where Hillary was to thank her supporters, I congratulated her backstage.

"Senator!" I exclaimed as we embraced.

"Admiral!" Hillary responded, with a broad smile. "Who would have thunk?" We both laughed in disbelief at our new titles.

The remainder of the evening I spent glued to the television set in my room, watching the presidential returns. The networks were uncertain as to the real winner, and the country was thrown into confusion. The medical unit wondered who would be our next first patients. Either way, it would be a family familiar to us: the Gores, who had been at the White House for the past eight years; or the Bushes, whose father I had taken care of in his last year in office. We finally learned a month later, while I was in London with Clinton, that Bush was declared the winner of the election. I was relieved that the uncertainty was over, and that the medical unit could now prepare for the next administration.

With the election of a new president, Bill Clinton would be leaving office. It seemed like yesterday that I had watched him win the White House for the first time. When Clinton left office the day George Bush was sworn in, my job would be done. I pondered the symmetry of life: I reported to the White House under the Bush administration, and I would leave under the Bush administration.

"Sure you don't want to stay on, boss?" Dick Tubb asked me half teasingly, half seriously one afternoon in my office, as I was going over the checklist of transition items to pass on to him.

"It's time for me to move on." I smiled at my loyal deputy of five years. "No other White House physician has been as prepared as you to take over the medical unit."

Tubb nodded humbly. "Thank you for believing in me, Connie." Then to change the topic, he asked, "So have you decided what you want to do next?"

"My future is in God's hands. And, believe me, I've had plenty of signs where I'm supposed to go next," I admitted. I knew that Tubb, a deeply spiritual man, understood what I meant.

Some people call them "coincidences." Others use the word "serendipity" or "synchronicities." But my family and I began to call them "SFGs" or "signs from God." After my detailer had offered me the position of force surgeon, I wrestled with the possibility of staying in the Navy. I didn't bring it up with Richard because he had his heart set on my retirement. But there were times that the idea of accepting another military assignment would come up and tempt me. That is, until I received an airborne answer.

I was daydreaming one morning, sitting in traffic inching its way across the 14th Street Bridge into Washington. For a fleeting moment, I saw myself wearing a khaki uniform with my bright shiny star on my collar, being piped aboard a ship in Pearl Harbor. But that vision was thunderously erased when an America West jetliner flew directly over my car as I looked up in the sky. America West? The company headquarters are in Phoenix, Arizona.

There had been other SFGs after my promotion ceremony. The proposal to set up the Center for Executive Medicine at George Washington University failed in the negotiations. One afternoon when I was thumbing through a medical journal, my eyes were drawn to an ad at the back of the magazine. I had never glanced at the employment ads in the medical journals because I always had a job in the military. But the words jumped out at me: "Executive Health Physician" and "Mayo Clinic Scottsdale." I knew of the Mayo Clinic from visits to Rochester, Minnesota, to see King Hussein of Jordan when he was hospitalized there. The Clintons had asked me to assist in facilitating his care, and I flew to Rochester to meet with the royal couple. While I was there, I met the executive health physicians, who were impressive and friendly, and who eagerly invited me to return to speak at their Grand Rounds.

I knew Scottsdale was also a nice place in which to live. A medical school classmate of mine, Linda Strand Leiber, had left the military and worked for a radiology group in Scottsdale. She raved about the comfortable lifestyle and how it was a wonderful place to raise a family. It was also an hour's flight from our hometown of San Diego. And Arizona had a reputation for having good Mexican food, similar to what we ate in San Diego. I knew Richard would consider that a selling point.

When I called my friends at the Mayo in Rochester about the Scottsdale clinic, they confided in me and said that they wanted me to join them in Minnesota.

"I'm very flattered to be asked to join you," I told them. "But, sorry, I don't do winter."

"Then you'll love Arizona. We'll call the guys there on your behalf," my friend in Rochester promised.

After I sent in my résumé, I was invited to Scottsdale for an interview. I left D.C. on a cold, rainy, wintry morning and landed in sunny, 72-degree Phoenix where palm trees swayed in the breeze. The interview went well; I knew I could do the job. I would be performing annual examinations on corporate executives. I would not be in charge of anything, and I would be going from queen bee to worker bee. But after nine years being the queen, I was ready to step down from my throne and disappear into the beehive.

When I returned from Scottsdale, I didn't hear from the Mayo group for a few weeks, as interviews were being concluded. During that time, it seemed like everywhere I turned, I heard the name "Scottsdale." Driving my sons to school one morning, the radio blared, "Win two free weeks on a dude ranch in Scottsdale." Walking into a ladies' dress shop in Alexandria, the two women at the counter were talking about a similar dress shop in Scottsdale. In the mail arrived an ad for a luggage tag. The advertisement showed a tag that had Richard's last name and an address on Overlook Trail in Scottsdale. My sons would look at me whenever Scottsdale was mentioned.

"Another SFG, Mom," my boys would tease, both of whom wanted to move to sunny Arizona.

The final SFG came at lunchtime at the California Pizza Kitchen in Pentagon City, where Jason and I had dropped by one Saturday afternoon.

Fully aware of all the SFGs that had occurred in the weeks after I interviewed for the job in Arizona, Jason noticed that the servers had their city of origin on their name tags.

"Wouldn't it be neat, Mom, if our server is from Arizona?" Jason asked smiling, as we were seated at our table by the window.

"Oh, Jason, that may be pushing it a bit too far," I said to him with a laugh, eyeing the diverse wait staff who buzzed around from table to table.

We looked down at our menus and within a few minutes, a tall, thin young man came over to take our order.

Jason looked up and his mouth dropped open. I looked at Jason first and then to the man's name tag.

The initials R.C. were on the first line, and Scottsdale was engraved on the second. Coincidence? Or SFG?

"Oh, hello," I said to the young man, who must've wondered why
my son and I were suddenly silent. "I noticed you're from Scottsdale."

The young man glanced at his name tag. "Oh, yeah." He grinned.
"Actually, more like Fountain Hills than Scottsdale."

I almost choked. "Oh," I remarked. "I was just in Scottsdale at the
Mayo Clinic."

"Oh, yeah," the waiter said again. "My parents live in Fountain
Hills, just a mile from that clinic."

I *had* to move my family to Scottsdale, Arizona. When God sends
a jetliner with the message "America West" to fly over your car, your
fate is indicated. But when God then sends you a friendly waiter who
grew up a mile from the Mayo Clinic in Scottsdale, it's time to pack
your bags and head west.

3.

It was a cold and rainy inauguration morning in 2001 as I stood shivering in my dark blue winter coat on the North Portico. President-
elect and Mrs. George Bush had arrived and were whisked from their
armored vehicle onto the State Floor, where they would have breakfast tea with the Clintons before proceeding to the Capitol for the
swearing-in ceremony.

The dreary weather set a mournful tone for me as President Clinton was about to leave office. It was hard to believe eight years had
passed since Clinton's arrival at the White House, and nine had
passed for me. There were times when my assignment there felt like
a life sentence in which time dragged on interminably. And then
other times, when the months flicked by so rapidly that I couldn't
believe nine years had elapsed. I had lived in the time warp of the
White House. Perhaps it was from the perpetual jet lag. But I

This black-and-white portrait of Bill Clinton hung in my White House office. It was taken by photographer Ralph Alswang and was signed by the president on his last night at the White House:

To Dr. Connie,
Who kept me well
With thanks,
Bill Clinton 1-19-01

chalked it up to living in the kill zone, where one becomes so focused on the moment that I'd lost my ability to accurately gauge time's passage.

At the White House, time was measured in "events," "movements," "RON" (remain overnight) stays, "OTR" (off-the-record) excursions. I had grown used to the announcer's voice on the Oscar frequency that whispered the whereabouts and activities of my first patient. This would be the last time I would monitor that traffic, wear the annoying earpiece, bear the heavy radio strapped to my belt, and lug the medical bag that strained my back and neck and had put me in the hospital. I was ready to relinquish all the accoutrements of my office.

The weeks leading up to January 20 had sped by quickly. The president had his final physical exam at Bethesda Naval Hospital and bid farewell to the hospital staff there. I packaged the personal medical records of the first family and gave it to them for safekeeping. For their future care, I interviewed and selected civilian physicians close to their homes. As a senator, Hillary would receive her care from the Office of Attending Physician to Congress, run by my friend Rear Admiral John Eisold. Although my patients would no longer be in my care, they would be in good hands. Despite my transfer of their care to other physicians, the Clintons and their personal aides kept my private cell phone number.

"Eagle, Evergreen, Energy moving to stagecoach," the male voice on Oscar frequency announced. I jumped into the spare limousine. Doug Band, Clinton's personal aide, got into the car and sat in his usual place beside me. He reached over and gave me a hug. "One more ride, Doc," he spoke with a sentimental lilt to his voice.

"And we've had a lot of good rides together, Doug. Haven't we? It's been quite a trip." I tried not to get teary-eyed from the emotion building up on my last day of duty. I had to do my job, cover the president, and ensure he made it through one more day. Then my mission would be accomplished.

Meanwhile, Dick Tubb had taken his place in the motorcade and began to shadow the president-elect. When George H. W. Bush was president, I had met his eldest son, "Junior," at Camp David over a spirited game of "walleyball," which was volleyball but you could play the ball off the wall as well. Friendly, witty, and disarmingly macho, I knew that the man about to become the forty-third president would instantly approve of Dr. Tubb. I was pleased that my role as presidential matchmaker had succeeded in lining up the new president with a physician who complemented his personality. Tubb would earn the endearing presidential moniker "The Tubbster," and be named physician to the president, remaining at the White House thirteen years, surpassing my record. His humility and kindness never changed during his tenure there.

The inaugural ceremony at the Capitol was a blur of activity. I went into duty-physician mode and assumed my position offstage, in a small corridor close to the Capitol's steps. As George Bush stepped out to take the oath of office, he paused for a brief moment a few feet away from me. His bright eyes, reminiscent of his father's, teared up as he surveyed the setting's awesome panorama and the august assembly that awaited his arrival. I said a silent prayer for him, wishing him well in his term of office. And then I offered a quiet prayer of thanks as Bush took his oath, with the presidency slipping from Clinton's into Bush's hands as the clock ticked past noon. My patient's term of office over, he had survived two terms, and never suffered the horror of assassination. I sighed in relief and thanks as Bush became president, freeing Clinton to become a former president and private citizen.

Once the ceremony was over, the next move was the exodus. Because of the rain and fog that morning, former President Clinton would not helicopter from the Capitol to Andrews. Instead, we drove. But it was no longer with the same package of vehicles, but a downsized version of our customary motorcade. I sat in a car that resembled the spare limousine, scrunched in the back with Doug Band. As the motorcade made its way to Andrews Air Force Base, we did something that we had never done when Clinton was president: we stopped at red lights. We no longer had intersection control; that was the privilege of presidents.

"I guess you can tell he's no longer president," Doug said with a sigh as he looked out the window as we paused at another red light.

The 747 jetliner that we knew as Air Force One was waiting on the tarmac. For a former president, it was called Mission 28000, with the Air Force One designation reserved only for when the president of the United States is onboard. I went to my medical compartment, realizing that this was my last trip to and from New York City on a plane that had been my home away from home for nine years.

Buddy, Clinton's chocolate Labrador retriever, padded softly into my compartment. Buddy and I were alone. I no longer had a nurse with me. I was the only medical personnel onboard to accompany the former president to New York, and then be brought back on the plane to Andrews.

"Hey, Buddy," I welcomed the first pet. He looked up at me with soulful, doleful eyes as though he knew his high-flying days were over. He made himself comfortable in the nurse's seat across from me. I smiled at him and said, "Okay, Buddy. If we have an in-flight emergency, you can be my first assist." He barked as though he knew I was teasing him.

I had more visitors to my compartment. The president's valets, Joe Fama and Fred Sanchez, came by to see me. They had been asked by the Clintons to help them set up their home in Chappaqua.

"Hey, Doc." Joe smiled as he sat in the middle seat of my compartment. "So you don't have to take care of the president anymore."

"I know, Joe," I agreed. "But I just took a job at the Mayo Clinic, where I have to take care of a lot of company presidents. I'm afraid they may be a lot harder to please than Clinton." I was simultaneously eager and dreading my new civilian job at the Mayo Clinic in Scottsdale. I would no longer have the familiarity and the authority of military rank. And I dreaded having to prove myself all over again, and this time in the civilian world. I pushed back those fears to focus on this final ride on my favorite plane.

The flight to New York was brief. We touched down and were greeted by a large rally in the airport hangar. After a rousing speech by Clinton, it was time to say farewell. But I didn't get a chance for a personal good-bye. There were so many people around Bill and

When I retired from the White House, one of the gifts I received was this caricature of me and President Clinton by Air Force One pilot J. Kausert. Clinton autographed it:

Connie,
You pulled me over the finish line in good health, though we ran hard all the way!
Thanks
Bill
1-11-01.

Hillary Clinton that I quietly took my place to the side, standing beside Sharon Farmer. The president's photographer was a beautiful, larger-than-life African American woman whose signature greeting was the two-finger peace sign and her mantra, "Baby, baby." I loved Sharon's earthiness and felt comfortable sharing this tearful moment on the tarmac. Sharon, like me, had spent eight years with her eye on the president. She, through her camera lens, captured historic and private moments in his life. Through my professional proximity, I witnessed many of those same moments, but through a doctor's lens of heartbeats, respiration rates, blood pressures. She recorded history; I kept Clinton alive to make it.

The Clintons' motorcade consisted of a handful of minivans and SUVs. The former president no longer sat in a stretch limousine with the presidential seal and flags fanning in the breeze. Instead, he and Hillary were ushered to a compact, generic minivan, suitable for carpooling children.

As the motorcade pulled away from the hangar, I stood on the tarmac in front of the 747, watching the minivan drive away with my former patients. I felt as though my children were going off to school for the first time. And for the first time in eight years, I no longer had the duty. I started to cry quietly as I watched the cars drive away. Embarrassed, I wiped away a tear. Sharon reached over and gave me a bear hug. "Baby, baby," was all she could say to console me, as she was also crying.

When I returned to Andrews that afternoon from New York, I had my own welcoming party waiting at the gate. Richard, Andrew, and Jason were standing by the terminal to meet me. I had said farewell to the first family and was greeted by my real family. It was January 20, inauguration day, my last day of duty, and Richard and my twenty-second wedding anniversary. It was a day of simultaneous celebration and sadness, of endings and new beginnings. I fell into the warm embrace of my family and we drove home.

"Are you the new school nurse?" the little girl asked me as I stood in the closet-sized medical office in my sons' school in Springfield, Virginia. Since Clinton left office, I was still assigned to the White House Medical Unit. However, I had saved up ninety days of terminal leave before I would be officially retired. So I took that time to do something I had never done before: be a stay-at-home mom. I cooked the meals, cleaned the house, took care of the boys, and drove them to and from school. I also volunteered. The school needed someone with a health-profession background to cover for the school nurse a few hours a week. Although I had a medical degree, I nervously volunteered to fill in for the nursing position.

"Sorry, I'm a doctor not a nurse," I apologized to the tow-headed tiny waif who stood twitching nervously in the hallway. "But maybe I can help you?"

She was soon joined by two other little girls her same height and size. One of the girls, a little red-haired imp with wavy short hair, spoke up for the gang of three, "WE have a headache."

I suppressed a laugh. "You ALL do?"

They all nodded their heads.

"Must be a rough class you're taking. How about some Tylenol?"

It was a glorious Saturday spring morning in Virginia, and I was watching television with my sons in the family room. I sat on the couch with my sons snuggled beside me. They laughed over the Saturday morning cartoons.

I looked at their happy faces. They had grown up since we first arrived in Virginia nine years earlier. Andrew was now fourteen and Jason was twelve. They had been accepted to a private Christian school in Scottsdale and were looking forward to moving there in the summer, where we would have a new house with a swimming pool.

As my sons chuckled over a television show, I commented to them, "I'm so happy to finally be home with you guys. I know you really missed me a lot when I was away." I thought of Jason's journal entry in which he had written that when I was away, it was as though I was dead. "It's nice to be home with you all the time now."

Jason responded, "Yeah, Mom, when you were away, we really missed you. But now that you're here all the time, we're starting to get sick of you!" And the boys both laughed as I embraced them and tousled their hair.

EIGHTEEN

Doctor's Progress Notes

The blond-haired, young uniformed division guard barely looked up from his paperwork behind the glass window.

"Driver's license," he muttered, not even making eye contact with me as I and my companion, John Weber, stood trembling in the November cold outside the northwest visitor's gate. Had the young man looked up, perhaps he would have recognized the former physician to the president. But I realized that I was expecting too much. It had been over seven years since I left my position at the White House. The guard at the gate hadn't even finished high school then, let alone set foot on the eighteen acres.

It was November 22, 2008, forty-five years from the day that President John F. Kennedy had been assassinated. It was odd but not unusual for me to remember that date, having medically prepared every day for an assassination during my nine years following the president. When Kennedy had been shot, I lived with my family in Navy housing at Anacostia, across the river from D.C. I remembered that day well. I was eight years old, attending parochial school. I sat quietly in class when one of the nuns interrupted the teacher to an-

Looking back at my White House years, seven years later, I am in awe of how my life has changed.
(SILVIO RONE)

nounce that the president had been shot.

"Children, we must pray for our president," the nun, in her black and white habit, intoned. That afternoon, as the students were lining up to go home, the nun announced that the president had died. "You didn't pray hard enough," she blamed us under her breath as she rushed back to the chapel, her long black skirt whipping past the lines of students.

I thought of that day as I handed the guard my Arizona driver's license. I also thought about prayer. I had prayed a lot while I was at the White House, but even more since I retired from the Navy in June 2001. In some ways my prayers were answered, but not as I had expected. After a while, I began to get used to, and even welcome, the unexpected. As I stood patiently waiting to be cleared into the compound where I had spent almost a decade of my life, I thought of how I had embraced the unexpected in recent years. Today's visit was because of an unexpected call from an old friend.

"Hey, boss," Brigadier General Dick Tubb's cheery voice on the phone greeted me. His tone camouflaged any stress he may have been experiencing while taking care of President George W. Bush in the final days of his eight-year term. "I know you and John will be in town for the Bocelli concert this weekend. Can you drop by your old office to pick up a gift?"

I was surprised and delighted to receive Tubb's call. I kept in touch with him through the years as he took over the medical unit and assumed the care of President Bush. Tubb was nearing almost thirteen years at the White House, surpassing my nine. I always felt my time there should have been counted in dog years because of the conflict and controversy associated with the Clinton presidency. But when I thought of Dick Tubb's tour as physician to President Bush, the 9/11 president, then the tough times under Clinton appeared trivial by comparison.

"Tubbster," I said with a smile, invoking the nickname President Bush had affectionately bestowed on his doctor. As I caught up on recent events in Dr. Tubb's busy life, I sat comfortably in my clinic in North Scottsdale, admiring the bright blue sky through the large picture window of my private office. "John and I will be in D.C. that weekend. I wouldn't pass up a chance to visit the old office at least one more time before you leave. But tell me, what's this about a gift?"

"That's my surprise for you!" Tubb chuckled. I could see him tossing his head back, his signature cowlick sticking up from the back of his shock of thick hair, now graying. "All I can say is that it's something from the past that you probably forgot about."

A blast from the past? Tubb had piqued my curiosity. I was looking forward to visiting my old office, but now even more so because there would be a surprise gift waiting for me. The past year had been full of surprises and the unexpected. So, why not an unexpected gift from the White House?

When we moved to Scottsdale in 2001, my family had settled into a comfortable lifestyle. Andrew and Jason enjoyed their new school, where they excelled in their classes and made many friends. I was relieved that the move to Arizona had gone well, timed before our sons started high school, where friendships were crucial.

Richard loved Arizona because the climate and food reminded him of his beloved San Diego. He maintained his ties with the law firm in D.C. and would take on project work, performing depositions and writing briefs. I was relieved to see him happy at last, experiencing moments of "percolated joy" as he drove in the Arizona sunshine.

As for me, I loved the beauty and comfortable lifestyle of Arizona but wasn't too certain about the job I accepted. I was hired by the Mayo Clinic in Scottsdale to work in their Executive Health Division performing annual examinations on corporate executives. Regular hours, good pay, and a predictable workday: the antithesis of my previous life. I didn't have to run the program, and wasn't in charge of anything. After a career in the military, especially being in charge of the White House Medical Unit, and admittedly a lifetime of being the responsible one, I welcomed the chance to be the worker bee. But after a few months on my new job, I missed being the queen bee. I needed to be in charge again.

So in October 2005, I left the Mayo Clinic and formed my own medical concierge practice in North Scottsdale, the Center for Executive Medicine. In my new practice, I got a chance to implement many of the ideas that I had proposed to George Washington University Medical Center when I was searching for the next duty station after the White House. My new practice quickly grew to three hundred patients, many of whom answered to the title president and CEO.

I loved having my own private practice. My schedule was as I had desired it: flexible, and allowing time to spend with my patients, never rushed. I was on call 24/7 just like at the White House. Patients had my personal cell phone number and e-mail address. And to further duplicate the medical unit atmosphere, I hired my former "black cloud" medic from the White House, Mac McLeod, who retired from the Air Force and joined me in October 2005 as my office-practice manager. There were times when we first started that I would pick up the phone, glance at Mac, and catch myself before instinctively answering, "White House Medical Unit." McLeod evoked memories of the good old days taking care of the president.

And we were going to create the good new days, I hoped and prayed.

But as my medical practice thrived, my marriage unfortunately died. I realized later that after I had left the military, to which I had been wed longer and owed a stronger allegiance than to my husband, I didn't know how to be a wife. I also grew to become another person from the one Richard married eight years after we met in high school. Like many couples who separate, we found that we simply had grown apart, not together. My work in the military and my life in the kill zone for nine years widened the distance between us. When I formed my practice, I poured my time and passion into running my own business. It was the final death knell for my marriage. And when our two sons left home for college, our nest went from an empty to a shattered one. It was time for me to say good-bye to my marriage.

My flashback of the past seven years zipped by in the blink of an eye, long enough for the guard to examine my driver's license, check his computer, and then toss my ID and "A" guest pass to me through the slit in the window. I remembered the days when I had the coveted blue pass that allowed me access anywhere on the compound, even into the inner sanctum of the second floor of the residence. Now I required an escort to walk me from the gate to my old office.

The guard took John's Indiana driver's license and gave it the same scrutiny. "Hey, can we wait inside?" John asked the young officer, who sat in the heated guardhouse. It was 40 degrees and windy, and I huddled against the warmth of John's woolen coat, missing the sunshine and sultry breeze of Arizona. "It's really cold out here."

"Sorry," the guard said unsympathetically, tossing John's driver's license back with his "A" pass. "You can't come inside until your escort arrives from the doctor's office." So much for being a retired rear admiral and former physician to the president.

White House Nurse Karey Dufour soon greeted us at the guardhouse. Only when Karey arrived were John and I allowed into the warm security booth where we passed through the magnetometers. Karey then walked with us along the driveway of the North Portico. She had been assigned to cover tours that Saturday morning. Dr. Tubb, who was in Peru with President Bush, had instructed her to carry out the mission of my visit. I was hoping to see Tubb before Bush left office but wasn't surprised that he would be on the road again. Been there, done that.

I introduced Karey to John, whom I had known since 2002 when he was a patient of mine at the Mayo Clinic. John at that time was running a company in Phoenix and would go to the Mayo Clinic for his annual physical exams. Because of his frequent travel in 2002, he had to reschedule his physical. When he called for a new appointment, his usual doctor's calendar was full. Mine was not and the scheduler asked if he would mind having a woman physician. John agreed, and I was assigned to be his doctor. When I formed my own private practice, John signed up even after he had moved to Indianapolis to run another company.

When John flew to Scottsdale the year before for his annual exam, we sat in my office going over his recent medical and social history. We talked about his job in Indiana, his twins, who would be graduating from college, and the status of his social life. After confiding in me the horrors of dating in the modern world, he turned the tables on me and asked me how I was doing.

"Well, after listening to you," I told my patient, "I have no intention whatsoever of dating."

"What do you mean?" John was puzzled. "I thought you were married." Throughout my entire time as his physician, John, who had been divorced for four years, knew that I was married with two children.

"This is a rough time for me," I confessed. "I'm going through a divorce."

Perennially cheerful and irreverent, John instantly spoke up. "Then marry me!"

I almost fell out of my chair. "Don't be ridiculous!" I scoffed. "I'm your doctor!"

John shot back with his brilliant smile, "Heck, I'll get another doctor."

I responded, "You'll never find a better doctor."

We both laughed over our friendly banter, and I sent him back on his way to Indiana. But John charmed me with his warmth, wit, and wisdom, and we started dating, but only after he found another doctor. Soon we discovered that we were amazingly compatible and happy together.

As the White House nurse escorted us down the North Lawn driveway, I couldn't help but reminisce once again. I had walked this path countless times, admiring the view of the portico. We took the side-door entrance into the Palm Room and from there through the double doors to the ground floor of the residence. The Uniformed Division guard outside the Map Room stood up when he saw me and yelled, "Hey, Doc! You're back. Are you going to be the new president's doctor?"

I shook his hand and my head simultaneously. "No, my White House doctor days are done. I'm happy in my new life."

Barack Obama had just been elected president a few weeks prior to our visit. The Bush White House was in its final days and Obama's team was picking its players, many of whom were from the Clinton administration, including Obama's chief of staff, senior advisors, and most familiar of all to me, his secretary of state, Hillary Clinton. I found it interesting that the new administration looked more like the old one, before Bush. It was ironic that some things changed by remaining the same.

"Welcome back, Admiral Mariano," Stephanie Ansell, Dr. Tubb's friendly executive assistant, greeted us as Karey flung open the door leading into the doctor's office.

As soon as I stepped into the reception room, I saw the gift that Tubb had been saving for me. And the sight of it made me laugh out loud.

It was my old baby blue IBM Selectric typewriter. Tubb had planted a red ribbon on top of it and included a witty letter reuniting me with my old, faithful scribe. I had used the typewriter for writing out the president's progress notes and medical entries in the days before we started using laptop computers in the medical unit. I liked the old-fashioned typewriter, which reminded me of my civil service days when I was once timed typing 175 words per minute, often overriding the machine itself. But the typewriter also provided secure records, with no computer to be hacked. With the old-fashioned machines, the ribbon cartridges that bore the evidence of the printed word were routinely destroyed. Tubb's letter explained that the typewriter had been found in my old cabin at Camp David and was to be junked, when he realized it was the one I had used. "If only these keys could talk," Tubb wrote cleverly in his missive to me. I thought, how true. Perhaps one day they will.

John found the gift amusing, and I shared the letter Tubb had written with him, Karey, and Stephanie as we stood in Dr. Tubb's office. Before we left, I had to look at my old office one last time. It was clearly no longer mine; it had been renovated, decorated, and was destined to be passed on to another physician after Tubb would vacate it in January 2009.

"Can we take a look at the house one last time?" I pleaded with Stephanie as John and I were preparing to leave. Karey had to leave us for a moment, having been summoned to check out a visitor on the State Floor who had become light-headed.

Stephanie was accommodating and offered to take us toward the West Wing. As we walked the Colonnade, I thought of the hundreds of times I had strolled, marched, or dragged my feet along the worn path that led to the Oval Office. But I never ran through that walkway. As I used to tell my staff, "Never run or let them see you sweat."

As we entered the West Wing, we were met by one of the mess specialists. "Hey, Admiral," the young African American man greeted me, "good to have you back."

"Good to see you," I spoke, trying hard to remember the man's name. "Just passing through one last time."

"Wanna see the Mess again?" he offered, before I had a chance to ask.

We poked our heads into the newly renovated White House Mess, with its polished walnut-paneled walls, beautiful oil paintings of Navy vessels, and delicate floral arrangements. I remembered the times I sat in the Mess having breakfast or lunch, meeting with Dr. Tubb and the other physicians or privately counseling a troubled nurse or physician assistant. We followed the mess specialist into the kitchen, and I was reunited with my past once again. The familiar scents of cooking, the stocked supplies, the pots and pans. And the smiling faces of a handful of Filipino mess specialists. It was my farewell visit to the Mess, where my career at the White House had started in the home of an admiral many years ago.

As we made our way back to Dr. Tubb's office to retrieve my typewriter, we toured the State Floor for me to see it one last time.

I showed John the State Dining Room, where I had been promoted to admiral eight years earlier. As we admired the portrait of Lincoln that hung over the fireplace, I read again the inscription carved into the mantel:

I pray Heaven to Bestow the Best of Blessings on THIS HOUSE and on All that shall hereafter Inhabit it. May none but honest and Wise Men ever rule this roof.

The inscription was taken from a letter written by President John Adams on his second night at the White House. How true and good were those words. And I would have added a postscript that would say ". . . and may none but honest and wise *doctors* care for those who live under this roof."

As we returned to my old office one last time, I thought how this visit orchestrated by Dick Tubb was a gift itself. It was a final farewell to my past. I had visited not only my office but the Mess, kitchen, and State Dining Room, where some of the happiest moments of my life had taken place both as a Navy brat and naval officer.

"Thank you so much," I said, hugging Stephanie and Karey as John and I prepared to leave. John took the heavy typewriter into his arms easily as Karey led us toward the East Wing to the exit facing the Treasury Department.

As we dropped our guest passes into the turnstiles at the guard gate, I looked back one last time at the White House. That chapter in my life was now finally over. And as John and I walked to the hotel nearby, I thought about the future. *If only these keys could talk.* I recalled the words by Dick Tubb in his letter. That phrase became my next challenge. I was now determined to make those keys speak again. And I would not be alone doing so. I would be with the man walking beside me who was destined to make my heart sing a new song.

INDEX

A

Adams, Abigail, 113

Adams, John, 113, 286

Adams, Michelle, 233–34, 235, 236, 237

Air Force One, 8–9

bomb threat, 130–31

Dr. Connie Mariano and, **8**

Albright, Madeleine, **131**

Alswang, Ralph, 137–39, 141, 167

Ansell, Stephanie, 284, 285, 287

APEC (Asia-Pacific Economic Cooperation) Summit

Jakarta, Indonesia, 167–72, 172–73

Manila, Philippines, 114–15, 157

toilet incident, 148–49

Vancouver, B.C., 146–49

Ashby, Craig, 131, 132

B

Bachar, Steve, 107

Baker, James, 116, 118

Band, Doug, 272, 273

Bautista, Lito, 7, 41, 87, 109–10

Beatty, Deb, 178–79

Begala, Paul, 219–20

Bennett, Bob, 214

Bittman, Robert, 216–17

Blythe, William, 163

Boone, Joel T., 174

Brady, James, 55, 128, 129

Britannia (royal yacht), 150, 167

Buddy (Clinton's dog), 249, 263,
    273–74
Burkley, George, 124–25
Bush, Barbara, 25
    Christmas dinner in the White
        House (1992), 110–14
    final days, 72–76
    Boris Yeltsin's state arrival,
        50–52
    White House, accident when
        leaving, 75–76, 99
Bush, George H. W., 20, **76**
    and the Band-Aid incident,
        43–44, 47–49
    Christmas dinner in the
        White House (1992),
        110–14
    final days, 72–76, **73**
    reelection bid (1992), 72–73
    King Hassan II of Morocco's
        funeral, 116, 118
    King Hussein of Jordan's
        funeral, 7–12
    Dr. Connie Mariano, meeting,
        44–47
    State Dinner in Japan, incident
        at, 106–7
    Walker's Point
        (Kennebunkport, Maine),
        60–63, 63–70
    Boris Yeltsin's state arrival, 39,
        50–56
Bush, George W., 267, 270, 272,
    279–80

C
Canada
    APEC (Asia-Pacific Economic
        Cooperation) Summit
        (Vancouver, B.C.), 146–49
Carter, Jimmy
    King Hussein of Jordan's
        funeral, 7–12
Chandler, Mary Ann, 50, 54, 55,
    75, 112
Chitwood, John, 224–25
Christmas dinner in the White
    House (1992), 110–14
Christopher, Warren, 116
Clinton, Bill, **80**, **140**, **159**, **271**
    allergy shots incident, 88–93
    Henry Oren "Buddy"
        Grisham's funeral, 162–63,
        164–65, 165–67
    mother (Virginia Kelley),
        death of, 97
    personality, 4–5, 12, 179
    quadriceps surgery, 128–29,
        197–98, 199–203,
        206–7
Clinton, Bill (as president)
    APEC (Asia-Pacific Economic
        Cooperation) Summit
        (Jakarta, Indonesia), 167–72,
        172–73
    APEC (Asia-Pacific Economic
        Cooperation) Summit
        (Manila, Philippines),
        114–15, 157

APEC (Asia-Pacific Economic
    Cooperation) Summit
    (Vancouver, B.C.), 146–49
King Hassan II of Morocco's
    funeral, 115–21
King Hussein of Jordan's
    funeral, 4–6, 6–12
impeachment proceedings,
    189–90
John Kluge's yacht (Biscayne
    Bay), 151–52
Macedonia, bomb threat on
    flight to, 130–31
presidential trips overseas, 4–6,
    6–12, 114, 115–21, 130–34,
    266
sailing on the *Fortuna* (coast of
    Palma de Mallorca),
    135–41
Secret Service code name
    for, 5
Summit of the Americas
    (Miami), 142–46, 147–49,
    150–55
trip to Australia, 156–62
unpredictability of, 85
in the White House, 77–80
White House, departure from,
    267, 273–75
Boris Yeltsin, meeting in
    Helsinki, 203–4
Clinton, Bill (and Monica
    Lewinsky), 190, 208–11,
    218–20

amorous reputation, 191–93,
    193–95
drawing blood for DNA
    sample, 215–16, 216–17
gossip concerning, 183
Map Room interview,
    218–20
and Ken Starr, 5, 109–10, 189,
    215, 218–20
TV broadcast of confession,
    220–21
Clinton, Bill (and Dr. Connie
    Mariano), *xiii–xiv*
caricature, **274**
ceremony for Connie's
    promotion to admiral,
    260–65, **264, 265**
meeting, 83–84
military promotion to captain,
    attending, **143, 144**
photos with, **80, 143, 144, 159,
    186, 193, 194, 195, 199,
    200, 203, 204, 205, 206,
    209, 210, 211**
Clinton, Chelsea
sailing on the *Fortuna* (coast of
    Palma de Mallorca), 135–41
in the White House, 77
Clinton, Hillary Rodham, 77,
    206
ceremony for Connie's
    promotion to admiral,
    260–65, **264, 265**
fashion sense, 151

Clinton, Hillary (*continued*)
 King Hassan II of Morocco's
  funeral, 116, 118
 health of, 188–90
 King Hussein of Jordan's
  funeral, 6–12
 John Kluge's yacht (Biscayne
  Bay), 151–55, **154**
 Dr. Connie Mariano, meeting,
  82–84
 personality, 83, 189–90, 266
 and Hugh Rodham, Sr., 80–84
 sailing on the *Fortuna* (coast of
  Palma de Mallorca), 135–41
 as Secretary of State, 284
 senator, election as, 266, 27
 State Dinner in Tokyo, 106–9
 trip to Australia, 156–62
 in the White House, 77, 83–84
 White House, departure from,
  273–75
 and Whitewater, 212
Corbett, Dr. David, 45–46

D
Day, Doris, 249
Dufour, Karey, 282–83, 287
Dunham, Gary, 50, 54, 55, 112

E
Eisold, John, 271
Emanuel, Rahm, 219–20

Eschbach, Dr. Jeff, 158, 159, 161,
 234–35, 236, 237
Estrada, Joseph, **242**

F
Fama, Joe, 5, 41, 109–10, 162, 274
Farmer, Sharon, 275
Flynn, Don, 235, 237
Ford, Gerald, **140**
 King Hussein of Jordan's
  funeral, 7–12
Fortuna
 sailing on the coast of Palma
  de Mallorca, 135–41
Friendly, Andrew, 106, 107, 150

G
Gaugham, John, 38, 96–98,
 181–82
George Washington University
 Law Center, 57
Goodwin, Eleanor, 26, 33
Goodwin, Hugh, 26, 33
Goodwin, Hugh, Jr. (son), 33
Goodwin, Sydney (daughter), 33
Gore, Al
 Achilles tendon repair, 228–31,
  231–32
 election campaign, 266
Gore, Tipper, 230–31
Grant, Mike, 229
Green, Phil, 263

Grisham, Henry Oren "Buddy"
   funeral of, 162–63, 164–65,
     165–67

H
"Hail to the Chief," 52
Hassan II of Morocco
   funeral of, 115–21
Healy, George P. A., 260
Hinckley, John, 128
Hoertz, Gary, 159, 160
Holy Hills golf course, 43–49
Hope (Arkansas)
   Henry Oren "Buddy"
     Grisham's funeral, 162–63,
     164–65, 165–67
Hosack, Jim, 3–4
Hotel Okura (Tokyo), 103
Hussein of Jordan, 268
   funeral for, 4–6, 6–12

I
Idone, Barbara, 133–34, 263
Indonesia
   APEC (Asia-Pacific Economic
     Cooperation) Summit
     (Jakarta), 167–72, 172–73

J
Jackson, Mary, 45, 46
Jakarta (Indonesia)

APEC (Asia-Pacific Economic
   Cooperation) Summit,
     167–72, 172–73
Jingco, Placida, **29**
John Paul II, Pope, **141**
Johnny (White House cook)
   illness and death of, 238–40,
     240–41
Johnson, Lyndon, 230
Jones, Paula, 214
Juan Carlos I of Spain, 135–41
   sailing on the *Fortuna* (coast
     of Palma de Mallorca),
     135–41
Jordan
   King Hussein's funeral, 7–12
Julius Caesar (Shakespeare), 198

K
Kausert, J., 274
Kelley, Dick, 177
Kelley, Virginia (Clinton's
   mother), 175–77, 221
   blood transfusion, 178–81
   death of, 97
   funeral of, 96–98, 181
Kelly, Shirley, 37
Kendall, David, 214–16, 216
Kennebunkport, Maine, 60–63,
   63–70
Kennedy, John F., 21
   assassination, 124–25
   funeral, 53, 276–77

Kerwin, Timmy, 9, 10
Kiefer, Gina, 146
kill zone, 55, 122–25, 125–27, 128–29, 129–30
Kluge, John, 150
Koroscil, Tom, 21
Krapohl, Greta, 195, 196, 198, 198–99, 202

L
Lang, Bill, 196, 200, 201
Lee, J. Burton, III, 20, 22–25, 35, 37, 38, 40, 45, 46, 47, 56, 61, 62, 72, 75–76, 221–22
  incident of the allergy shots, 88–93
Leiber, Linda Strand, 268
Lewinsky, Monica, 190, 208–11, 215, 218–20
Lincoln, Abraham, 260, 265, 286
Luminati, Ed, 143–44, 145, 146

M
McBride, Tim, 38–39
McCurry, Mike, **204**, 249
Macedonia
  bomb threat on flight to, 130–31
McGee, Bill, 98, 100, 230
McLeod, Jim "Black Cloud," 115, 117, 118, 160, 223–25, 281

McPartlin, Brian, 235, 236, 237
Maguire, Frank, 189–90, 262, 263, 264
Manila (Philippines)
  Asia-Pacific Economic Cooperation Summit, 114–15, 157
Mariano, Angel C. (father), 26, **27**, 27–28, 33, 53, **143**, **144**, 163, 254–55, 261, 263
Mariano, Dr. Connie
  achievements and career, *xiii–xiv*, 13–17, 250–51
  admiral, promotion to, 251, 252–55
  admiral, promotion ceremony, 260–65, **264**, **265**
  childhood and education, 15, 26–33, 33–34, 163–64
  children (Andrew and Jason), 57–59, **58**, 71, **143**, **144**, 187, 244–48, 276–77, 280
  divorce and remarriage (John Weber), 278, 280, 282, 283–84
  domestic life, 57–59, 71, 187, 244–48, 248–49, 276–77, 280–82
  health problems, 181–83, 183–84, 184–88
  John F. Kennedy's funeral, 53, 276–77
  marriage (to Richard Stevens), 19–20, 36–37

marriage, career stress and, 244–48, 255–59, 282

Mayo Clinic, working at, 242–43, 268–70, 274, 280–81

private practice, 281–82

racism and racial assumptions, 85–88, 163–65

sense of humor, 46

USS *Prairie*, service on, 18, 62, 64, 140, 156, 262

White House, return to, 278, 280, 282–87

See also Stevens, Andrew; Stevens, Jason; Stevens, Richard

Mariano, Dr. Connie (White House Medical Unit, G. H. W. Bush administration)

appointment, 16, 17–19, 20–25

Barbara Bush, treating, 75–76

George H. W. Bush, meeting, 44–47

Christmas dinner in the White House (1992), 110–14

golf duty (Band-Aid incident), 43–44, 47–49

Heimlich maneuver, 112, 113

at Kennebunkport, Maine, 60–63, 63–70

and J. Burton Lee, III, 35, 37, 38, 40, 45, 46, 56, 61, 62, 72, 75–76, 221–22

J. Burton Lee, III, interview with, 20, 22–25, 48

and the Secret Service, 61–63, 63–70

security clearance, 20

training exercise, 63–70

unit commander meeting, 37–40

Boris Yeltsin's state arrival, 39, 50–56

Mariano, Dr. Connie (White House Medical Unit, Clinton administration)

allergy shots incident, 88–93

APEC (Asia-Pacific Economic Cooperation) Summit (Jakarta, Indonesia), 167–72, 172–73

APEC (Asia-Pacific Economic Cooperation) Summit (Manila, Philippines), 114–15, 157

APEC (Asia-Pacific Economic Cooperation) Summit (Vancouver, B.C.), 146–49

captain, promotion to rank of, 142, **143**, **144**, 145

Bill Clinton's quadriceps surgery, 197–98, 199–203, 206–7

Hillary Clinton, health of, 188–90

Dublin trip, potential suicide on, 233–36, 236–38

Mariano, Dr. Connie (*continued*)

drawing blood for DNA sample, 215–16, 216–17

existing procedures, questioning and improving, 95–96

King Hassan II of Morocco's funeral, 115–21

head of Unit, appointment to, 97–98, 181–82

King Hussein of Jordan's funeral, 4–6, 6–12

Johnny (White House cook), illness and death of, 238–40, 240–41

and J. Burton Lee, III, 88–93

Macedonia, bomb threat on flight to, 130–31

president of Guatemala, treating, 146, 147, 148–49

presidential trips overseas, 4–6, 6–12, 114, 115–21, 130–34, 156–59

succession plan, 132–34

sultan of Brunei and ChapStick, 146–47

Summit of the Americas (Miami), 142–46, 147–49, 150–55

Tokyo, Clinton's visit to, 103–6, 106–10

tourist overcome in State Dining Room, 1–4

transition, 85–88, 93–98

trip to Australia, 156–62

and the White House Military Office, 98–102

Boris Yeltsin, meeting in Helsinki, 203–4

Mariano, Dr. Connie (and the Clintons)

and Bill Clinton, 208–11

Bill Clinton on, *xiii–xiv*

and Hillary Clinton, 211–12

Henry Oren "Buddy" Grisham's funeral, 162–63, 164–65, 165–67

the Robert Talbott tie, 208, 210, 214

and Hugh Rodham, Sr., 80–84

Mariano, Dr. Connie (photos), 8, 75–76, **279**

and Air Force One, **8**

Annhand pin, **212**

with Madeline Albright, **131**

with George H. W. Bush, **73**, **76**

captain, promotion to rank of, **143**, **144**

children (Andrew and Jason), **58**

of Bill Clinton, **271**

with Bill Clinton, **80**, **159**, **186**, **193**, **194**, **195**, **199**, **200**, **203**, **204**, **205**, **209**, **210**, **211**

with Bill Clinton (caricature), **274**

with Bill and Hillary Clinton,
    206, **264**, **265**
with Bill Clinton and Gerald
    Ford, **140**
with Bill Clinton and Pope
    John Paul II, **141**
with Bill Clinton and
    Philippine President Joseph
    Estrada, **242**
with Hillary Clinton on John
    Kluge's yacht, **154**
graduation, **31**
with grandmother, **29**
Burton Lee's autograph, **40**
and the Navy Achievement
    Medal, **18**
Secret Service training
    exercise, **68**
at Uninformed Services
    University School of
    Medicine, **16**
uniforms, **17**
Mariano, Diane (Rocky's wife),
    21
Mariano, Jose, Jr. (brother), **29**,
    262
Mariano, Lorie (sister), 262
Mariano, Lourdes Jingco
    (mother), 53, **143**, **144**,
    254–55, 261–62
Mariano, Marciano "Rocky"
    (cousin), 21, 53, 221
Mariano, Remy (sister), **29**,
    261

Mariano, Tessie (brother), **29**,
    261
Mayo Clinic (Scottsdale,
    Arizona), 242–43, 268–70,
    274, 280–81
Merletti, Lew, 143–44, 148
Miguel (White House cook),
    238–39, 241
Miller, Kitty, 248
Miller, Rich, 60–61, 95, 125,
    248
Millie (Bush's cat), 47
Millikin, Tom, 75
Mitas, John A., II, 17, 17–20,
    262
Mohammed VI of Morocco, 118
Mohr, Larry, 21, 74–76, 96
    incident of the allergy shots,
    88–93
Morocco
    King Hassan II's funeral,
    115–21
Myers, Dee Dee, 91–93

N

Nash, Dr. Barry, 225–26, 227
Nelvis, Bayani, 41
Norman, Greg, 128, 196,
    197–98

O

Obama, Barack, 284

P

Panetta, Leon, **204**

Philippines
  Asia-Pacific Economic
    Cooperation Summit
    (Manila), 114–15, 157

Powell, Glenn, 166

Presidential Emergency
  Operations Center
  (PEOC), 37

Pulliam, Morris "Bud,"
  185–86

Q

Quayle, Dan, 51

Quayle, Marilyn, 51

R

Rabat (Morocco)
  King Hassan II's funeral,
    115–21

Ramsey, Bob, 74
  and Bill Clinton's blood type,
    96–97
  reassignment, 96–97, 98

Ranger (Bush's dog), 47

Reagan, Nancy, 230

Reagan, Ronald, 128, 230

Reeve, Christopher, 185,
  186

Ridenour, Dick, 250–52, 253,
  255

Ridenour, Leslie, 250–52,
  253

Roberts, Al, 21, 22, 25, 34–35,
  62

Rodham, Hugh, Sr., 80–84

Rogers, Mark, 183–84

"Ruffles and Flourishes," 54

S

Sanchez, Fred, 7, 274

Santa Cruz, Susan, 89

Scowcroft, Brent, 47

Secret Service
  kill zone, 55, 122–25, 125–27,
    128–29, 129–30
  training exercise, 61–63,
    63–70, **68**, 122–24

Semper Gumby, 93–94

Shakespeare, William, 198

Shorsch, Rusty, 175–76

Socks (Clinton's cat), 5, 263

Sofia of Spain, 135–41
  sailing on the *Fortuna* (coast of
    Palma de Mallorca),
    135–41

Starks, Vince, 4, 9–10, 11, 130,
  132, 224–25

Starr, Ken, 5, 109–10, 189, 215,
  218–20

State Dining Room, 286
  ceremony for Connie's
    promotion to admiral,
    260–65, **264, 265**

Stevens, Andrew (Connie's son),
    57–59, **58**, 71, **143**, **144**, 187,
    248–49, 262, 264, 275,
    276–77, 280
    and chicken pox, 245–46
Stevens, Jason (Connie's son),
    57–59, **58**, 71, **143**, **144**,
    187, 247–48, 248–49, 259,
    262, 264, 275, 276–77,
    280
    and chicken pox, 244–45
Stevens, Richard (Connie's
    husband), 19–20, 20,
    36–37, 57–59, 187,
    244–48, 248–49, 255,
    257–58, 262, 264, 275,
    280–82
Sudduth, Debbie, 75
Summit of the Americas
    (Miami), 142–46, 147–49
    John Kluge's yacht,
    150–55

T
Tailhook investigation, 39–40
Taipei, 114
Taiwan, 115
Toiv, Barry, 249
Tokyo, Clinton's visit to, 103–6,
    106–10
    preparations, 104–6
    State Dinner, 106–9
Travell, Dr. Janet, 174–75

Tubb, Dr. Richard, 131, 132,
    203, 263, 267, 272, 279–80,
    285, 287

U
Uninformed Services University
    School of Medicine, 15
    Dr. Connie Mariano at, **16**
    Semper Gumby, 93–94
USS *Prairie*, 18, 62, 64, 140, 156,
    262

V
Valdez, Dave, 75
Van Dyke, Wendy, 142, 145,
    168–71, 172–73
Vancouver, B.C.
    APEC (Asia-Pacific Economic
    Cooperation) Summit
    (Canada), 146–49

W
Weber, John, 278, 280, 282–87
West Wing (TV series), 40
White House
    at Christmas, 20–21
    Christmas dinner (1992),
    110–14
    staff and servants, 35–36,
    41–42
    See also State Dinning Room

White House Medical Unit
  existing procedures,
    questioning and improving,
    95–96
  Connie Mariano appointed as
    head of Unit, 96–98
  succession plan, 132–34
  and the White House Military
    Office, 98–102
  political partisanship in, 74

White House Military Office,
    98–102
Wissler, John, 252–53

Y
Yakeley, Jay, 39
Yeltsin, Boris, 203–4
    state arrival, 39, 50–56
Yeltsin, Naina, 51–52